Women in Philosophy

Women in Philosophy

WHAT NEEDS TO CHANGE?

Edited by
Katrina Hutchison and Fiona Jenkins

OXFORD
UNIVERSITY PRESS

OXFORD

UNIVERSITY PRESS

Oxford University Press is a department of the University of Oxford.
It furthers the University's objective of excellence in research, scholarship,
and education by publishing worldwide.

Oxford   New York

Auckland   Cape Town   Dar es Salaam   Hong Kong   Karachi
Kuala Lumpur   Madrid   Melbourne   Mexico City   Nairobi
New Delhi   Shanghai   Taipei   Toronto

With offices in

Argentina   Austria   Brazil   Chile   Czech Republic   France   Greece
Guatemala   Hungary   Italy   Japan   Poland   Portugal   Singapore
South Korea   Switzerland   Thailand   Turkey   Ukraine   Vietnam

Oxford is a registered trademark of Oxford University Press
in the UK and certain other countries.

Published in the United States of America by
Oxford University Press
198 Madison Avenue, New York, NY 10016

Library of Congress Cataloging-in-Publication Data
Women in philosophy: what needs to change? / edited by
Katrina Hutchison and Fiona Jenkins.
pages cm
Includes bibliographical references and index.
ISBN 978–0–19–932561–0 (pbk.: alk. paper)—ISBN 978–0–19–932560–3 (alk. paper)—
ISBN 978–0–19–932562–7 (updf)   1. Women philosophers.   I. Hutchison, Katrina,
editor of compilation.
B105.W6W63 2013
190'.82—dc23
2013001689

1 3 5 7 9 8 6 4 2
Printed in the United States of America
on acid-free paper

{ CONTENTS }

{ ACKNOWLEDGMENTS }

This book would not have taken shape without the support and input of many people.

It was initially motivated by a symposium held at the Australian National University (ANU) in August 2009. This symposium was funded by the Australasian Association of Philosophy (AAP) and supported by the ANU College of Arts and Social Sciences. Participants in the symposium highlighted the ongoing relevance of the questions posed by this volume. Of particular note was a keynote paper by Moira Gatens, as well as papers by Kristi Giselsson, Kyleigh Langrick, Hannah McCann, and Fiona Webster, that starkly highlighted some of the problems female students in philosophy can face. Although these papers are not included in the volume for a range of reasons, they shaped the thinking of both editors and contributors.

We would also like to thank a number of individuals and organizations for assistance with data collection. The AAP allowed us to use their data on women's participation in philosophy in Australia and provided some assistance from Eliza Goddard in her capacity as executive officer. Adriane Rini collected data from New Zealand to supplement the AAP's Australasian data. Helen Beebee collected data on the situation of women in philosophy in the U.K. on behalf of the British Philosophical Association (BPA). Katherine Norlock was very helpful in providing us with her own and others' data collection on the situation of women in philosophy in the U.S.A., much of which was done in conjunction with the American Philosophical Association (APA). Canadian data were accessed from material published on the Canadian Philosophical Association (CPA) website, and we are grateful to those who compiled it.

The people who read some or all of the chapters of the manuscript suggested changes and revisions that have made this a better book: many thanks to Gillian Brock, Havi Carel, David Chalmers, Joanne Faulkner, Rod Girle, Alan Hájek, Helen Keane, Rosanne Kennedy, Jeanette Kennett, Justine Kingsbury, Marguerite La Caze, Norva Lo, Mark Nolan, Pam Roberts, Kim Rubenstein, Emma Rush, Inge Saris, Marian Sawer, Susanna Schellenberg, Undine Sellbach, and Scott Wisor. Lorraine Code provided valuable advice on various matters, as well as reading and commenting on some chapters.

Sally Haslanger offered great encouragement and practical support for this project from the outset. We would also like to thank Peter Ohlin, our commissioning editor, for his invaluable enthusiasm for the project, and David Chalmers, who encouraged us to approach Oxford University Press in the first place. We are grateful to the three anonymous referees from OUP who provided helpful feedback through two rounds of review and did much to influence the final structure of the manuscript. Our departments, the School of Philosophy in the Research School of Social Sciences at ANU and the Department of Philosophy in the Faculty of Arts at Macquarie University, generously facilitated the time spent working on this book.

Finally, we each thank our lovely families for sharing the journey of discovery with us, through what has inevitably been a personal as well as a professional project of research.

Women in Philosophy

Introduction

SEARCHING FOR SOFIA: GENDER AND
PHILOSOPHY IN THE 21ST CENTURY

Fiona Jenkins and Katrina Hutchison

It is not uncommon in certain fields of study that when academic women come to talk among themselves about their careers, powerful feelings of frustration, hurt, and annoyance at their experiences start to surface. Sally Haslanger phrases it forcefully when she writes in an influential piece published in the feminist philosophy journal *Hypatia* in 2008: "There is a deep well of rage inside of me; rage about how I as an individual have been treated in philosophy; rage about how others I know have been treated; and rage about the conditions that I'm sure affect many women and minorities in philosophy, and have caused many others to leave" (210). In the discussion that ensues, this sense of rage should not be forgotten, although it gives way in the essays collected here, as in Haslanger's own essay, to careful reflection on how to make sense of such experience, how to find an articulation of its form, structure, causes, and potential remedies. For women initiating and pursuing these discussions in philosophy, training in the discipline becomes a resource for careful analysis of the questions at stake. As has often been the case with the best feminist scholarship, reflection on lived experience, as well as the evidence of statistical data, becomes a stimulus for asking searching questions that probe broad social and institutional conditions. What may have begun, for individuals sharing their stories, as the paradoxically welcome discovery that it was not they *alone* who felt slights and disappointments, hostility, or simple lack of encouragement, becomes the emergent capacity to articulate the often subtle forms of injustice that shape persistent trends of exclusion.

One of the questions this book addresses is what it is about philosophy—the *über*-rational discipline—that has left it, along with several of the science, technology, and engineering (STEM) disciplines and a couple of the social science ones (notably economics and political science), lagging well behind a general trend toward improvement in women's representation and standing in academia.

There are considerable differences in patterns of change between areas of study and disciplines over the last 30 years or so, and progress in improving women's representation has been very uneven. As Virginia Valian pointed out in her 1999 book *Why So Slow?: The Advancement of Women*, a crucial dimension of this problem lies with the quite general cultural tendency to rate men's achievements more highly than those of women, an observable phenomenon that has been given substantive backing by a range of experiments in social psychology. Such judgments are supported by common gender schemas, that is, hypotheses shaping expectations about performance and behaviour that vary for men and women. Although such schemas shape judgment across a wide range of social interactions, they can become intensified in certain settings where the expectations are supported, often in unremarked ways, by determinations of the salience or importance of features that make a person 'belong' to one group rather than another. Valian's analysis of the importance of unconscious reliance upon gender schemas is important for several of the essays collected here, and it joins forces with a well-developed feminist argument that western philosophy was formed around an overlapping series of conceptual oppositions—reason/emotion, mind/body, culture/nature—coding a hierarchical understanding of the relationship of masculine and feminine that can be discerned throughout the 2,500-year history of the subject.[1] The gender schemas that shape the history and practise of the discipline may thus form a problematic nexus with the particular institutional forms that philosophy takes in the 21st century, including elements of its social significance, pedagogic practices, research priorities, privileged methods, and ways of engaging with feminist critique.

The contributors to this volume give shape together to a story about how women figure and fare in an ancient discipline, as it is constituted at the beginning of the 21st century. In view of the long history of the discipline, it is indeed only very recently that women have appeared as would-be equals in a field that has in the past actively and systematically disparaged women's very capacity for its key qualifying attribute—the possession of reason itself. Such disparagement is evident, for example, in Kant's suggestion that men and women have different intellectual strengths, "the understanding of the man and the taste of the wife" (Kant, 2011:249), and Schopenhauer's view that women "remain big children, their whole lives long: a kind of intermediate stage between the child and the man, who is the actual human being, 'man'" (Schopenhauer, 1970:81). Yet in view of the wide changes toward greater gender equity that have accelerated throughout society and academia since the last strong wave of feminist activism in the 1970s, it is also necessary to consider why philosophy should lag so badly in including women. The perspectives offered here allow us to develop a case study of one academic area in which progress toward gender equity seems, if not completely stalled, at least unduly stagnant. They also allow some

---

[1] On this, see Beauvoir (1989); Lloyd (1993); Le Dœuff (1989, 1990, 2003); Gatens (1991).

light to be shed upon women's testimonies of their often painful experiences in pursuing the subject. Such experiences, as catalogued in the disturbing and provocative blog, "What is it like to be a woman in philosophy?"[2] are sometimes of overt sexism and discrimination; but they further chart the sense of there being a profound degree of misunderstanding of the perspectives of women in the profession. Thus the blog's title plays on a famous essay by Thomas Nagel titled "What is it like to be a bat?" to suggest that it may be anticipated that the experiences of women in philosophy are sufficiently different that they will appear to many men as those of an alien species. This may record a situation in which women's experiences are treated as 'deviant' from the norm (see Beebee, this volume) or, where negative, as somehow attributable to not fitting in with a given culture (see McGill, this volume), and forms part of the wider set of issues for women in philosophy analysed by our contributors.[3]

The problems faced by women in philosophy today require us to think beyond the terms of such liberal agendas as securing formally equitable procedures for new appointments and promotions, vital as these have been in enabling change. That is in part because the argument to ensure fairness in the workplace through legal measures and codes of conduct seems largely to have been won. Where overt discrimination or sexism occurs, measures exist to combat it; and although the demonstration of wrongdoing, as well as the implementation of such measures, is not always easy to carry out, academic institutions do have well-developed frameworks for individuals seeking redress. Moreover, concerns about the underrepresentation of women are not solely advanced by feminists, but are recognised as problematic issues by many universities and government agencies, as well as by national representative bodies.[4] In this respect, the formal acknowledgment of equity goals is largely uncontested at the 'top' level and provides an important framework for discussion, as well as targets for improving workplace and student gender profiles. With what are now strong procedural guarantees of equity generally in place, and evidence that women are appointed to jobs in philosophy at the rate at which they apply for them, attention should rightly turn to the problems endemic in

---

[2] http://beingawomaninphilosophy.wordpress.com/.

[3] See also the collection of women philosophers' stories in Alcoff (2003).

[4] Evidence of this concern includes the publication of reports on the issue by the Australasian Association of Philosophy (http://aap.org.au/women/reports/index.html); initiatives such as "Women and Men in Globalizing Universities" by the International Alliance of Research Universities (http://www.iaruni.org/women/women); and government initiatives such as the Australian Federal Government's Office for Women, the role of which includes increasing women's leadership and representation opportunities (http://www.fahcsia.gov.au/sa/women/progserv/equal/Pages/LeadershipRepresentationOpportunities.aspx). In general, however, in the academic context, the perception of a problematic gender gap is only focused on the STEM disciplines, while areas perceived as less socially important, such as philosophy, slip under the radar and lack targeted responses from wider agencies despite having highly comparable underrepresentation and lack of seniority of women.

certain disciplinary cultures and identifying the many factors that continue to stop women entering professional philosophy in numbers proportional to their representation in the population, cause them to drop out at high rates, or leave them stuck at low levels of the profession with careers that are 'going nowhere'.

This suggests a set of problems that are somewhat different from the overt sexism prevalent in the past and which may have taken on forms within academia that allow them to be readily overlooked. For instance, despite wide acknowledgement of equity goals, these are in practise typically conceived as fully separable from the values appropriate to core academic pursuits and virtues. The pursuit of truth or objectivity has often been framed as an aim that requires a disregard for 'who' pursues it, or indeed for the direct relevance of equity of access to engagement in pursuing it—a view that can appear 'gender-blind' but may in effect simply express the prevalence of one group's vision over other, more plural, ways of seeing. Past inequities may have shaped the present discipline in ways that merely formal attention to averting discrimination fails to address. Moreover, if a discipline is conceived as presently successful according to a range of indicators other than those of equal representation of women, the very successes of the discipline may serve to insulate it from the need to change (as Jenkins argues in her chapter). Other social and institutional pressures may also act strongly to shape disciplinary profiles and employment practises. Philosophy has survived some difficult times in recent years with the rise of the 'corporate' university and increasing pressure on the humanities arising from an instrumental conception of education.[5] And yet philosophy, although sometimes targeted for cuts, has in many institutions fared surprisingly well in defending its status as an 'elite' discipline that no respectable university would wish to be without. Is it possible that this too has impacted the current conception of the discipline as one that builds on particularly masculine—and thus more readily convincing—markers of value and achievement? In a climate of intensive 'performance' evaluation, has it become easier to defend continuing with 'business as usual' in already heavily male-dominated disciplines (as Rini argues in this volume)? Certainly it makes sense to look at how what have been labelled 'micro-inequities', small harms that fall beneath the radar detecting discrimination, can combine to generate powerful effects of exclusion (see Brennan, this volume).

Here we have taken for granted the value of thinking about how philosophy has been shaped as a discipline over its long, as well as its more recent, history. We look at the kinds of work it fosters and promotes, the cultures it encourages, and the ways in which contributions are evaluated, alongside questions about

---

[5] A number of philosophers have engaged with this issue recently, including Martha Nussbaum (2010), who argues forcefully against purely instrumental conceptions of education, and John Armstrong (2011), who calls for reform of humanities disciplines in light of the perceived irrelevance of their research and teaching outputs.

the exclusions it sustains, the contingency of its contemporary form and how things might be done—and better—otherwise. Moreover, we are concerned by how a discipline with a strong claim to a core place among the humanities, as well as high standing among the social sciences, is impoverished by its ongoing record of exclusion. If wisdom—Sofia—has historically been represented as a woman, how does philosophy's claim to represent a kind of cultural and human wisdom fare in view of the still narrow representation of humanity in the ranks of its practitioners, and the class, race, and gender composition of its elite? How indeed, does this impact its claim to represent, criticise, or interpret the theoretical dimensions of the social sciences? Should we care to ensure that women come to practise philosophy in numbers comparable to men, for reasons that go beyond equity goals (though they include them), to invoke the good of the discipline itself?

If women continue to be underrepresented in philosophy, the situation is even more dire for a range of other minority groups in a discipline that, despite its claims to speak on behalf of 'humanity', in fact speaks with a voice composed primarily from white, middle-class, and masculine sources. There are very broad equity and diversity issues that would share aspects of the problems discussed in the essays collected here: the exclusion of people of colour or indigenous groups, of the differently able, or of those with discernable accents that are socially marked as indicating lesser intelligence (on this, see Alcoff and Potter, 1993:3). But although these wider exclusions are touched on by several essays, we believe they may well also raise their own distinct issues, ones that are different from those raised by gender non-parity. Rather than take on the full range of equity and exclusion issues here, our narrower focus in this project lies with a particular problem that *despite* being made the target of some considerable efforts to bring about a changed demographic and equitable career paths, and despite some significant improvements in these, nonetheless continues to make a person's gender a strong marker of likely success or failure, as well perhaps as interest or disinterest, in the pursuit of philosophy. Our argument, moreover, builds on data collected over recent decades on the representation of women in philosophy; and unfortunately there are only very patchy data presently available on the underrepresentation of other groups.

Figures on women's underrepresentation in the discipline of philosophy have been collected by national representative bodies for philosophy, sometimes over several decades (the available data are discussed in much fuller detail in the appendix to this volume). To give an indicative sample, in Australia, according to data collected by the AAP (Australasian Association of Philosophy), women held only 28 percent of continuing positions in philosophy in 2009, and there is an inverse relationship between gender and seniority (Bishop et al., this volume). The AAP has collected data over more than 30 years, and this suggests that there has been little change in the composition of the discipline since the late '80s or early '90s. In the United States, the American Philosophical

Association (APA) reported figures indicating that women comprised only 21 percent of U.S. academic philosophers in 2003, and an update based on 2009 figures shows that the percentage has remained stable (Norlock, 2006, 2011). Haslanger gives data suggesting that women are disproportionately underrepresented at elite institutions, and indeed that publishing patterns can be analysed to show that the 'top' journals publish articles by women at rates significantly lower than even the levels of women who have made it into tenure at elite universities (Haslanger, 2008). Recent figures from the CPA (Canadian Philosophical Association) equity survey show that in the 2008–2009 academic year, about 21 percent of full professors in philosophy were women and 46 percent of associate professors were women, indicating that there too women are underrepresented in the discipline, but particularly noticeably, that women are not being proportionally *promoted* in the discipline, remaining at low levels and not accessing markers of success, such as nationally awarded research professorships (Boileau and Daigle, 2009), a result that chimes with experience in the other countries we look at here. Other Anglophone regions that are represented in this volume lag behind Australia and North America in terms of the collection of data. However, there too evidence has stimulated renewed interest in the issue, and data has begun to be collected in the United Kingdom and New Zealand indicating that women are underrepresented, particularly severely at the senior levels in the profession (Bishop et al., this volume).

Again, given the limitations of present datasets, in this volume, we concentrate on Anglophone philosophy. Although interesting work could no doubt be done to compare Anglophone philosophy with the situation in continental Europe and other locations, this further research lies beyond the scope of the present project. Anglophone philosophy, however, is a highly interrelated field, with many similarities in terms of the areas of inquiry that are taken to constitute the discipline, and it is also interconnected through factors such as recognition of qualifications, high mobility in the job market, and common philosophy journals. It provides an intriguing case study of how a particular configuration of a discipline has stabilised internationally in a form that remains highly male dominated in all the countries we examine. With varying levels of detail, depending on what information is being collected by different organisations, it enables us to look at trends in gender balance in philosophy and to see the evident drop-off in numbers participating at different levels of engagement from undergraduate to post-graduate study and at different levels of seniority.

Yet as Dodds and Goddard persuasively argue in their chapter, the idea that we simply have a 'pipeline problem' such that, as numbers reach parity at lower levels, there will be a gradual 'feed-through' to more senior levels, has proved to be an unfounded optimism. Moreover, it has fostered the sanguine belief that the problem will gradually fix itself as obvious blockages are removed, displacing the need to take more active measures. In the appendix of this volume, statistician Glenys Bishop and a number of the contributors of the national data discuss in greater depth what the data can show us and what their current limitations are as a body of evidence. The appendix also gives indications of the kind of data that would be useful for national organisations to be collecting in the future, so that the situation for women can be more accurately monitored and any changes or progress identified. These chapters, nonetheless, present a compelling picture of philosophy's particularly problematic relation with gender as judged against the presumption that women have equal capacity for the subject and therefore should be equally represented at all levels of rank, barring impediments that deserve further explanation. There is reason to think that it would be useful to collect further information on the intersection of gender inequity with other minority groups, as well as collecting data that are sensitive to the gendered patterns of different areas of specialization.

Here it also seems significant that philosophy is most akin to the STEM disciplines when it comes to the representation of women in its ranks—much closer than it is to other disciplinary areas that one might think have more in common with it. For example, in the United States, women make up 21 percent of academic philosophers based on figures from 2003 and 2009 (Norlock, 2006, 2011). This is comparable to their representation of 20.6 percent in the physical sciences and 22.2 percent in the life sciences in 2009 (Hill et al., 2010:18).[6] In contrast, Norlock reports that in 2003, women made up 41 percent of academics in the humanities as a whole (Norlock, 2006). Indeed, the broad comparison with other disciplines is instructive. History and sociology, for example, have dramatically improved their gender profile over the last 30 years, from not dissimilar starting points to philosophy. This has occurred through forms of feminist activism and scholarship that not only asserted the entitlement and capacities of women to enter and rise within disciplinary ranks, but also led to the enlargement of the scope of disciplinary knowledge by including attention to women and gender issues. Although there are ongoing debates within these fields about how well integrated feminist perspectives have become (Alway, 1995; England, 1999; Williams, 2006, Stacey, 2006; Osler, 1994; Lerner, 1999; Rupp, 2006), there has very clearly been considerable evolution in the terms on which disciplinary knowledge is formed with reference to an understanding of the profound and socially constitutive role of gender (a perspective, indeed, that as it developed drew significantly on feminist work in philosophy). If, as compared with those in philosophy, women in these other fields have achieved better representation and higher status, this might suggest the importance of speculation on the interconnections between the questions, methods, and modes of reasoning legitimated and fostered within a discipline, and the scope it allows for renegotiating the social boundaries constituted by gender.

---

[6] These STEM figures represent the percentages of *tenured* academic women in STEM fields in 2009. For more detailed figures including the representation of women in non-tenured academic positions in these fields, see Hill et al. (2010:18).

The fate of feminism in philosophy is touched upon in several of the essays collected here (see Bastian, Dodds and Goddard, Jenkins). The entry of women to philosophy saw the flourishing of feminist and gender scholarship from the early 1980s. In a survey conducted by Haslanger for the APA,[7] feminist philosophy appeared as the subject area identified with by more women than any other, while it figured for men as the subject area with which they least identified. Yet in recent journal rankings,[8] this area of publication boasted only one A* journal (*Hypatia*), whereas many of the most prestigious 'general' philosophy journals to make this grade publish extensively in analytic metaphysics and epistemology, but publish little or no feminist philosophy.[9] Although these rankings were subsequently abandoned by the Australian Research Council, they continue to be used to rank departments and academics in New Zealand (Rini, this volume). If sophisticated gender scholarship poses challenges to dominant conceptions of the discipline, it is worth asking how this challenge has been received. Have the presence of women in philosophy and the questions they have raised about how gender has inscribed thought made a difference to the subject? Are there conceptions of knowledge and reason at work that contain implicit bias, or simply highly persistent masculine images of who 'the philosopher' is that block women from advancing in this subject (see Friedman)? Certainly it is noteworthy that feminist philosophy, although a well-recognised field and one that many women identify as working within, nonetheless often has a more significant presence in areas categorised as specific 'gender studies' than in philosophy departments.

The questions posed by feminist philosophers may seem to have simply resulted in such scholarship becoming marginalised or a separate field of study. What would philosophy look like today if feminist scholarship had succeeded in transforming our contemporary understanding of the discipline through its challenge to authoritative and male-friendly norms? At its most radical, this leads to questions about the deep gendering of philosophical categories and intuitions. When we conceptualise experience, including the experiences of women in philosophy, do we tend to privilege the masculine frameworks that, as some of the most radical feminist philosophers argue, have delimited our fundamental metaphysical ideas, even such seemingly neutral elements of our

---

[7] "Preliminary Report of the Survey on publishing in Philosophy", APA Committee on the Status of Women in the Profession, December 2009, available at http://www.mit.edu/~shaslang/papers/HaslangerPRSPP.pdf, accessed Dec. 27, 2012.

[8] See the Australian Research Council's ERA 2010 journal rankings (http://www.arc.gov.au/era/era_2010/archive/era_journal_list.htm#1).

[9] Of the seven highly regarded general philosophy journals that Haslanger surveyed, five (*Journal of Philosophy, Mind, Noûs, Philosophical Review, Philosophy and Phenomenological Research*) were ranked A* by the Australian Research Council. According to Haslanger's data, between 2002 and 2007, none of these five journals published any work in feminist philosophy (Haslanger, 2008:220).

sense of reality as the dimensions of space or time? And how does this impact the experiences of women engaged in studying philosophy? These latter questions are forcefully taken up by Michelle Bastian in this volume, identifying in particular a way of thinking about time that, she argues, differentially shapes men's and women's lived experiences of doing philosophy.

Approaches that see masculinisation affecting fundamental categories of thought suggest that change will require entirely remaking the discipline. But there are other less radical approaches to the question of what would have to change within the discipline for women's representation and status within it to improve. For many of our contributors, the best approach is a piecemeal engagement with the many daily ways in which gender schemas can exert an influence in philosophy. They advocate a range of strategies to redress bias that is often unconscious, but which can be countered to the extent that its operation is acknowledged. Among the factors limiting change discussed in this volume are the influence of unconscious biases and the impact this has on women who internalise them (Saul), the cumulative effect of micro-inequities (Brennan), the tendency to identify women's differences from men with deviance from an uncritically adopted norm (Beebee), undergraduate teaching curricular (Friedman) and methods (Hutchison), as well as systemic failures to recognise women as partners to discussion, leading to their effective 'silencing' within the discipline (McGill).

Yet despite the importance of finding practicable solutions that leave intact much within the current practise of the discipline, the long history of gender bias in philosophy remains irreducibly important. Although significant work on this topic, perhaps beginning from Simone de Beauvoir's *The Second Sex*, might seem to belong to an earlier phase of feminist thinking, these writings instead prove relevant again and again to questions that women in the discipline find themselves wrestling with today. Certainly some key texts, including Genevieve Lloyd's study *The Man of Reason* (1993) and Moira Gaten's *Feminism and Philosophy* (1991), are frequent points of reference for the essays collected here. What apparently continues to need thought, some 20 or more years after these works were written, is how the exclusion of women, or, put differently, the fostering of men, might be playing a part in the ongoing formation of particular institutionally based disciplines, a question that demands interrogation of cultures, modes of judgment, schemas of bias, and patterns of reward *alongside* philosophical investigation of the gendering of fundamental metaphysical, ethical, and epistemological categories.

Such issues could readily lend themselves to sociological analysis or other ways of looking from an 'external' perspective at the factors shaping disciplinary formation and history. Local knowledge and experience, however, are invaluable assets. Here we have asked female philosophers to draw on their own experiences and internal knowledge of the discipline, its culture and institutional forms, to develop analyses of what lies behind the data and offer suggestions for what needs to change if philosophy is to become a discipline both more hospitable to women *and* more able to benefit from the contribution that including women will make to its future. Without combining internal knowledge of the subject matter, a deep understanding of philosophical reasoning, and the kinds of challenges feminists' contributions have thrown out to professional philosophy, as well as the workings of disciplinary decision-making and the typical cultures of classroom, seminars, or hiring committees, a key 'internal' dimension of analysis of what these statistics show would be missing. Moreover, women's participation in analysing the problems they face from the standpoint of actually encountering a range of negative experiences is surely a vital step toward a solution. Sharing experiences, analysis, and recommendations must aim to change the broader culture, addressing male, as well as female, colleagues, university leadership, and education and research agendas. As a crucial step, it also creates a sense of solidarity among women who are too often solo in their departments and prone to understand their experiences as attributable only to their individual circumstances or personal limitations. Perhaps it is only then that the sense of rage Haslanger speaks of can become part of a renewed momentum to build real and effective changes toward a more just and egalitarian future.

In the past few years, there have been a number of symposia and panel sessions on the participation and status of women in philosophy,[10] and these are exemplary of this kind of starting point, providing opportunities to share experiences, build solidarity, and generate momentum for change. Just such a symposium was held at the Australian National University in 2009 and provided the initial impetus to this project. Some common themes that emerged there have been reiterated in many other online forums[11]: experiences of a lack of encouragement or mentoring, of combative styles of argument at seminars and conferences, and of encountering narrow conceptions of disciplinary philosophy or of the value of pursuing certain topics, often seeming to disqualify areas that are of interest to women. If many had tales to tell along with these about where they had found support or about the palpable differences between 'friendly' and 'unfriendly' environments, too often it seems that established

---

[10] For example, the 2007 panel "Why are Women only 21% of Philosophy" at the APA's central division meeting in Chicago (see Kourany, 2009, for a discussion of this event); the 2009 symposium at the Australian National University (ANU) sponsored by the AAP, "Women in Philosophy: A Reflective Symposium"; and the conference on "Underrepresented groups in philosophy" presented by the Society of Women in Philosophy UK (SWIP-UK) and the British Philosophical Association (BPA) in Cardiff, Wales, 2010.

[11] Such as the blog, "What is it like to be a woman in philosophy?" (http://beingawomaninphilosophy.wordpress.com/); the women-in-philosophy category on the feminist philosophers blog (http://feministphilosophers.wordpress.com/category/women-in-philosophy/); and Leiter Reports: A Philosophy Blog (http://leiterreports.typepad.com/) where there is no specific category on the topic, but many posts and comments can be found with a simple search on 'women in philosophy'.

practitioners of philosophy lean toward the dismissive and savage criticism of work that is not well understood or assumed to fall beneath some mark of rational or argumentative rigour, the validity of which is taken for granted. One woman who had recently completed a Ph.D. gave a painful rendering of the dismissive and disrespectful way in which her thesis review had been handled, and how, upon complaining of this, she had been advised simply to "toughen up". Another recent graduate drew attention to the difficulties of justifying the choice to study philosophy to friends and family as a single mother occupying a social position associated with certain clear (and heavily morally weighted) practical responsibilities. As McKenzie and Townley comment in this volume, the association of philosophy with impractical and unworldly pursuits may be deterring to many students, to the disadvantage of themselves, as well as to the disadvantage of philosophy. Again, such aspects of the contemporary institution of philosophy raise significant concerns that it too often constitutes narrow and masculinist cultures, ones that are no doubt unfriendly to many men, as well as to many women and other marginalised groups.

Given these testimonies, one might wonder why women stay in philosophy at all. A significant refrain of discussions such as these has been the experience of finding a real passion for the discipline. Some indeed enjoy the scope it gives women to argue out theoretical positions with a robust indifference to 'feminine' protocols of compliant behaviour or 'niceness'. The tipping line between this agonism and situations where argument becomes a desire to undermine or trip up one's opponent deserves further thought (Beebee, Jenkins, and McGill all comment on it in this volume). The love of philosophy is for many women no doubt conjoined with irritation or disappointment in its dominant institutional forms and, interestingly, as documented by Haslanger (2008), it appears to be the case that many women with Ph.D.s in philosophy may pursue this interest and develop their capacities in friendlier cognate fields (such as linguistics, comparative literature, gender studies, or cognitive science), rather than remain within philosophy itself. Here, indeed, it is worth noting another frequent set of comments, recounted in this volume by Hutchison and Bastian, about the difficulty of *identifying* oneself as a philosopher. Cheshire Calhoun (2009) has argued that becoming a philosopher is not something many women contemplate because of the difficulty for women in identifying *as* a philosopher; even after years in the profession, she remarks on the difficulty of saying 'I *am* a philosopher' instead of 'I *teach* philosophy'. As other contributors here might put it, following Valian's approach, the schema for being a philosopher and the schema for being a woman still do not sit readily together. How then can we promote conceptions of philosophy that will not only give women a valid 'place' within it, but also better reflect women's experience of its value and importance, challenging narrow understandings of its role? Can we collectively build practices of philosophy that are not only formally inclusive but perceived by women themselves as a vitally important and worthwhile dimension of human life?

The essay that opens this volume begins from this last issue. The question of what philosophy is, indeed how it may continue to claim to be the love of wisdom, while being, as Nietzsche held, irreducibly reflective of one's perspective and situation, frames Marilyn Friedman's discussion. If the identity of the person who does philosophy has an effect on the questions raised and the answers reached, then it should concern all involved that women participate in and shape it. Exploring how women may be discouraged from doing so, Friedman examines the contemporary presentation of the character of philosophy and the philosopher, particularly as given in introductory undergraduate textbooks. To care about the participation of women in philosophy, she argues, is to revise gendered conceptions of who the philosopher must be, but also to consider the intrinsic benefits to philosophy. Here Friedman considers both the effect on current students and academic staff and the potential for improving philosophy's realisation of two of its aims: offering practical wisdom to help us in our lives and turning a critical eye upon other disciplines.

One might equally make the argument that it vitally matters to philosophers themselves, in a sense intrinsic to their discipline, that they look to eliminate bias in their judgments. Jennifer Saul puts forward this argument and then goes on to note two problematic phenomena that have been the subject of considerable recent research in social psychology. First, bias can be shown to be much less readily available to rational reflection and correction than most philosophers have imagined; rather, it continues to shape reactions and judgments regardless of views that might be held explicitly and consciously—for instance, that women should be treated equally. Second, Saul points to the phenomenon of stereotype threat, such that stereotypes are 'active' in environments, regardless of whether the stereotype is actually overtly held to be true by other parties or not. For instance, a stereotypical schema that suggests girls are poor at math will lead to girls underperforming whenever they encounter 'reminders' of it. Philosophical writings and also ordinary situations such as the department seminar can be full of such 'reminders' of stereotypical ideas, such as those that link women to emotion and not reason. Saul explores how this generates environments experienced as hostile by women and undermines their ability to perform well, in ways that men who are present may be blithely unaware of, and indeed in ways that women who are affected may also be unaware of.

Helen Beebee, like Saul, looks to psychology for an explanation of the underrepresentation of women in philosophy. Her primary focus, however, is on the specific issue of deviance and the way that a group responds to a deviant individual or minority. Because women are a minority in philosophy, any ways in which they differ from men will tend to be cast as 'deviant'; and it is those cast in this way who are expected to change to fit in with the 'typical' individuals. Applying this to two aspects of philosophical practice, the combative seminar room or discussion and the role of intuitions as philosophical data, she argues for the need to examine and change teaching practices. If combative behaviour is the norm in the philosophy classroom, and women are less comfortable or less likely to engage in this manner, the interpretation most likely to be given is that women need to change (perhaps just to 'toughen up', as in the advice given to the graduate student). People's intuitions are often at the centre of classroom discussion, as well as broader work in analytic philosophy. Beebee reflects on the likelihood that in the classroom environment, philosophy tutors and lecturers might read one set of intuitions (the 'typical' or majority set) as 'right' and the other 'deviant' (minority) set of intuitions as 'wrong' and thereby alienate those who are persistently given the feedback that their intuitions are 'wrong'. If these happen to disproportionately be women or non-white students, then these students might, unsurprisingly, be made to feel stupid, tend to lose interest, and abandon further study.

The observations Beebee makes about intuitions are especially interesting insofar as they hint at important future revolutions that might occur within epistemology and in philosophy more broadly to accommodate this sort of finding. One might think of the influence in the field of ethics of Carol Gilligan's work (Gilligan, 1982) on differences between male and female intuitions about moral questions, which has served to throw doubt on the gendered nature of assumptions about 'mature' judgment, as reflected in the theoretical work of Kohlberg (1981). When developmental 'maturity' in fact turned out to be a way of codifying typical or normative masculinity, this finding lent a significant piece of evidence to the feminist argument that fields of study are strongly shaped and inflected by the particularistic biases of those generating their findings (such as Harding, 1991). If to some, it is still not obvious why it matters that science or philosophy is done by women as well as men, this is often because of a view that pursuing objective truth is work that goes beyond any question of the contexts that shape the social identities of truth-seekers. Yet that is an idea that has been strongly challenged by standpoint epistemology (Code, 1991; Harding, 1991; Hartsock, 1983; Smith, 1974), which points not only to the irreducibly situated character of inquiry, but also to how removing serious contestants in shaping an understanding of the world, by excluding the perspectives of those differently situated, allows the particular to pose as universal and omits the often superior insight of the marginalised. This worry, however, leads to the need to examine the political contexts in which certain views become entrenched and uncontestable while other voices are silenced.

Fiona Jenkins takes up this question as integral to the problems women face in getting their contributions valued as highly as men, and discusses how a situation emerges in which promoting disciplinary excellence and promoting equity goals come to seem disjunct and often competing agendas. She argues that meritocratic selection for academic positions, which is charged with ensuring that bias is removed, can in fact appear as a particularly powerful site where this separation between disciplinary excellence and equity goals occurs. Even as it seems that the assessment of the 'best' work and 'best' people should be an important avenue for overturning established hierarchies, placing too much faith in meritocratic mechanisms can paradoxically be an obstacle to women seeking change. Entrenched privilege is preserved insofar as received standards of excellence, which reflect the past of the discipline, persistently shape entry into and promotion within the discipline in ways that will tend to reproduce masculine dominance. This in turn reflects a social landscape that is wider than philosophy alone and exercises distinctive contemporary pressures. The nature of the 'gendered academy' suggests that changing philosophy will require a broader intervention into the ways and means by which elite status is established for institutions and disciplines. Yet philosophy also needs to foster pluralism and to seriously integrate feminist critiques of power. The good of philosophy (its excellence) and the good of women working within it must cease to be seen as rival goals.

Philosophy is under many sorts of institutional pressure, including the 'performance' pressures of the corporate university and the need to increase student numbers in order to sustain the existence of departments. If women are leaving philosophy in the numbers indicated here, it becomes a matter of survival to make philosophy more hospitable to women's interests and to reflect critically on what philosophy risks by virtue of its common public perception as an irrelevant and leisurely occupation, rather than a discipline that is creative and innovative, working at the limits of ideas. One wager of this book's discussion of women in philosophy is that issues of gender representation are not unrelated to the frequently narrow and conservative conceptions of the discipline that are dominant in many departments of philosophy, as well as the wider society. Within this, however, there is a particular problem that philosophy has, as compared with many other disciplines, in establishing the nature of its claims to knowledge, or more broadly, the character of authority within the discipline. Katrina Hutchison addresses this by examining the problem of how students and early career philosophers establish their credibility in the field, and how they come (or fail to come) to exercise theoretical authority as philosophers. She offers an analysis of the nature of philosophy that contrasts it with other disciplines to support an argument that attributions of theoretical authority within philosophy are more subject to distortion than in some other disciplines. Nonetheless, she argues that it is possible to identify some of the ways in which philosophers do establish their credibility—through the ability to use a range of methods. Such methods thus form important areas for future research and teaching focus. Understanding the methods that philosophers in fact use to establish their credibility will better equip students (including female students) to progress according to acknowledged criteria, rather than foundering, as many currently do, within the 'mystique' of tacit understandings that lend themselves to masculine bias.

The question of how work is assessed as being of value, what kinds of academic credibility it has, and what the gendered implications of this may be is further developed by Adriane Rini. Her discussion begins from the startling fact that between July 2005 and April 2013, 20 men were appointed to positions in philosophy in New Zealand, but only one woman was. Exploring the possible background to this, Rini draws attention to the context of rubrics for assessing work that relies upon highly problematic assumptions about how excellence and achievement are to be measured. Like a number of other countries surveyed here, New Zealand has introduced journal rankings as a proxy for evaluating the quality of work, and these rankings powerfully shape appointments and promotions. Yet there is little or no justification given for why journals publishing predominantly on certain subject areas of the discipline figure so highly in these rankings while those focused on other areas of specialization, notably those where women are better represented (including feminist philosophy and history of philosophy), are given only low ratings. By drawing on Haslanger's work on women's representation in 'top journals' (2008), further evidence emerges that the favoured areas are also those where men are most intensely concentrated. Rini contemplates the dilemma that women must face when they are advised that in order to do well in professional terms they must conform to norms established by existing success and achievement in this hugely male-dominated field. Deploying Plato's famous allegory of the cave, Rini throws doubt on how current standards of perception are forged and asks who are the true philosophers here—those who remain wedded to the values and perceptions forged in the sanguine life of the cave, or those who, moved by a genuine spirit of inquiry and love of wisdom, find themselves at an uncomfortable critical distance from its privileges and assumptions?

In their chapter, Susan Dodds and Eliza Goddard also examine the institutional conditions of philosophy, focusing in particular on the kinds of pressure that representative national bodies are able—and willing—to place on individual philosophy departments to take up the recommendations of reports on the status of women. Through a careful analysis of several reports on the status of women by the AAP, undertaken over three decades, they identify a prevailing tendency to take up recommendations that follow from the "pipeline model" while ignoring the reports' recommendations for broader cultural change. Arguing that the pipeline model is deeply misleading and has been proven erroneous over time, they identify several features of contemporary philosophical culture that demand change, as well as the need for further research into student experiences, alternative pedagogies, and changing public understandings of the importance and relevance of philosophy.

These important questions also shape Catriona Mackenzie and Cynthia Townley's contribution. Specifically, they begin by unsettling the assumption that the success of philosophy departments should be measured by the number of Ph.D.s and eventually academic philosophers they produce, and instead consider what a philosophy department might look like if it took the needs of all its students seriously, expanding conceptions of success for graduates of philosophy. They recommend here the identification and advocacy of 'happy' outcomes other than that of becoming a professional philosopher. The conclusion does not shy away from the difficult question of who will hear this message, and the possibility that it will discourage more women than men from pursuing careers as professional philosophers (or, perhaps, encourage more women than men to pursue happy careers outside of philosophy). But the discussion raises crucial questions about how the value of pursuing philosophy is to be understood in relation to life possibilities. It builds on concerns voiced in several of the previous chapters about the narrowness of institutional philosophy and echoes some of the concerns Friedman raises about how, in substantive ways, we should take up the claim that philosophy is a study that is of value for what it *gives back* to life.

In the remainder of the chapters in this volume, the focus returns to analysing how subtle exclusions take shape, often in ways that seem all but invisible to everyone concerned. Samantha Brennan begins by asking why, in the face of goodwill and political commitment, we have failed to meet the goals of women's participation and gender equity to which we have so often previously committed. Her analysis points to the role of micro-inequities that Mary Rowe, commenting on her experiences in addressing gender bias at MIT, defines as "apparently small events which are often ephemeral and hard-to-prove, events which are covert, often unintentional, frequently unrecognized by the perpetrator, which occur wherever people are perceived to be 'different'" (Rowe, 2008:45). In the MIT investigation, it was discovered that men were systemically given more laboratory space than women, a seemingly trivial finding that in fact directly impacted women's ability to perform well, as well as reflecting hidden assumptions about their lesser 'needs'. Brennan looks at how feedback effects ensure that the higher expectations of masculine prowess in philosophy prove self-confirming, while responsibility for giving women equal opportunities to shine vanishes under the rubrics of paternalistic protection. The chapter draws attention to how hard it can be to see micro-inequities when people are focused only on detecting the 'big' and obvious examples of discrimination. Once again, this is an example of how feminist investigations might shape philosophy for the better, as Brennan argues that it is important for moral philosophy in general to attend to systemic micro-inequities, even in the absence of any intentional ill will or deliberate harm being perpetrated.

Looking to dramatise and demonstrate the significance of experiences that might well be attributed to the order of micro-inequities, Justine McGill investigates how women 'fall silent' in philosophy. McGill hypothesizes that one can find oneself silenced through the repeated experience of the failure of one's speech acts, as tacit assumptions on the part of the audience of an intended communication intervene to nullify, misrepresent, or interrupt a woman's meaning. Women's participation in conversations may be blocked from the outset by the presumption that the other party already 'knows' what they are saying, and McGill defends the strong claim that this may constitute a form of violence. This is a point she draws out with reference to Langton and West's (1999) application of speech act theory to the pornographic power to silence women, a power that seems capable of turning a 'no' into a 'yes' by nullifying the force of the former. If women are expected to perform within a language game carried on among men, they may find themselves disqualified as participants and are reminded of a vulnerability that follows from having one's capacity to speak seriously eroded under prejudicial conditions of reception. McGill considers how this situation might improve and argues for the patient exposition and critical unveiling of the unexamined presuppositions that shape silencing, arguing both that the presence of these in philosophy is properly a cause of disciplinary shame and that *realising* this shame might bring about change. Framing her discussion through careful analysis of the writings of a Buddhist nun, she also stages the retrieval from exclusion of writings that have never formed part of an acknowledged philosophical canon and thus may stand for a deep level of silencing in the constitution of tradition.

This last point not only draws attention to the problematic issue of how male voices dominate the history of philosophy, but also suggests that fundamental dimensions of experience for men and women in philosophy may be constituted in profoundly different ways. These claims receive a distinctive direction in Michelle Bastian's chapter through an exploration of philosophy and time. She foregrounds the common assumption that time is an objective and neutral backdrop to experience, one on which men's and women's differences have no bearing. Contesting this, she examines how time operates as social modality and an explanatory discourse, producing profound disjunctions between gendered roles, such as that of 'mother' and 'philosopher'. Indeed, within the temporal inheritance of philosophical legacies, exclusions are carried into the future by uncritically assuming that 'what has been' will shape the present and the future. Bastian illustrates how this occurs for women of colour who encounter in others the 'impossibility' of imagining such a being as a black female philosopher. Adapting Christine Battersby's important work contesting the Kantian account of space and time as 'containers' of bodies (Battersby, 1998), Bastian develops the idea that we should attend to the lived time and social temporality of different bodies, and thus focuses the question of how what is 'timely', 'too late', or 'to come' shapes gendered expectations, explanations, and contradictions. Her call is for philosophers to become aware of the need to negotiate multiple speeds and subtle differences of rhythm, as well as becoming more attuned to how social constructions of time can be understood as supportive of some ways of life over others. If the transformations in the discipline that will make room for women are truly to come about, Bastian argues, temporality itself demands a deconstruction.

Bastian's idea that philosophy should not already be "colonised for a particular kind of philosopher" but rather that it should have "a conception of the future as unpredictable and surprising" forms a leitmotif for this volume. It is worth noting that in spite of the many differences among the contributions, one of the most recurring themes in the collection is suggested by these words—almost all contributors have called for an expansive conception of philosophy, for plurality both topical and methodological. The implications of this are significant. Several factors dominate institutional philosophy at present that might work against the goals of pluralism. These include the trend to create smaller departments with narrower research specialisations that are developed to be competitive in excellence rankings, but create disciplinary spaces in which it is difficult to encourage breadth of teaching and learning, and as such are also unable to support diverse cohorts (as Mackenzie and Townley advocate). More research is surely needed on how women have been impacted by the adaptations of the discipline to contemporary conditions. But beside this, we need to re-imagine the futures of philosophy, no longer as the practise of a highly restricted set of members, fractured by gender, race, and class, but as capable of incorporating a wider wisdom, the true *Sofia* of its proper name.

References

Alcoff, Linda Martin, ed. (2003) *Singing in the Fire: Stories of Women in Philosophy*, New York: Rowman & Littlefield.

Alcoff, Linda Martin, and Elizabeth Potter (1993) *Feminist Epistemologies*, London and New York: Routledge.

Alway, Joan (1995) "The Trouble with Gender: Tales of the Still-Missing Feminist Revolution in Sociological Theory", *Sociological Theory*, Vol. 13, No. 3, 209–228.

Armstrong, John (2011) "Reformation and renaissance: New life for the humanities", *Griffith Review*, Edition 31, 13–51.

Battersby, Christine (1998) *The phenomenal woman: Feminist metaphysics and the patterns of identity*, New York: Routledge.

Beauvoir, Simone de (1989) *The Second Sex*, trans. Parshley, New York: Vintage.

Boileau, Laura, and Christine Daigle (2009) "Summary of the Equity Survey for the CPA (2007–2009)" published on the Canadian Philosophical Association's Equity Committee website (http://www.acpcpa.ca/documents/Surveypercent202009percent20Finalpercent20Reportpercent20En.pdf).

Calhoun, Cheshire (2009) "The Undergraduate Pipeline Problem", *Hypatia*, Vol. 24, No. 2, 216–223.

Code, Lorraine (1991) *What Can She Know? Feminist Theory and the Construction of Knowledge*, Ithaca, NY: Cornell University Press.

England, Paula (1999) "The Impact of Feminist Thought on Sociology", *Contemporary Sociology*, Vol. 28, No. 3, 263–268.

Gatens, Moira (1991) *Feminism and Philosophy: Perspectives on Difference and Equality*, Bloomington, IN: Indiana University Press.

Gilligan, Carol (1982) *In a Different Voice: Psychological Theory and Women's Development*, Cambridge, MA: Harvard University Press.

Harding, S. (1991) *Whose Science, Whose Knowledge? Thinking from Women's Lives*, Ithaca, NY: Cornell University Press.

Hartsock, Nancy (1983) "The Feminist Standpoint: Developing the Ground for a Specifically Feminist Historical Materialism" in Harding and Hintikka, eds., *Discovering Reality: Feminist Perspectives on Epistemology, Metaphysics, Methodology, and the Philosophy of Science*, 283–310, Dordrecht, NL: D. Reidel.

Haslanger, Sally (2008) "Changing the Ideology and Culture of Philosophy: Not by Reason (Alone)", *Hypatia*, Vol. 23, No. 2, 210–223.

Hill, C., C. Corbett, and A. Rose (2010) "Why so Few?: Women in Science, Technology, Engineering and Mathematics" published by the American Association of University Women (http://www.aauw.org/learn/research/upload/whysofew.pdf).

Kant, Immanuel (2011) *Observations on the Feeling of the Beautiful and Sublime and Other Writings*, ed. and trans. Frierson and Guyer, Cambridge, UK: Cambridge University Press.

Kohlberg, Lawrence (1981) *The Philosophy of Moral Development: Moral Stages and the Idea of Justice (Essays on Moral Development Volume 1)*, New York: Harper and Row.

Kourany, Janet A. (2009) "Why are Women only 21% of Philosophy?: Introduction to the Panel Presentations", *APA Newsletter on Feminism and Philosophy*, Vol. 8, No. 2, 9–10.

Langton, Rae, and Caroline West (1999) "Scorekeeping in a pornographic language game", *Australasian Journal of Philosophy*, 77(3): 303–319.

Le Dœuff, Michèle (2003) *The Sex of Knowing*, trans. Hamer and Code, New York and London: Routledge.

Le Dœuff, Michèle (1990) *Hipparchia's Choice: An Essay Concerning Women, Philosophy etc.*, trans. Trista Selous, Oxford, UK: Blackwell.

Le Dœuff, Michèle (1989) *The Philosophical Imaginary*, trans. Gordon, London and New York: Continuum.

Lerner, Gerda (1999) "Women among the professors of history: the story of a process of transformation", in *Voices of women historians: The personal, the political, the professional*, 1–10, Eileen Boris and Nupur Chaudhuri, eds., Bloomington, IN: Indiana University Press.

Lloyd, Genevieve (1993). *The Man of Reason: "Male" and "Female" in Western Philosophy*, Minneapolis: University of Minnesota Press.

Norlock, Kathryn J. (2011) "Update on the Status of Women" published on the American Philosophical Association's Committee for the Status of Women website (https://docs.google.com/viewer?a=v&pid=sites&srcid=ZGVmYXVsdGRvbWFpbnxhcGFjb21taXR0ZWVvbnRoZXN0YXR1c29md29tZW58Z3g6NzkxYmU5NGU0NzRjNjk1Nw).

Norlock, Kathryn J. (2006) "Women in the Profession: A more formal report to the CSW" published on the American Philosophical Association's Committee for the Status of Women website (https://docs.google.com/viewer?a=v&pid=sites&srcid=ZGVmYXVsdGRvbWFpbnxhcGFjb21taXR0ZWVvbnRoZXN0YXR1c29md29tZW58Z3g6MTBkMjEyYmExMDg2NDZjjYQ).

Nussbaum, Martha C. (2010) *Not for Profit: Why Democracy Needs the Humanities*, Princeton, NJ: Princeton University Press.

Osler, Audrey (1994) "Still Hidden from History? The representation of women in recently published history textbooks", *Oxford Review of Education*, Vol. 20, No. 2, 219–235.

Rowe, Mary. (2008) "Micro-affirmations and micro-inequities", *Journal of the International Ombudsman Association* 1: 45–48.

Rupp, Leila J. (2006) "Is the Feminist Revolution Still Missing? Reflections from Women's History", *Social Problems*, Vol. 53, No. 4, 466–472.

Schopenhauer, Arthur (1970) *Essays and Aphorisms*, trans. Hollingdale, London and New York: Penguin.

Smith, Dorothy E. (1974) "Women's Perspective as a Radical Critique of Sociology", *Sociological Inquiry*, Vol. 44, No. 1, 7–13.

Stacey, Judith (2006) "Feminism and Sociology in 2005: What Are We Missing?", *Social Problems*, Vol. 53, No. 4, 479–482.

Valian, Virginia (1999) *Why So Slow? The Advancement of Women* Cambridge, MA: MIT Press.

Williams, Christine (2006) "Still Missing? Comments on the Twentieth Anniversary of 'The Missing Feminist Revolution in Sociology'", *Social Problems*, Vol. 53, No. 4, 454–458.

{ 1 }

Women in Philosophy

WHY SHOULD WE CARE?

Marilyn Friedman

1. Introduction

Why should we care whether women participate in professional philosophy in roughly equal numbers to men? Would philosophy be better for it? Would *women* be better for it?

Philosophy has not always been regarded in a favorable light. Nietzsche, for one, regarded philosophy and philosophers "half suspiciously, half mockingly" and suggested that philosophers lied about the deepest matters (1966:12). What each philosopher presented as truth and the result of logic and reason, wrote Nietzsche, was "at bottom" nothing more than "an assumption, a hunch, indeed a kind of 'inspiration'—most often a desire of the heart that has been filtered and made abstract" and defended "with reasons they have sought after the fact." Despite pretensions to the contrary, "in the philosopher...there is nothing whatever that is impersonal; and above all, his morality bears decided and decisive witness to *who he is*—that is, in what order of rank the innermost drives of his nature stand in relation to each other." All was not lost, in Nietzsche's view, for philosophical deceptions might be a foolishness[1] that was "necessary for the preservation of just such beings as we are." To grasp this, it might, Nietzsche suggests, be useful to suppose that "not just man is the 'measure of things'" (1966:11–14).

Borrowing Nietzsche's words, though not his meaning, we might say that this volume is devoted to the idea that "not just *man* is the measure of things." Philosophy should certainly reflect that insight. Even if philosophical works express merely the "innermost drives" of philosophers, there may still be good reasons to promote women's increased participation in the field. I return to my

---

[1] Nietzsche uses the French word *niaiserie* (stupidity) (1966:11).

original question: Would philosophy or women benefit if women participated in equal numbers to men?[2]

Sally Haslanger has recently written of the rage she feels about the treatment of women and minorities in the field of philosophy (2008:210–212). Haslanger's recent discussion and others like it are highly critical of professional philosophy.[3] One wonders: If philosophy is riddled with such problems for women, why should we bother to enter the field? Why not simply abandon it and encourage women to go into fields that welcome us and value our work properly? Haslanger suggests that her "deep love for philosophy" kept her in the field despite the disrespect, devaluation, and mistreatment she either endured or witnessed (2008:210). This is a crucial point to mention. If we are warranted in encouraging more women to enter professional philosophy and changing the field to make it more welcoming and respectful toward women, then there must be something worth salvaging about professional philosophy. One way to encourage more women to join the field is to tell them what there is about the activity of philosophy that is worth their while.

I will not try to tell that story here. Instead, I try to single out aspects of philosophy that may be sources of the *problems* that Haslanger and other women have experienced in philosophy. In the next section, I comment briefly on what I term the "business" side of philosophy, and the extent to which difficulties faced by women can be attributed to it. In section 3, I survey some introductory philosophy textbooks and articles that discuss the nature of philosophy in order to see whether there are hints of anti-female bias in what philosophers say about our discipline when reflecting on what it is that we do. In section 4, I return to the question of whether we should care if philosophy marginalizes women, and if so, how we might go about changing those exclusionary practices.

2. The Business of Philosophy

Philosophy is the love of wisdom. But, in what sense is it this today?

In the *Republic*, Plato draws a famous distinction between what people do in their roles as the particular tradespeople and professionals they are from what they do to earn *income* from their trades and professions. Philosophers as income-earners are not acting in their capacities as lovers of wisdom. Instead, today, they are acting as ordinary paid employees who work for non-profit but

---

[2] It can also be asked of any other group that is currently underrepresented in philosophy whether its members should participate at near the rate of its percentage in the surrounding population. This chapter concentrates on the category of women, assuming this group to contain ethnic, racial, and other forms of population diversity.

[3] See, for example, the essays in the "Symposium: Women Philosophers, Sidelined Challenges, and Professional Philosophy," *Hypatia*, Vol. 20, No. 3 (Summer 2005), 149–213.

still corporate-like enterprises, usually colleges and universities. This is the business side of philosophy, complete with its own corporate (in this case, academic) politics. The environment is competitive, and everyone's self-interest is at stake.

Many of the criticisms levelled at the professional field of academic philosophy are about the business side of the field. Much of the discrimination against women in philosophy occurs in the course of the business practices that maintain the philosophy profession. These include hiring, firing, salaries, promotions, tenuring, adding new positions, cutting old positions, teaching assignments, departmental budgets, departmental administration, and the conversational dynamics of departmental life.

Unfortunately, the business side of philosophy is unavoidable for nearly all those who enter the field. To be sure, people can do philosophy without academic employment. Philosophy is not a strictly regulated profession like medicine or law. Anyone, whether employed in a school or not, whether holding a post-secondary degree or not, can legally engage in the activity of philosophy and try to publish or broadcast their ideas somehow to the wider world. However, philosophy has an informally closed nature that is apparent to anyone who wants to practice philosophy in the academy. Existing members of the profession determine who else will be admitted to academic employment, granted tenure, and published in refereed publications. Thus current members of the philosophy profession act as de facto gatekeepers who largely determine which persons do—or do not—carry on the future academic work of the field.[4]

The business side of philosophy gives people power over the careers of those lower than they are on the academic totem pole, and tempts the more powerful players to use that power in ways that serve their own interests and desires. It is tempting to criticize or vote against someone whose philosophical perspective threatens one's own, who espouses a philosophical position one detests, who outshines one as a teacher, or whom one simply does not personally like. In making these decisions, philosophers as employees, or in some cases as administrators or program heads, can be as cutthroat as employees at any large for-profit corporation.

Discrimination against women, prompted by the business side of philosophy, may be a large part of what discourages women from continuing in the field. It is certainly not as an income-earning activity that there is anything special to love about philosophy, nor does anyone love the academic politics of professional philosophy, unless they are a bit demented. Unfortunately, the academic rat race of philosophy will not go away anytime soon. (Of course, this does not provide an excuse to ignore the problem of discrimination, and the subsequent discussion does not ignore it.)

---

[4] Some commentators on this issue have suggested that women are more disadvantaged than men by this aspect of philosophy. See the chapters by Hutchison, Jenkins, and Rini in this volume.

3. Methods of Philosophy

The problems with philosophy as a business cannot be the whole explanation, however, for women's underrepresentation in the field. There are other academic fields that are equally business-like yet in which women participate in roughly equal numbers to men or even in greater numbers than men (see Walker, 2005:158). Also, students of philosophy do not typically become aware of the business side of philosophy before graduate school. So this aspect of the field would not help to explain why women as undergraduate students do not pursue advanced studies in philosophy in particular. It is legitimate to wonder whether something about the nature of philosophy itself is also at the root of the problem of women's relatively low numbers in the field.

Of course, things have changed over time for women in philosophy. After 2,400 years of philosophical practice, the lovers of wisdom no longer formally exclude women from the field of philosophy, including its business side. As noted earlier, women amount to about a quarter of professional philosophers now in some countries. Writings by women are published, cited, discussed, and sometimes influential. Yet women remain underrepresented in sheer numbers and in their publication rates in "top-ranked" philosophy journals (see Haslanger, 2008:220–221). Thus, it still makes sense to wonder whether features of the practice of philosophy as such are covertly (or overtly) inhospitable to women.

It is not hard to find aspects of philosophy, unrelated to the rat race of academia, that provide an inhospitable environment for women. As Margaret Walker explains, women have tried to participate in philosophy in all historic periods in which the field has existed, but their male philosophical contemporaries seem to have paid little attention to them and did not take up the women's concerns as important philosophical issues (Walker, 2005:154). Many men in philosophy, like many men everywhere, have historically not engaged respectfully and attentively in serious intellectual interchanges with women. This practice seems connected to the informally closed nature of philosophy and the way those already in the profession act as gatekeepers who determine who gets to enter and stay in the academic field, whose voices are heard in prestigious refereed publications, and so on. Most of the historically acclaimed men of the philosophical canon, in their philosophical writings, criticized women's abilities to reason and do philosophy (see Tuana, 1992). Philosophy has a small but very resilient canon, so the misogynist attitudes of these important historical figures remain alive in the philosophical canon today.

We are looking for at least two sorts of problems. First, some features of philosophy might lead philosophical gatekeepers to devalue women or otherwise make it difficult for women to engage in philosophical work. Second, some features of philosophy might alienate women from philosophy and prompt them to avoid the field. These two sorts of problems might coincide but they need not. The likeliest aspects of philosophy that might deter or alienate women are (1) the contents of philosophy, its distinctive questions, issues, and ideas; (2) the methods, broadly construed, that are used in philosophy to deal with that content; and (3) the way in which philosophy is taught and communicated. The canonical philosophers, as noted above, who deprecated women's philosophical or rational abilities were thereby contributing to the contents of philosophy. In the rest of this discussion, I focus on the second and third of the three areas: philosophical methods, and the way in which philosophy is taught and communicated.

Stephen Toulmin discusses what he calls a "familiar" characterization of philosophers, one that seems to reveal a philosophical method or approach that could alienate women from the field. According to this characterization described (and disparaged) by Toulmin, philosophers are

> just logic-choppers and paradox-mongers who trade on the confusions produced by playing word games with tricky abstract nouns; hence their claim to achieve profound insights, whether into the nature of the world or into the workings of people's minds, is simply presumptuous rubbish. They ought, rather, to leave the material cosmos to the physicists, mental activities to the psychologists, and keep their pointless word games to themselves. (Toulmin, 1976:11)

If this is philosophy, no wonder women have relatively little interest in entering the field. It is not clear why men would enter the field either, unless men were more enamored than women of "logic-chopping" and "paradox-mongering."

However, we should keep in mind that philosophy is not well understood in the popular imagination, as any philosopher can report who has ever tried to tell a non-academic group of people what she does for a living. The characterization that Toulmin rejects is merely a caricature. Philosophers in general do not accept Nietzsche's view that their philosophies are nothing more than rationalizations for their "innermost drives." Similarly, they reject the caricature of their reasonings as "pointless word games." Philosophers, for the most part, continue to advertise their theories as the results of reason. In that case, however, the age-old schema of woman as defective in reasoning ability could be working its evil magic still today. It could be a major part of the explanation for the underrepresentation of women in philosophy.

I suggest, however, that this is not a helpful insight. It is too crude. The ways of reason are many, complicated, and nuanced. It might be more helpful to see if there are *specific images* of reason and reasoners in philosophy that are discouraging women from entering the field and leading those already in the field to regard and evaluate women as less than fully capable of philosophical activity. Perhaps there are particular manifestations of reasoners and reasoning ability in philosophy that are especially antithetical to women (see, for example, Rooney, 2010).

Introductory philosophy textbooks provide illuminating windows into the views of professional philosophers about the methods of reasoning in philosophy. Consider Robert Solomon's textbook, *Introducing Philosophy: Problems and Perspectives* (1977).[5] In his introduction to the book, Solomon makes the familiar claim that philosophy "is a critical approach to all subjects." It is "a life of ideas or the life of reason. It is thinking, about everything and anything. But mainly, it is living thoughtfully." So far, so good. Solomon also suggests that philosophy enlarges "our view of ourselves and our knowledge of the world, allowing us to break out of prejudices and harmful habits which we have held since we were too young or too naïve to know better." Philosophy enables us to defend our positions with arguments and learn about alternatives to them. We secure our positions "on intellectual ground in place of the fragile supports provided by inherited prejudices, fragments of parental advice, and mindless slogans borrowed from television commercials and televised demagogues" (Solomon, 1977:7–8). This view, too, is not particularly troublesome, as long as we do not equate problematic "parental advice" with "old wives' tales."

A possible problem arises, however, with what Solomon's says is his particular approach to philosophy, namely, that it is focused on "the autonomy of the individual person." He elaborates:

> This means that each of us must be credited with the ability to ascertain what is true and what is right, through our own thinking and experience, without the usual appeal to outside authority: parents, teachers, popes, kings or a majority of peers. Whether you believe in God or not must be decided by you, by appeal to your own reason and arguments which you can formulate and examine by yourself.... This stress on individual autonomy stands at the very foundation of contemporary Western thought. We might say that it is our most basic assumption. (Accordingly, we shall have to examine it as well; but the obvious place to begin is to assume that we are—each of us—capable of carrying out the reflection and criticism that philosophy demands of us.) (Solomon, 1977:10)

Further elaborating his view, Solomon writes that Descartes is "the ideal starting point" for "anyone beginning to study philosophy today" because he helped to inaugurate the modern version of the emphasis on individual autonomy by locating the "ultimate authority" to decide matters of belief and rightness "in our own thinking and experience, nowhere else" (Solomon, 1977:11).

Perhaps an emphasis on individually autonomous reason, not reason as such, has been a factor that has discouraged, and continues to discourage, some

---

[5] Although this textbook dates from 1977, the textbooks of that era might provide especially useful clues as to why women are underrepresented at advanced ranks in philosophy today.

women from entering philosophy. Feminist philosophers have recently challenged the ideal of autonomy, particularly its individualist version. Social, relational, or intersubjective accounts of autonomy have become common among feminists (see, for example, Mackenzie & Stoljar, 2000). To be sure, not all female philosophers are feminist, and not all feminist philosophers are female. There probably were female students of philosophy who were not put off by a Solomonic emphasis on individual autonomy. Some women did enter the field of philosophy in recent decades, so an emphasis on individual autonomy might have discouraged only some women from entering the field. Yet perhaps this sort of emphasis is *part* of the explanation why there are fewer women than men in philosophy today.[6]

Granted, only some philosophers and textbooks in recent decades have emphasized Solomon's individually autonomous approach. A quick survey of other textbooks of the same period as Solomon's does not turn up other mentions of autonomy or the image of the isolated philosophical reasoner.[7] Other textbooks give more emphasis than Solomon does to engaging in dialogue with others. Robert Paul Wolff's textbook, *About Philosophy*, for example, refers to philosophy explicitly as "a dialogue between two people" (Wolff, 1976:7). So the image of an isolated reasoner appealing to her "own reason and arguments" cannot be the whole story about why many women might have found philosophy unappealing.[8]

Yet, even the textbook references to philosophical dialogue might seem inhospitable to women. Wolff focuses specifically on the Socratic method in philosophy, which he characterizes as a *hierarchical* dialogue between a "novice" and a philosopher, in which the philosopher must use irony and other "tricks" to get around the "enormous" resistance each novice will put up to learning what "he needs to learn" (Wolff, 1976:7). This model of asymmetric, competitive dialogue sounds more like a contest of wills, a verbal smackdown, than a mutually supportive or respectful interchange.

This image leads us to perhaps the most important and pervasive feature of philosophical practice that could be alienating women: the adversarial style of philosophical dialogue. Many years ago, Janice Moulton chastised philosophers for their adversarial style and for treating this style as the single most important paradigm of philosophical method (Moulton, 1980, 2003). According to this paradigm, philosophical work is to be subjected to the strongest possible criticism, and only the work that can survive such opposition is to be considered philosophically worthwhile. Moulton does not reject

---

[6] Diana Meyers summarizes research that suggests that traditional female socialization makes women less likely than men to achieve autonomy competency; see Meyers, 1989, Part 3.

[7] See the references below to other philosophy textbooks.

[8] I should say that it may not be part of the story at all. My suggestions are speculative and intended to encourage dialogue among philosophers about the causes of women's underrepresentation in the field.

the adversarial method entirely. However, she argues both that there are other methods that should not be neglected and that the adversarial method may distort our understanding of the issues involved in any philosophical interchange (Moulton, 1980:419–421).

What is of special note about the adversarial method in the present context is that it operates by way of criticism and opposition. Philosophical dialogue in the adversarial mode consists of objections and counterexamples to which the best responses are *refutations* of objections and counterexamples followed by *more of the same*. The competitive attacks are unending. Fledgling philosophers have to learn the hard lesson of "not taking it personally" when their favourite theory is destroyed by others. They have to learn not to invest themselves too heavily in a particular philosophical position lest it be shot out from under them in the next philosophical go-round. They have to learn to distance themselves from their philosophical positions and not to care about them too much if they are to avoid regarding a philosophical defeat as a personal humiliation. This promotes a superficial and shallow attitude toward philosophical ideas. All that matters is the gladiatorial skirmish.

To be sure, there are other fields in which scholars criticize each other's work and are expected to be responsive to objections to their own work, fields such as those of art and literature. However, in those fields, the actual work done does not itself have the nature of critical reflection in an adversarial style. The actual work is a painting or a poem, say. In philosophy, by contrast, the actual work done features a great deal of dialectical engagement with objections raised by others. This is a substantial part of the ground-level work that philosophers do. Students are taught that an important part of the presentation and defense of their view is to rebut objections. Advanced students are taught that a typical philosophy paper ends with a section on "Possible Objections to My View." This constant responsiveness to objections and criticism, integrated into the very nature and presentation of philosophical work, may promote an atmosphere in which philosophers tend to avoid investing themselves too deeply in their philosophical positions lest they have to give those up at the next go-round. In this way, it is easy to regard philosophy as a game or contest rather than a genuine search for wisdom.

Apart from its effects on philosophers' commitments to their work, the adversarial style of philosophy likely contributes also to an inhospitable atmosphere in philosophy for any persons who do not enjoy combat and have not been raised to fight. Does this not evoke a familiar gendered script? Although some women clearly engage in and enjoy the adversarial style in philosophy, the pervasiveness of this practice may well account for the relatively low numbers of women who find the field appealing. To be sure, it is possible that recent changes in gender roles are promoting a more adversarial character in young females today than females used to have. Girls' involvement in competitive sports is certainly increasing as is that of adult women.[9] However, female sports are usually played by female individuals or all-female teams against all-female opponents. It is an open question whether females are becoming generally more combative toward all potential opponents in general, as they would have to be in philosophy.

The adversarial style underlies another familiar image of philosophical reason presented by Haig Khatchadourian, who argues that philosophers should strive to do work that is relevant to the world's people by becoming social gadflies; by critically examining people's fundamental values, attitudes, assumptions, and lifestyles; and by developing an "enlightened secular-humanistic, normative ethic and moral code" that would promote human rights and social justice (Khatchadourian, 2005:326). In this otherwise benign account of philosophy, the image of the gadfly is what I wish to single out. The gadfly does not seem gender-neutral.

The gadfly appears also in William P. Alston and Richard B. Brandt's textbook, *The Problems of Philosophy*, where they tell us that the gadfly is one of two "popular images" that people already have of the philosopher (Alston & Brandt, 1974:9). (The other image is the "sage." More on that in a moment.) The gadfly, according to Alston and Brandt, is

> the philosopher as the skeptic, the man who questions basic assumptions and concepts. The gadfly goes around asking people what they mean by "good" or "know." He challenges comfortable common-sense assumptions.... This is the clever reasoner, the man with a sharp eye for distinctions, and a quick wit for objections. He is more adept at tearing down than at building up, and he delights in reducing his interlocutors to confusion. (Alston & Brandt, 1974:9–10)

For those who do not see themselves as social gadflies, there is the image of the philosopher as sage:

> the man of wisdom, he who by dint of long reflection and deep experience has attained a synoptic view of things, a profound understanding of the universe and of the good for man. (Alston & Brandt, 1974:10)

Alston and Brandt write that both these images are "deeply imbedded in the philosophical enterprise" and that "the greatest philosophers have always exemplified both to a high degree" (1974:10).

Gadfly or sage? In Alston and Brandt's portraits, both are described in terms of male nouns and pronouns, but that is not a decisive point, as the use of male nouns and pronouns to stand for all people was the norm in the 1970s when their textbook first appeared. (Such uses are regrettably not gone yet.)

---

[9] See, for example, American Association of University Women, "Position on Equity in School Athletics," http://www.aauw.org/act/issue_advocacy/actionpages/titleix_athletics.cfm; accessed 21 January 2011.

It is the contents of the images that are more revealing. A gadfly is someone who has a "sharp eye for distinctions," "a quick wit for objections," tears down rather than builds up (arguments? people?), and "delights in reducing his interlocutors to confusion." These specific uses of reason are not parts of any common schemas for women. That is, they are not included in the expected traits by which women tend to be represented or to represent themselves. Nor does the image of sage match the schemas for women any better. Women are not associated with "long reflection," a "synoptic view of things," or a "profound understanding of the universe and the good" for human beings. This is not to say that women should not be regarded in those terms. The point is descriptive, not normative. Female students and their (male or female) teachers may have more trouble seeing women than men as gadflies or sages. This could account for Walker's comment, noted earlier, that men through the centuries have failed to pay attention to women's philosophical contributions.

It should be noted, of course, that not all philosophers advocate the adversarial method. Bernard Williams, for example, suggests more modest methods for philosophy, such as "offering arguments and expressing oneself clearly" (Williams, 2000:477). Williams does suggest that the discipline of philosophy is characterized by right and wrong ways of doing it. However, Williams rejects "the well known and highly typical style of many texts in analytic philosophy which seeks precision by total mind control, through issuing continuous and rigid interpretative directions." Williams cautions against this style of philosophy, which "tries to remove in advance every conceivable misunderstanding or misinterpretation or objection, including those that would occur only to the malicious or the clinically literal-minded" (Williams, 2000:480).

Thus, these various contingent features of solipsistic or adversarial philosophical practice are not utilized by all philosophers. As well, their impact on both male and female students is surely a matter of degree. Not all women will be alienated by them, and not all men will be drawn to them. I propose them merely as possible (and partial) explanations for women's lesser participation in philosophy compared to that of men.

In this section, I have suggested that women might not be turned off by the image of philosophy as the activity of reason generally conceived. What women might find inhospitable, however, are the specific manifestations that philosophical reason might take or the social roles in which it might be expressed. These include individually autonomous reason, the role of social gadfly, the role of sage, and the adversarial style of philosophical dialogue.

A final thought about method: Sometimes philosophers deride ordinary non-philosophical ways of thinking as riddled with problems such as vagueness, ambiguity, and self-serving bias. Here, for example, is Bertrand Russell:

> I regret to say that all too many professors of philosophy consider it their duty to be sycophants of common sense, and thus, doubtless

unintentionally, to bow down in homage before the savage superstitions of cannibals. (Russell, 1958:145)

If these attitudes become known to students, would women be more put off by them than men? Do women feel more identified than men with "common sense"? Those are questions for further thought.

In the final section, I discuss why we should care if the conceptions of reasoning that are associated with philosophy and reflected in undergraduate textbooks are alienating to women.

4. Arguments for Increasing the Number of Women in Philosophy

All persons should be evaluated fairly and respected equally in all classrooms and workplaces. We should not need to argue that outright discrimination against and exclusion of women are wrong. Intentionally denying jobs and tenure to people who have earned those rewards fairly is unjust. However, suppose that women's relatively low participation in philosophy is due substantially to unconscious bias on the parts of current philosophy faculty or to methods of philosophy that alienate women. Some studies show that in general, women's achievements are judged to be of lesser worth than identical achievements thought to be done by men (Haslanger, 2008:213; Valian, 2005:202–204). Suppose the evidence suggested that unconscious bias against women by philosophers is likely. Such evidence would call for positive effort to examine all assessment practices in philosophy to determine whether bias actually is present and, if so, to eliminate or compensate for it.

If philosophical methods are what tend to alienate women from the field, these methods should be assessed to see if they are worth the cost. We would have to balance the costs and benefits of increasing women's participation in philosophy against the costs, benefits, and necessity of the methods in question. I have already suggested that there are alternative methods (as defended by Williams) to the pervasive adversarial style of doing philosophy. I will not say anything more about whether current philosophical methods are beneficial or necessary. In this remaining section, I consider the other part of the equation by asking: What are some of the counterbalancing benefits of promoting women's greater participation in professional philosophy?

First, current female students in philosophy classes might be more likely to be attracted to the field if women were recognizably present in substantial numbers, most importantly as teachers and authors.[10] Valian argues that we should increase the number of women who are professional philosophers in order to have more female teachers of philosophy. This would lead to more classroom

---

[10] I owe a great debt to my own first philosophy teacher, Sandra Bartky.

environments in which female students will feel that philosophy welcomes their participation. The result would be that more female students would be drawn to enter the field in the future (Valian, 2005:208).

Second, most women who are already professional philosophers would likely benefit from an increase in their numbers in the field. Female philosophers isolated in their departments often tire of being the lone woman at department meetings who has trouble being heard or taken seriously by her colleagues. With more women in the field, there would be less likelihood that departments would have only a single woman on the faculty. Thus an increase in the numbers of women will probably increase the professional confidence, standing, and regard for women who are already in the field, as well as those who can join them subsequently.

The first and second reasons above are not yet independently relevant answers to the question about why to care whether women's participation in philosophy increases. Those reasons tell us that having more women in philosophy will both attract still more women to the field and improve the professional standing of those who are in the field. Thus, the first two reasons argue in a circle, already presupposing that it is valuable to increase the numbers of women in philosophy. We still need *independent* reasons for thinking that an increase in the number of women in philosophy will, at the very least, improve philosophy and, it is to be hoped, also be good for women.

My third and most important suggestion is thus presented as an independent reason to increase the number of women in professional philosophy, namely, that doing so would improve philosophy.[11] This suggestion has two parts. Improvement would arise, first, from the particular contribution that feminist philosophy makes to philosophy and, second, from the general methodological improvement to philosophy that would arise from (the continuing expansion of) gender diversity.[12]

First, feminist philosophy makes a particular contribution to philosophy as a sub-specialization. Feminist philosophy has opened philosophical thought in many philosophical areas to issues of gender and the moral and political standing of women. And feminist philosophy is very largely the product of female philosophers. As Margaret Walker observes, had it not been for the numbers of women in philosophy reaching a minimal critical mass, there probably would have been no feminist philosophy (Walker 2005:159). Feminist philosophical contributions include the introduction and/or substantial development of work on care ethics (Held, 1995, 2006; Slote, 2007; Noddings, 2002; Robinson,

---

[11] The same can obviously be asked and answered with regard to ethnic, racial, and religious groups, among other significant social categorizations.

[12] As indicated in the preceding note, other sorts of population diversity are also beneficial for philosophy. My focus on gender diversity certainly does not rule out the value of those other sorts.

1999), ecofeminism (Warren, 2000; Cuomo, 2002), feminist bioethics (Scully et al., 2009; Mahowald, 2006; Donchin & Purdy, 1999; Sherwin et al., 1998), embodiment (Butler, 1990; Butler, 1993; Grosz, 1994; Young, 2005), intersectionality (Collins, 2003; Bilge, 2010), standpoint epistemology (Alcoff & Potter, 1993; Harding, 2004, 2009), and feminist science studies (Kourany, 2010; Harding, 2008; Longino, 2001; Creager, 2001). This list is by no means complete. Philosophers will not all agree with these contributions, but they nevertheless represent critical expansions and enrichments of philosophical thinking in their respective subfields. A further increase in the numbers of women in philosophy promises to extend these developments and their contributions to the field.

Second, the (continuing expansion of) the gender diversity of philosophy, like any kind of socially significant group diversity, promotes a general methodological improvement in philosophy. To appreciate this point, let us consider the overall nature of philosophy. Many philosophers consider it the special role of philosophy to reflect on the foundations of human thought. J. N. Findlay, for example, characterizes philosophy as

> a critical examination of fundamental concepts and principles, that is, concepts and principles which structure all or nearly all of our experience, all of our language and its essential grammar and every thing or fact or theme that we can know or think of: It also in some of its exercises attempts to revise and to simplify and tidy up such fundamental concepts and principles, so as to rid them of unclarities and ambiguities—and also to free them of inner conflicts.... (Findlay, 2005:141)[13]

Haig Khatchadourian suggests that philosophy today should reinvigorate its ancient tradition of offering wisdom to human beings in the living of their lives. Philosophical wisdom should concern the "ends that humankind ought to strive to realize" and "insight into who and what we really are" (Khatchadourian, 2005:325).[14] Bernard Williams suggests that philosophy is "part of a more general attempt to make the best sense of our life, and so of our intellectual activities, in the situation in which we find ourselves" (Williams, 2000:479). Williams suggests that "philosophy might play an important part in making people think about what they are doing," that it is part of the "whole humanistic enterprise of trying to understand ourselves..." (Williams, 2000:495–496).

Broadly speaking, there are at least two different ways in which philosophy can examine our fundamental concepts and principles, explore human

---

[13] This essay was based on full notes by Findlay from a course he taught in the 1970s.

[14] As a reviewer of this chapter pointed out, these remarks and some of those that follow could fit the model of philosopher as sage. None of my previous comments was intended to suggest that the model of the philosopher as sage was inherently problematic. Rather, my worry was that it is not a model women tend to associate with themselves as thinkers.

ends, and promote human self-understanding. First, philosophy can seek a direct connection to the daily practical concerns of ordinary people. Some areas of philosophy, ethics for example, seek to understand ordinary human beings and the everyday world they face and to explore how ordinary people can best live in that world. Philosophy is in part the search for the practical wisdom of how to live human lives in the world as we find it, given humanity as we find it. In this way, philosophy aims at preparing human beings to make the best they can of their lives. Whatever else it does, philosophy should do this job of aiming at deep understandings and practical guidance for the whole panoply of ordinary lives that people can live. Toward this end, philosophy should be translatable into common discourse, and philosophers should spend some time on "applied" issues that have direct relevance to everyday lives.

The second way in which philosophy can examine fundamental concepts and promote human ends is to play a critical and foundational role with respect to other specialized fields and professions. This philosophical aim connects with philosophy's age-old capacity to give birth to empirical sciences (Williams, 2000:495–496). In this role, philosophy should include critical assessment and foundational understanding of the scientific enterprise, medicine, law, the arts, and the other professional fields and disciplines to which philosophy connects. Among other things, the philosophers of science, the arts, and so on should engage in critical inquiry to be sure those fields are not distorted by bias and are otherwise serving the interests of diverse segments of society. Toward this end, questions and challenges are not out of place; however, they can be rendered in a collaborative spirit that is free of hostility and personal acrimony.

Allen Wood recognizes both of the above philosophical roles when he argues that philosophy should be continually engaged with "the results of the sciences," "the practical life of society," and "its own history." It should hold all social practices and belief systems to "the proper rational norms and standards that apply to them," as well as subjecting those norms to continual re-examination. Philosophy should not represent human life simply as people wish it to be or as authorities dictate. Conceived in this way, Wood writes, "philosophy is a painful, anxiety-provoking, and socially dangerous, and often thankless activity" (Wood, 2006:135). Against the prejudices and superstitions of today, philosophy represents critical thinking, which is "very much in decline" (Wood, 2006:136).

Whether by connecting directly with ordinary lives or indirectly through critical reflection on other professional fields, philosophy seeks to understand profound matters. Borrowing somewhat from Nietzsche, I suggest that, in either case, the philosopher's own personal perspective plays a crucial role in shaping her philosophical work. Philosophers work from their own perspectives, however filtered and reconfigured these are by the collective interchanges of the field. Nietzsche speculated that philosophers expressed their "innermost drives," which he thought might be necessary for "such beings as we are." Some contemporary philosophers agree that philosophers' standpoints have a perspectival nature. Bernard Williams, for example, rejects the idea that there could be a perspectivally independent conception of the world (Williams, 2000:483–484). Our history made not only our outlook; it also made us, argues Williams. We are no less contingently formed than our ideas (490). Williams also notes that it makes a great difference who the "we" is for which the philosophical enterprise is carried on. Contemporary ideas can often seem to be timeless and "simply there" (493–494). Williams thinks we should abandon the illusion that we can find ideas "which would be the best from an absolute point of view, a point of view that was free of contingent historical perspective" (491).

John Ryder, similarly, writes that both geographical and historical conditions determine the way in which philosophy is done (Ryder, 2007:389). If these sorts of conditions affect the way philosophy is done, it does so through the perspectives of the persons who are engaged in professional philosophical work. If philosophers' methods are affected in significant ways by the time and place in which they live, then it is a small step to the conclusion that other determinants of human perspectives, such as gender, are also determinants of how philosophy is done.

If there are major social groups that are underrepresented in philosophy, then the collective understanding achieved by philosophy will express the perspectives only of those groups that are well represented. When seeking *direct* practical wisdom for the living of ordinary lives, philosophy might easily miss the concerns or interests of many ordinary people if it does not adequately represent the diversity of its public. Critically exploring the foundations of *other* professional fields is another task in which philosophy might fail to represent the significant diversity of its public. The underrepresentation of women could thus lead to a serious gap in the collective understanding of a society. The diverse interests and perspectives among women themselves are especially likely to be overlooked when women in the aggregate are not well represented in professional philosophical activity.

I have suggested three reasons why it matters to increase the numbers of women in professional philosophy. It is crucial for philosophers to strain toward the ideal of increased female participation and against the "business" side of philosophy that, as noted earlier, constantly tempts its practitioners to act out of self-interested other-disregarding profit motives. Against these tendencies, an increase in the numbers of women would be likely to (1) further increase the number of female students who would be attracted to the field; (2) promote a more hospitable environment and enhanced professional standing for women who are already in the field; and, most important, (3) improve the quality of philosophy both by promoting more work in feminist philosophy and by enriching the philosophical quest for the wisdom to guide the enormous variety of human lives.

Acknowledgment

Thanks to Fiona Jenkins and Katrina Hutchison for comments on an earlier draft of this chapter.

References

Alcoff, Linda, & Potter, Elizabeth (eds.) (1993) *Feminist Epistemologies*, New York/London: Routledge.

Alston, William P., & Brandt, Richard B. (1974) *The Problems of Philosophy*, 2nd ed. Boston: Allyn & Bacon.

Bilge, Sirma (2010) "Recent Feminist Outlooks on Intersectionality," *Diogenes*, Vol. 57, No. 225, 58–72.

Butler, Judith (1993) *Bodies that Matter: On the Discursive Limits of Sex*, New York: Routledge.

Butler, Judith (1990) *Gender Trouble: Feminism and the Subversion of Identity*, New York: Routledge.

Collins, Patricia Hill (2003) "Some Group Matters: Intersectionality, Situated Standpoints, and Black Feminist Thought," in *A Companion to African-American Thought*, ed. Tommy L. Lott, Malden, MA: Blackwell, 205–229.

Creager, Angela N. H., et al. (2001) *Feminism in Twentieth Century Science, Technology, and Medicine*, Chicago: University of Chicago Press

Cuomo, Chris (2002) "On Ecofeminist Philosophy," *Ethics & the Environment*, Vol. 7, No. 2, 1–11.

Donchin, Anne, & Purdy, Laura M. (eds.) (1999) *Embodying Bioethics: Recent Feminist Advances*, Lanham, MD: Rowman and Littlefield.

Findlay, J. N. (2005) "Philosophy as a Discipline," *The Philosophical Forum*, Vol. XXXVI, No. 2.

Grosz, Elizabeth (1994) *Volatile Bodies: Toward a Corporeal Feminism*, London: Routledge.

Harding, Sandra (2009) "Standpoint Theories: Productively Controversial," *Hypatia*, Vol. 24, No. 4, 192–200.

Harding, Sandra (2008) *Sciences from Below: Feminisms, Postcolonialisms, and Modernities*, Durham, NC: Duke University Press.

Harding, Sandra (ed.) (2004) *The Feminist Standpoint Theory Reader*, New York: Routledge.

Haslanger, Sally (2008) "Changing the ideology and Culture of Philosophy: Not by Reason (Alone)," *Hypatia*, Vol. 23, No. 2, 210–223.

Held, Virginia (2006) *The Ethics of Care: Personal, Political, and Global*, Oxford, UK: Oxford University Press.

Held, Virginia (ed.) (1995) *Justice and Care: Essential Readings in Feminist Ethics,* Boulder, CO: Westview.

Khatchadourian, Haig (2005) "How I See Philosophy in the Twenty-First Century and Beyond," *Metaphilosophy*, Vol. 35, No. 3, 321–326.

Kourany, Janet (2010) *Philosophy of Science after Feminism*, Oxford, UK: Oxford University Press.

Longino, Helen (2001) *The Fate of Knowledge*, Princeton, NJ: Princeton University Press.

Mackenzie, Catriona, and Stoljar, Natalie (eds.) (2000) *Relational Autonomy: Feminist Perspectives on Autonomy, Agency, and the Social Self*, New York: Oxford University Press.

Mahowald, Mary B. (2006) *Bioethics and Women: Across the Lifespan*, New York: Oxford University Press.

Meyers, Diana (1989) *Self, Society, and Personal Choice*, New York: Columbia University Press.

Moulton, Janice (2003) "A Paradigm of Philosophy: The Adversary Method," in *Discovering Reality: Feminist Perspectives on Epistemology, Metaphysics, Methodology and Philosophy of Science*, eds., Sandra Harding and Meryl Hintikka, 2nd ed., 149–164.

Moulton, Janice (1980) "Duelism in Philosophy," *Teaching Philosophy*, Fall 1980, 419–433.

Nietzsche, Friedrich (1966) *Beyond Good and Evil: Prelude to a Philosophy of the Future*, trans. Walter Kaufman, New York: Random House.

Noddings, Nel (2002) *Starting at Home: Caring and Social Policy*, Berkeley, CA: University of California Press.

Robinson, Fiona (1999) *Globalizing Care: Ethics, Feminist Theory, and International Relations*, Boston, MA: Beacon.

Rooney, Phyllis (2010) "Philosophy, Adversarial Argumentation, and Embattled Reason," *Informal Logic*, Vol. 30, No. 3, 203–234.

Russell, Bertrand (1958) "Mind and Matter," in his *Portraits from Memory* (London: George Allen & Unwin, 1925/1958), 145. Quoted in Daniel Z. Korman, "Eliminativism and the Challenge from Folk Belief," *Noûs*, Vol. 43, No. 2 (2009), 242.

Ryder, John (2007) "The Making of Professional Philosophy," *Transactions of the Charles S. Peirce Society*, Vol. 43, No. 2.

Scully, J. L., et al. (eds.) (2009) *Feminist Bioethics: At the Centre on the Margins*, Baltimore, MD: Johns Hopkins University Press, 2009.

Sherwin, Susan, et al. (eds.) (1998) *The Politics of Women's Health: Exploring Agency and Autonomy*, Philadelphia: Temple University Press.

Slote, Michael (2007) *The Ethics of Care and Empathy*, London: Routledge.

Solomon, Robert C. (1977) *Introducing Philosophy: Problems and Perspectives*, New York: Harcourt Brace Jovanovich.

Toulmin, Stephen (1976) *Knowing and Acting: An Invitation to Philosophy*, New York: Macmillan.

Tuana, Nancy (1992) *Woman and the History of Philosophy*, New York: Paragon House.

Valian, Virginia (2005) "Beyond Gender Schemas: Improving the Advancement of Women in Academia," *Hypatia*, Vol. 20, No. 3, 198–213.

Walker, Margaret (2005) "Diotima's Ghost: The Uncertain Place of Feminist Philosophy in Professional Philosophy," *Hypatia*, Vol. 20, No. 3, 153–164.

Warren, Karen (2000) *Ecofeminist Philosophy: Western Perspectives on What It Is and Why It Matters*, Lanham, MD: Rowman & Littlefield.

Williams, Bernard (2000) "Philosophy as a Humanistic Discipline," *Philosophy*, Vol. 75, No. 4, 477–496.

Wolff, Robert Paul (1976) *About Philosophy*, Englewood Cliffs, NJ: Prentice-Hall.

Wood, Allen (2006) "Philosophy—what is to be done?" *Topoi*, Vol. 25.

Young, Iris Marion (2005) *On Female Body Experience: 'Throwing Like a Girl' and Other Essays*, New York: Oxford University Press.

2

Implicit Bias, Stereotype Threat, and Women in Philosophy

Jennifer Saul

Chapters in this volume and elsewhere show that the number of women in professional philosophy is much lower than the number of men. However, this does not on its own show that there is a problem to be addressed by philosophers. It could be that women just don't like (or aren't good at) the sorts of reasoning philosophers engage in or the sorts of problems philosophers discuss, either as a result of their innate nature or as a result of their socialisation. If either of these is the case, then it's far from clear that *philosophers* should feel the need to do anything about women in philosophy. These hypotheses are very difficult to adequately study, and so difficult to decisively rule out.[1] Some move from this to the thought that we shouldn't try to do anything about women in philosophy because we don't *know* that these hypotheses are false.

I take this to be a mistake. The reason that I take it to be a mistake is that there is another hypothesis that we have good reason to believe is true. This hypothesis is that women's progress in philosophy is impeded by the presence of two well-documented psychological phenomena, implicit bias and stereotype threat. In this chapter, I argue that we have good reason to take this to be true, and that this gives philosophers good reason to want to do something about the underrepresentation of women in philosophy—both for reasons of justice and for the sake of philosophy. Moreover, there would be good reason to do this *even if* it were also true that there were some differences of the sort hypothesised by those who suggest that philosophers should not worry about women in philosophy.

By focusing on the phenomena that I discuss in this chapter, I don't mean to suggest that bias as traditionally understood (e.g., the conscious belief that

---

[1] Though for some evidence against such generalisations, see Fine 2010 and Jordan-Young 2010.

women are bad at philosophy) is a thing of the past.[2] Unfortunately, it does still exist.[3] But the phenomena that I discuss here are less well known, and they may also be more widespread.

1. Surprising Psychological Results

Here I focus on two psychological phenomena: implicit bias and stereotype threat. The implicit biases that we are concerned with here are unconscious biases that affect the way we perceive, evaluate, or interact with people from the groups that our biases "target".[4] Stereotype threat is sometimes consciously felt but also sometimes unconscious,[5] and it concerns ways that a person's (awareness of their) own group membership may negatively affect their performance. So, in the case of women in philosophy, implicit biases will be unconscious biases that affect the way we judge (for instance) the quality of a woman's work, leading us to evaluate it more negatively than it deserves; while stereotype threat may lead a woman to genuinely underperform in philosophy.

1.1 IMPLICIT BIAS

Psychological research over the last decades has shown that most people—even those who explicitly and sincerely avow egalitarian views—hold what have been described as implicit biases against such groups as blacks, women, gay people, and so on. This is true even of members of the 'targeted' group (see, e.g., Moss-Racusin et al. 2012; Steinpreis et al. 1999; Vedantam 2005). So, for example, women as well as men are biased against women. These biases are manifested in, for example, association tasks asking subjects to pair positive and negative adjectives with black or white faces: Most are much speedier to match black faces with negative adjectives than with positive ones.[6] They are also, it has

---

[2] Nor do I mean to suggest that biases are the only factors involved in the underrepresentation of women in philosophy. Other factors may well also play a role, like the gendered differences in intuitions suggested by Buckwalter and Stich (2010). Though also see Louise Antony's critique of this work (Antony 2012).

[3] Those who doubt this are invited to browse the blog www.beingawomaninphilosophy. wordpress.com.

[4] One may also use the term 'implicit bias' in a more general way, to refer to unconscious associations more generally. Even in the more specific way that I am using the term here, implicit biases need not have negative effects: One might unconsciously associate groups with different flavours of ice cream without this having any negative effects. However, my focus here is on implicit biases that may have negative effects.

[5] Steele (2010) discusses both conscious and unconscious stereotype threat. For conscious stereotype threat, see, for example, his chapter 5; for unconscious stereotype threat, see, for example, his chapter 7.

[6] To take one of the tests, go to <https://implicit.harvard.edu/implicit/>. The Implicit Association Tests (IATs) are not without critics. See, for example, Blanton and Jaccard 2006. But see also the replies in Greenwald et al. 2006 and Jost et al. 2009. And note, as discussed in Jost et al., that the IATs represent just one paradigm for demonstrating the existence of implicit bias.

been argued, manifested in behaviour: Studies have shown that those with anti-black implicit biases are less friendly to black experimenters and more likely to classify an ambiguous object in a black person's hand as a gun while classifying it as harmless in a white person's hand.[7]

Academics are clearly affected by implicit bias, even if (as seems likely) explicit commitments to egalitarianism are widespread. First, take the case of journal submissions. Anonymous review[8] is apparently only rarely practiced in ecology and evolution journals. But one such journal, *Behavioural Ecology*, recently decided to do it. They found that it led to a 33 percent increase in representation of female authors (Budden et al. 2008).

Next, take the case of CVs. It is well established that the presence of a male or female name on a CV has a strong effect on how that CV is evaluated. This is true both inside and outside of academia. Philosophers have not specifically been studied, but we do know that those academics most likely to be aware of the existence of unconscious psychological processes—psychologists—exhibit just this bias. In Moss-Racusin et al.'s 2012 study, faculty participants rated the same CV as more competent and hireable, and deserving of a higher salary if a male name was at the top of it. They were also more willing to mentor the males. These effects were equally strong for both male and female evaluators, of all ages. They were also shown to correlate with preexisting "subtle" biases against women.

What data like these seem to show is that people—including academics, including those with explicit egalitarian beliefs, and including those who are themselves women—more readily associate the sorts of traits valued in CVs and in articles with men than with women. Research indicates that traits like originality, excellence, leadership, and intellectual ability seem to be more readily associated with men than with women (Valian 1999).

1.2 STEREOTYPE THREAT

Stereotype threat is a very different sort of phenomenon. Rather than affecting the way that members of a stigmatised group are *perceived or evaluated*, stereotype threat affects the way that members of that group actually *perform*. Victims of stereotype threat underperform[9] on the relevant tasks because they are unconsciously preoccupied by fears of confirming the stereotypes about their group—so preoccupied that they show elevated heart rates and blood pressure (Steele 119–120, 149). Rather tragically, the effect is strongest with those most committed to

---

[7] For an excellent overview of this research, see Jost et al. 2009.

[8] By 'anonymous review,' I mean a process in which the author's name is not made available to referees.

[9] The term 'underperformance' may be a bit misleading, as using it could seem to involve a commitment to the idea that there is some *right* level of performance for each individual that represents the truth about them. It should not be read in this way. Instead, the idea is that some people face barriers that impede their performance. These people underperform in the sense that their performance is negatively affected by these barriers.

doing well in the area in question. Victims of stereotype threat are often, though not always, unaware of what is happening.[10]

The effects of stereotype threat are dramatic. When in a threat-provoking situation, blacks perform worse than whites on standardised tests; girls perform worse than boys in math; white people perform worse than blacks at sports (Steele 2010). But when the threat is removed, performance from the stigmatised group improves dramatically—often to the point of equality.[11]

Obviously, the notions of "threat-provoking" and "threat-removing" situations are incredibly important. Stereotype threat is likely to be provoked when one is from a group that is negatively stigmatised in a certain context, one is in that context, and one's group membership is made salient. This can happen in many ways. For example, if you ask five-to-seven-year-old girls to colour in drawings of girls holding dolls before taking a math test, their performance is significantly reduced (Steele 170). You can also provoke stereotype threat simply through visual reminders of their group's underrepresentation (Steele 149). In some cases, one does not need to do anything to make the group membership salient enough to provoke stereotype threat—what's difficult is coming up with ways to dissipate it. This is the case, for example, with blacks taking tests that they believe to be tests of intellectual ability (Steele 51). We will discuss "threat-removing situations" later when we come to the topic of solutions.

2. Implicit Bias and Stereotype Threat in Philosophy

As we have seen, there is by now a well-established body of research in psychology showing that human beings are strongly influenced by a range of disturbing and often unconscious biases and dispositions related to categories like race, sex, age, disability, sexual orientation, etc. So far, there has been no empirical work on whether *philosophers* are influenced by these biases. But given that philosophers are human beings, it seems very likely that they are.

So what would one expect to find? The literature on implicit bias tells us that, if philosophers are like other human beings, including those in academia

---

[10] You may be wondering how psychologists could know that such victims of stereotype threat are preoccupied in this way, especially when the preoccupation is unconscious. Here's one compelling experiment showing that they are. If you place black subjects in a situation that provokes stereotype threat for them (and it doesn't take much to do this, as we'll see), then ask them about musical preferences, they will choose music stereotyped as white at a higher rate than white subjects will. But if you place them in a situation that doesn't provoke stereotype threat, they will choose music stereotyped as black (Steele 53). Clearly, *not confirming the stereotypes* is on their minds in the threat-provoking situations. For more, see Steele.

[11] It is actually to be expected (even by those who discount claims of biological difference) that performance wouldn't always equalize. Stereotype threat isn't, after all, the only manifestation of an unequal society. Racism, sexism, and the like abound—as do their effects in the form of reduced income, reduced encouragement, less access to certain opportunities, and so on.

(see, for example, Steinpreis et al. 1999; Valian 1999), we will find a range of unconscious biases against women that will affect behaviour in a variety of ways. Moreover, specific stereotypes about philosophy may lead to further biases. Both of these are discussed in more detail below.

The literature on stereotype threat tells us that we would expect to find underperformance by those stereotypically taken to be less good at philosophy. There has been no direct empirical research on stereotypes about gender and philosophy, but there is very good reason to believe that philosophy is stereo-typed as male. (As I write, however, I am in the process of conducting a study on this in collaboration with Sheffield psychologists, using an IAT for philosophy and gender.)

As other chapters in this volume attest, feminist philosophers have long argued that there is a tradition in philosophy of associating reason, objectivity, and philosophical thought with maleness, and emotion, subjectivity, and the non-philosophical with femaleness (see, e.g., Haslanger 2008). And although psychologists have not studied philosophers' stereotypes of philosophy,[12] they have extensively studied stereotypes of mathematics. Mathematics is strongly stereotyped as male (e.g., Nosek et al. 2002), and it seems reasonable to suppose that Anglophone philosophy, with its heavy use of logic, will inherit this stereotype. (It is true that not all Anglophone philosophy makes heavy use of logic, but nonetheless logical competence is generally viewed as a near-neces-sary condition for success in the field: Logic courses are widely required of both undergraduate and postgraduate philosophy students.)

It seems very likely then that philosophers will display implicit bias against women, and that women in philosophy will experience stereotype threat.[13] (The literature[14] on both these topics also tells us that people will often be unaware that either of these things is happening.) It would be very surprising if these forces did not play a role in the underrepresentation of women in philosophy.[15]

I have sometimes heard it suggested that philosophers would not be subject to implicit bias against stigmatised social groups because of their greater ability to be objective. Research has shown, however, that people systematically over-estimate their own ability to be objective (Uhlmann and Cohen 2007). Even more important, it turns out that being primed with objectivity (e.g., asked to

---

[12] The study I am currently involved with, noted above, is the one exception.

[13] One might worry that accepting the existence of stereotype threat would commit one to the thought that women are actually performing less well than men at philosophy—so we shouldn't be worried by (for example) all-male conferences, as these simply reflect the fact that women are producing inferior philosophy. But there is no reason to suppose that the women in philosophy are producing work that is less good than that produced by the men in philosophy. In fact, given the likely effects of implicit bias, we might suspect just the opposite. However, stereotype threat is likely to mean that at least some women are performing less well than they otherwise might, and that women are likely to leave philosophy. I discuss other issues related to this point later.

[14] E.g., Jost et al. 2009; Steele 2010.

[15] Sally Haslanger has also argued for this in her 2008 article.

tick a box rating one's own objectivity) increases susceptibility to gender bias in job applicant evaluation (Uhlmann and Cohen 2006). If that's right, then philosophers may be *especially* subject to implicit biases, rather than especially immune from them.

One might also object that philosophers are unlikely to hold the same sorts of views of women in philosophy as the public at large—after all, our views about philosophy are in general different from those in the broader population. Even if this is right, however, it would only cast doubt on claims about philosophers' stereotypes about women *philosophers.* It would have no bearing on the claim that philosophers are likely to make the same sorts of negative evaluations of women in general that other humans do. But I don't really see any reason to suppose that the objection is correct. Scientists, even women scientists, share the same sorts of biases about women in science that others do (Moss-Racusin 2012; Steinpreis et al. 1999; Vedantam 2005). So it is reasonable to suppose that philosophers share the same sorts of biases about women in philosophy. If what I have argued here is right, these factors very likely contribute to the fact that women's representation in philosophy drops off as women work their ways from undergraduate education to jobs in philosophy of various ranks.[16] Below I show how they may combine to produce this effect.

2.1 IMPLICIT BIAS, STEREOTYPE THREAT, AND WOMEN'S CAREER TRAJECTORIES

A female philosophy student will probably be in the minority as a woman in her department, and she'll almost certainly be in the minority as a woman if she takes classes in the more stereotypically male areas like (for example) logic, language, and metaphysics. As she continues on to higher levels of study, the number of women will be steadily diminishing. In any class she takes other than feminist philosophy, she's likely to encounter a syllabus that consists overwhelmingly (often exclusively) of male authors. The people teaching most of the classes are also very likely to be male. All of these factors calling attention to low numbers of women are known to provoke stereotype threat. Because stereotype threat has its strongest effect on the most committed students, this means that the most committed women are likely to underperform.

Those teaching undergraduates are human beings and therefore susceptible to implicit bias. Whatever their egalitarian beliefs and intentions (and even if they are themselves women), they are likely to be affected by implicit biases that lead to more negative evaluations of women's abilities. (If it's right that philosophy is stereotyped as male, this will only be heightened.) What will this mean for their teaching? It's likely to mean that when they're drawing up their

---

[16] See Beebee, this volume, and Calhoun (2009) and Haslanger (2008).

syllabi, the names that leap to mind as the best, most important authors will be male. As they conduct in-class discussions, they are likely to (unconsciously) expect better contributions from the male students. This may mean that they're more likely to call upon men.[17] If grading is not anonymous, men are likely to be given higher grades than women for the same quality of work. Finally, if a teacher unconsciously associates men more easily with philosophical excellence, they will be more likely to encourage men to major in philosophy and to go on to further work in philosophy after graduation. At the graduate level, supervisors may be more likely to encourage men to publish their work. Both graduate and undergraduate women are likely to get a weaker letter of reference than a similar man (Valian 2005: 201; Madera et al. 2009).

Eventually, women philosophers will try to publish their work. As we have seen, implicit bias can affect the review of articles submitted for publication. If refereeing is not anonymous, women's work is likely to be evaluated more negatively than men's. Even if refereeing is anonymous, 81 percent of philosophy journals allow editors to see names as they make the initial cut of how many papers get sent out for review. And editors reject up to 65 percent of submissions at this stage (the mean rejection rate is 22 percent).[18] If submissions are not anonymous to the editor, then the evidence suggests that women's work will probably be judged more negatively than men's work of the same quality.

Both stereotype threat and implicit bias may have strong effects on a woman's performance in the job market. CVs with women's names are likely to be seen as less good than CVs with men's names. As we have noted, letters of recommendation are likely to be weaker for women than for men. And women may well have had more trouble than men at getting publications. Women will also very likely face stereotype threat, often in the form of an overwhelmingly (or wholly) male team of interviewers adding to the stress of the already hideously stressful interview process.

Once a woman philosopher has managed to get a job, she will continue to experience the effects of implicit bias and stereotype threat in all the ways we have seen so far. But new aspects may also be added. Because women are more associated than men with interpersonal and helping skills, they're likely to be assigned more of the time-intensive student support and administrative/service tasks that tend to be poorly rewarded in terms of promotion.[19] This will take away from time that they could otherwise use for the research that could help them to obtain permanent jobs, tenure, or promotion. Women's experiences as teachers are also likely to be different from men's. For example, a recent study (Goodyear et al. 2010) suggests that they are more likely to encounter

---

[17] This asymmetry is well-documented. See Bartky 1990: 91; Sadker, Sadker, and Zittleman 2009.

[18] Lee and Schunn 2010: 3.

[19] See Link et al. 2008; Misra et al. 2011.

incivility in the classroom, ranging from sleeping or checking e-mail to aggressive and bullying interruptions. Examples of such behaviour in philosophy are recounted in Superson (2002) and Hanrahan and Antony (2005). Here is one from personal correspondence with Louise Antony:

> If students (or conference participants) challenge women more than they do men, women have to face choices that men do not, and these choices are likely to be double binds. So for example, when I taught a course to engineers that was usually taught by a male colleague, he advised me to brook absolutely no excuses for late papers, and to announce (as he always did) that students would simply be docked 5 points for every day late. When I found that I had over 40 late papers (in a class of 300+), and that many of them were so late they would have a failing grade before I even read them, I asked him what he did: did he disregard the announced policy, or did he let the chips fall where they may (leading to failing grades for quite a few students). His answer: that's never happened to me. Thus, he never had to face the dilemma of either undermining his own authority by not following his announced policy, or evoking the ire of 40 students in a class that didn't like you to begin with.

This behaviour, and the biases that produce it, is likely to also affect their teaching evaluation scores, which can be crucial for getting tenure. It can also affect whether they are chosen as supervisors, which can affect tenure and promotion prospects. If their first job is a temporary one (as it is increasingly likely to be), they will suffer all the effects of implicit bias and stereotype threat as they go on the job market again (and possibly again and again).

Women later in their careers will continue to experience many of the same problems. A new one, however, is that women at later stages may want (or need) to be taken seriously in leadership roles. They are likely to find this more difficult than men. In studies using actors trained to behave identically,[20] women in positions of leadership were judged far more negatively than men were—as "bossy and dominating" and less competent (Valian 131.)

One might speculate, however, that if a woman achieves success and security, she will at least cease to suffer from stereotype threat. And it probably is true that stereotype threat will be reduced and perhaps even eliminated for some. But, sadly, it probably won't completely disappear for many. I am a full professor, with plenty of publications and a job I love in a fantastic department that I love—and where I feel completely at ease. But this hasn't made me immune. I recently presented a paper at a department that had its own seminar room. Because they had their own seminar room, they'd decorated the walls by

---

[20] Interestingly, the actors didn't actually succeed in behaving identically. The non-actors in the experiments failed to pay attention to what the women leaders said, so the female leaders ended up having to speak more than the male leaders did.

filling them with pictures of famous philosophers. I noticed immediately that every picture I saw was a man. (Apparently there was a lone woman, but she was behind me.) I also noticed that everyone in the audience was a man. Two women then arrived, but the room was still overwhelmingly male. As I gave the paper, I felt that it was going poorly. I found myself feeling nervous, stumbling over words, and answering questions hesitantly and poorly. While doing this, I was aware of it—and surprised, as I'd given the paper very successfully several times before. I knew enough about stereotype threat to realise that this was what I was experiencing. But unfortunately, that awareness didn't keep it from happening. I now think of that room as "The Stereotype Threat Room." And I did tell some department members—all of them lovely people who were very supportive of feminist philosophy—that perhaps they might want to add some women to the walls.

2.2 OTHER STEREOTYPED GROUPS

Although women are underrepresented in philosophy, they are far from being the most underrepresented group. Blacks, Latinos, and other ethnic minorities are severely underrepresented, as are disabled people and members of many other stigmatised groups. All these groups will be subject to stereotype threat and implicit bias. People do not belong to just one social group: Some women are black, some black people are disabled, some white people are gay, and so on. Moreover, quite a lot of people will be subject to stereotype threat and implicit bias on the basis of more than one identity. Sometimes, one identity will be stigmatised and another not, in which case focusing on the non-stigmatised identity can at least sometimes be helpful for combating stereotype threat.[21] But having more than one stigmatised identity will both alter and magnify the implicit bias and the stereotype threat that one suffers.

2.2.1 Motherhood

It's worth, for instance, thinking about the workings of bias with regard to motherhood, which of course might impact women at any stage of their career. Shelley Correll and Stephen Benard (2007) have shown that there are very substantial biases against mothers in the workplace. Their study (of both undergraduates and employers in marketing and business) presented equivalent CVs with either male or female names, indicating parental status (through cues like "member of the Parent Teacher Association"). They found that mothers were less likely to be hired than other women, less likely to be judged as good candidates for promotion, judged to deserve lower salaries, considered less

---

[21] East Asian girls in the U.S. can improve their performance on math tests by colouring in pictures of chopsticks.

committed to their jobs, and held to higher performance standards (including a lower tolerance for late arrival at work). Fatherhood did not have any negative impact on candidates, and in fact had a positive impact: Fathers were likely to be judged more committed to their jobs, offered a higher tolerance for late arrival, and considered worthy of higher salaries than other men. If these effects carry over to philosophy, we would expect things to be much tougher for women philosophers who are also mothers. Given the underrepresentation of mothers in philosophy (and cultural associations of motherhood with emotion rather than reason), one would also expect mothers in philosophy to suffer from stereotype threat.

2.3 FEEDBACK LOOPS

It is important to note that all of these factors work together to create a kind of feedback loop. Women have trouble performing well and being fairly assessed when they are so underrepresented. But it is very hard to fight the underrepresentation when women are being unfairly assessed and impeded in their performance. In short, the underrepresentation that underlies implicit bias and stereotype threat is *reinforced* by the implicit bias and stereotype threat that it helps to produce.

3. Why Should Philosophers Care?

The sorts of problems posed by implicit bias and stereotype threat are ones that demand action from philosophers. Moreover, they demand action from philosophers simply on grounds of concern for either (a) fairness or (b) philosophy, even philosophy as traditionally conceived. No particular concern for women, for feminist philosophy, or even for enriching philosophy with a diversity of perspectives is needed in order to motivate action on the basis of these phenomena.

3.1 FAIRNESS

It seems reasonable to assume that most philosophers believe that it is important to be fair. They want to give work the mark that it deserves, to hire the best candidate, to judge submitted papers on their merits, and so on. Anyone who cares about doing these things should be very concerned about implicit bias—because implicit bias may well be unconsciously preventing them from being fair in this way. Even if they somehow become assured that they are not personally being affected in this way, they probably also want to be a part of a profession that is fair in these ways. So they should care about reducing or eradicating the effects of implicit bias on philosophy.

Many philosophers also believe, in one form or other, in equality of opportunity. There is a lot of debate over what this means. Most proponents of equal opportunity believe that we need to equalize that which stems from people's circumstances, but we need not equalize that which results from, roughly, *who the person is*. The problem, of course, is how to draw this all-important distinction. It's clear that whether one has access to nourishing food in early childhood is a matter of circumstance, and that having such food is important for the physical and mental development needed to have any real opportunities in life. But it's far less clear what to make of inequalities resulting from differences in effort. Whether one is hardworking seems initially to be a matter of *who one is*, but of course this will have been shaped by one's circumstances—for example, the attitudes toward effort that prevail in one's family or the prospects of success that one's society leads one to anticipate.

But the effects of implicit bias and stereotype threat are *not* difficult cases for the supporter of equal opportunity. First, take the case of implicit bias. The literature on implicit bias shows us that the marks one will receive for a piece of work, or its likelihood of publication, are affected by the marker's or referee's implicit biases. A man and a woman of equal abilities producing work that is equal in quality are likely to receive different marks and different referee reports. If this happens, the man is likely to have superior career opportunities. Because the variation is solely due to the assessor's implicit biases, there is no question that this is a failure of equal opportunity.

Now consider stereotype threat. This may at first seem like a trickier case, because stereotype threat will affect the actual performance of women, rendering it (in many cases) less good than it would otherwise be, and perhaps less good than men's. Consider the case of a female philosophy student who suffers from stereotype threat and a male philosophy student who does not. Suppose the woman and the man are equally philosophically talented (imagine for the sake of the example that we know what that means!). Suppose also that they are marked anonymously, so that the marker's implicit biases cannot influence the mark that they give. The woman may still get a lower mark than the man because the stereotype threat she suffers leads her to underperform and produce a piece of work that is less good than the man's, and less good than she is capable of producing. My contention is that this should be very worrying to the proponent of equal opportunities. Why? Because the woman's poor performance is due to her unequal circumstances. If she were in an environment that did not provoke stereotype threat—perhaps a department with ₁lots of women, in classes where women authors were well-represented on the syllabi—she would perform just as well as the man. Again, we have a clear case of an inequality caused by circumstances, just the sort of thing proponents of equal opportunities should want to eliminate.

3.2 BENEFITS TO PHILOSOPHY

One does not, however, have to care about either equal opportunities or fairness to think that something should be done about implicit bias and stereotype threat in philosophy. One only needs to care about philosophy. If implicit bias and stereotype threat are having the sorts of effects in philosophy that they have elsewhere, then women's work is being wrongly judged to be of lower quality than it actually is. This will lead to talented philosophers not being encouraged to continue, not getting grants, not getting jobs, not getting promoted, and not getting their work read. Moreover, talented and committed women philosophers are producing less good work than they otherwise would.

To get the best possible philosophy being done, we need the best philosophers to receive proper encouragement and good jobs, and to be working in environments where they can produce their best work. (See Helen Beebee's chapter in this volume for a discussion of stereotype threat and dropout rate.) Until we successfully do something about implicit bias and stereotype threat, this is not happening. The philosophy being produced is likely to be substantially worse than it would be in a fairer environment.

4. Remedies

So what should philosophers do to try to combat these problematic forces? The first thing to do is to note that one of the most widely used strategies—simply trying very hard to be unbiased—will do nothing to combat either implicit bias or stereotype threat. In fact, research shows that this may *increase* implicit bias (Stewart and Payne 2008: 1333).

4.1 BREAKING DOWN STEREOTYPES

This does not mean, however, that nothing can be done. One set of remedies stems from realising that both stereotype threat and implicit bias are due in part to the existence of stereotypes about women and about women in philosophy. Anything that can help to break these stereotypes down, then, will help to alleviate the problem. A clear way to break down the stereotypes is to make sure that people are exposed to excellent women in philosophy (Blair 2002; Kang and Banaji 2006). There are many ways in which this can be done: making sure to invite women speakers to departmental seminars and to conferences; including women in invited volumes; putting women philosophers' pictures up in departments and on websites; ensuring that reading lists include women philosophers.[22] These sorts of

---

[22] Given the workings of implicit bias and the state of philosophy, it may be difficult to think of female names. However, there are many options that could be tried, including Google Scholar, the Philosophers' Index, and Phil Papers. There are also new web-based resources for adding women to the syllabus being created as I write. It is worth seeking these out.

actions will help to break down stereotypes, but they will also help to overcome the effects of existing stereotypes. First, they will help to ensure that the work of excellent women is not overlooked, as it is likely to be due to implicit bias. Second, they will help to create a less stereotype threat-provoking environment.[23]

Mazarin Banaji, one of the leading scholars of implicit bias, has described her own efforts to expose herself to counter-stereotypical exemplars:

> For example, when she was recently asked to help select a psychologist for an award, Banaji says, she and two other panelists drew up a list of potential winners. But then they realized that their implicit biases might have eliminated many worthy candidates. So they came up with a new approach. They alphabetically went down a list of all the psychologists who were in the pool and evaluated each in turn (Vedantam 2005: 4).

Continuing along the same line of thought, it is also clear that it will be important and helpful to get more women into philosophy at every level in order to combat both implicit bias and stereotype threat. Exposure to counter-stereotypical exemplars helps to break down stereotypes and reduces one's tendency to be implicitly biased, and seeing more women who are philosophers reduces stereotype threat for women in philosophy. It is all the more important to do this when one considers that the current low numbers are likely to be partially the *result* of implicit bias and stereotype threat. But this is far easier said than done, at least partly due to the workings of implicit bias and stereotype threat. Hence, specific techniques are needed.

One very simple thing to do, at all levels, is to encourage women. Given the stereotypes of philosophy, women may need more explicit encouragement to think of themselves as good enough to go on in philosophy. This can take the form of simply encouraging those who are good at philosophy to continue: Monash University was able to increase (from around 20 percent to 50 percent) the number of women who continued on for an optional fourth year of philosophy simply by writing to *all* good students in the third year, encouraging them to continue. (This had the additional benefit of quadrupling the enrolment in the fourth year.)[24]

Including women and encouraging women can also go hand in hand. Stereotype threat can be reduced by exposing people from stigmatised groups

---

[23] One study asked math and science students to watch videos advertising a Maths, Science and Engineering Leadership Conference. In some videos, equal numbers of men and women were depicted. In others, there were three men for every woman. Experimenters monitored heart rate, blood pressure, and sweating. For men, none of these were affected by whether they saw a gender-balanced or unbalanced video. For women, all of these signs of stress were elevated by the gender-unbalanced video (Steele 149). Now think about the standard makeup of a philosophy conference, and reflect on the effects this might have on women philosophers. Bringing these conferences closer to balance could make an important difference.

[24] Personal communication from Rae Langton.

to narratives from other members of one's group who initially felt ill at ease, but then later became comfortable and successful. These narratives of success *despite* adversity can help to show both that the problems can be overcome and that the problems were due to something other than lack of ability. It might be worth trying to put together a book of these narratives in philosophy or a website. Further, women students can be told to remind themselves of these narratives before entering stressful situations. Research shows that "reminding women math students about strong women role models just before they took a difficult math test [eliminated] their typical underperformance on the test" (Steele 215).

When selecting graduate students or making hiring decisions, one should be aware of the ways that implicit bias may affect judgments. Many admissions and hiring committees have a commitment to improving gender balance and perhaps even to choosing a woman over an equally qualified man—but implicit bias may well prevent them from seeing which women are equally qualified.[25] It is often thought that putting women on these panels will be enough to correct for bias, but this is insufficient: Women may themselves be implicitly biased. What's most important is to have people on hiring panels who know about implicit bias and about techniques to keep it from wrongly disadvantaging candidates. Anyone can do this with the right knowledge and motivation. I was once on a panel where someone reported having heard that a female candidate was a very difficult and prickly person. A male panel member was the one who pointed out that women tend to be categorised as difficult and prickly when they engage in behaviours that are considered perfectly normal for men—and that we should therefore discount this. It is important to note, though, that women on panels in sufficient numbers may help to reduce stereotype threat for applicants at interviews.

4.2 BLOCKING THE EFFECTS OF STEREOTYPES

The remedies above are designed with the ultimate goal of undermining the stereotypes about gender and about philosophy that give rise to both stereotype threat and implicit bias. But another important kind of remedy is one that attempts to block the damaging effects of these stereotypes.

4.2.1 Anonymity

The most obvious such remedy is anonymising when possible. Implicit bias has nothing to work with if the person whose work is being evaluated is anonymous (unless they otherwise indicate their sex, race, etc.).

---

[25] There are some helpful suggestions here: <wiseli.engr.wisc.edu/docs/BiasBrochure_2ndEd. pdf>. This is a brief pamphlet that can easily be read by all members of a hiring committee.

Student work can and should be marked anonymously, as far as possible. This is now pretty much universal in the U.K., so it clearly can be done. This can readily be automated for institutions that use electronic submission. A quick low-tech alternative, suggested by Clea Rees,[26] is simply to have students put their identifying information on a cover sheet. Upon receipt of the essays, the marker can fold back the cover sheets of all essays before beginning to mark, thereby allowing the marker to avoid this identifying information until after grading is done. Obviously, in very small classes where drafts are read, it is very difficult to obtain anonymity. But this is no reason not to try in other classes.

Journal submissions should be anonymous, both to editor and to referees. Anonymous refereeing is widespread. Anonymity to editor does require the involvement of either an assistant or some good software. But it seems worth doing, given the costs of implicit bias both to justice and to the profession. It is worth bearing in mind that this will correct for a wide range of biases, including racial biases, biases against the less well known, those with foreign names or low-prestige institutions, and in favour of the famous.[27]

4.2.2 Altering Thought Patterns that Enhance the Effects of Stereotypes

It turns out that the pernicious effects of stereotypes—both in terms of implicit bias and in terms of stereotype threat—are much stronger in people who hold the view that intellectual ability is a thing that people possess to some fixed degree. It helps to set members of stigmatized groups up for stereotype threat (Steele 168–169), because it then becomes very easy to worry about whether one lacks intelligence (just as, stereotypically, other members of one's group do). More generally, the view that traits are fixed makes one more prone to stereotype endorsement (Levy et al. 1998) and to implicit bias. If intellectual ability is viewed as a more complicated set of abilities and skills, both of these problematic phenomena are reduced. And this latter view also has the benefit of being better supported by the psychological literature (Steele 168–169).

I think this is an especially important point for philosophers to reflect on, because it seems to me that philosophers are very prone to claims about "who's smart" and "who's stupid". I knew nothing of stereotype threat when I was in graduate school, but I do remember the terror I felt that I might someday be listed as one of the people who was "stupid" in the departmental lounge discussions. It could only be a good thing for the profession if philosophers stopped talking this way. (And this is so for reasons other than stereotype threat as well.

---

[26] Personal communication. Rees was not the originator of this idea, although she is not sure who was.

[27] Lee and Schunn (2010: 7) note that "a classic study found that when articles already published in highly prestigious psychology journals were resubmitted to the same journals, but under fictitious names with low-prestige institutions, nearly 90 percent were rejected." But the decisions were justified (no doubt sincerely) as being due to serious methodological flaws.

Fear of being labeled "stupid" undoubtedly makes everyone more hesitant to try out a really new and different idea, or to discuss one's work at an early stage, when it's still a bit inchoate but would really benefit from discussion.)

In addition, it is very likely that judgments of "who's smart" are affected by implicit bias. We've already seen plenty of reason to think that evaluative judgments are in general, but it seems likely to think that "smartness" judgments are especially susceptible to this. After all, they're judgments about what someone's capable of rather than their actual output: For example, "He's really smart, but it just doesn't come through in his work" is a perfectly normal sort of thing to say. The same is true of the negative judgments: For example, "She writes good papers, but that's just because she works so hard. I don't think she's really smart". The lack of sensitivity to actual results means that these judgments can be influenced *even more* by implicit biases.

Eric Schwitzegebel (2010) has written eloquently about the phenomenon of "seeming smart" in philosophy:

> I have been collecting anecdotal data on seeming smart. One thing I've noticed is what sort of person tends spontaneously to be described, in my presence, as "seeming smart". A very striking pattern emerges: In every case I have noted the smart-seeming person has been a young white male.... I would guess that there is something real behind that pattern, to wit:
>
> Seeming smart is probably to a large extent about activating people's *associations* with intelligence.... And what do people associate with intelligence? Some things that are good: Poise, confidence (but not defensiveness), giving a moderate amount of detail but not too much, providing some frame and jargon, etc. But also, unfortunately, I suspect: whiteness, maleness, a certain physical bearing, a certain dialect (one American type, one British type), certain patterns of prosody—all of which favor, I suspect, upper- to upper-middle class white men.

It would seem to me, then, to be a good idea in many ways for philosophers to forswear judgments of "who's smart" and "who's stupid".[28]

4.2.3 Creating Stereotype Threat-Reducing Situations

Another important way to block the effects of stereotypes is to create stereotype threat-reducing situations. We have already seen some ways of doing this: including more women (which also undermines the stereotypes) is an important method. But in addition there are some remedies directed specifically at stereotype threat that have been shown to make a difference. For example, reminding students—or oneself—that anxiety experienced may be

---

[28] On this topic, see also Beebee and Brennan, this volume.

the result of stereotype threat (Johns et al. 2005) has been shown to reduce the effects of stereotype threat. In addition, focusing on one's membership in groups that are not negatively stereotyped (e.g., those that have been accepted to a top Ph.D. programme) can reduce stereotype threat (Steele 2010: 170).[29]

4.3 RAISING AWARENESS

A longer-term important remedy is to raise awareness of implicit bias and stereotype threat among philosophers. It is only by implementing this remedy that philosophers will begin to understand these phenomena and work to overcome their influence. The picture of bias that seems to prevail among philosophers is the traditional one, in which (a) there are some very bad racist and sexist people who hold explicitly biased beliefs (e.g., "women aren't good at reasoning"); and (b) those who hold explicitly egalitarian beliefs don't need to worry about being biased. As long as this picture prevails, implicit bias cannot be fought in the ways that it needs to be fought, because people believe that their genuinely held egalitarian beliefs mean that they are not biased. Philosophers need to become aware that good people who sincerely hold egalitarian beliefs may still be unconsciously biased.

I think it is also important to abandon the view that all biases against stigmatised groups are *blameworthy*. My first reason for abandoning this view is its falsehood. A person should not be blamed for an implicit bias of which they are completely unaware that results solely from the fact that they live in a sexist culture. Even once they become aware that they are likely to have implicit biases, they do not instantly become able to control their biases, and so they should not be blamed for them. (They may, however, be blamed if they fail to act properly on the knowledge that they are likely to be biased—e.g., by investigating and implementing remedies to deal with their biases.)

My second reason is far more practical. What we need is an acknowledgment that we are all likely to be implicitly biased—only this can provide the motivation for what needs to be done. If acknowledging that one is biased means declaring oneself to be one of those bad racist or sexist people, we cannot realistically expect the widespread acknowledgement that is required. Instead, we'll get defensiveness and hostility. It's worth noting, though, that disassociating implicit bias and blame does not mean failing to insist that implicit bias is *bad*. It clearly is, and it is important to insist on this—even while insisting (accurately, it seems to me) that we should not be blamed for our implicit biases.[30]

---

[29] Further interventions can be found at reducingstereotypethreat.org.
[30] For a fuller discussion of blame and implicit bias, see Kelly and Roedder 2008.

4.4 EXPERIMENT

We don't know yet what will work in philosophy to combat implicit bias and stereotype threat. I've offered some suggestions, but they are only that: suggestions. And there are undoubtedly many more things that one might try. Fortunately, many of the strategies are fairly simple to implement, so uncertainty about their prospects for success shouldn't deter people from trying. For example, after reading a draft of this chapter, Helen Beebee has decided to discuss stereotype threat at the beginning of her logic classes at Birmingham University, as that's one place where stereotype threat is especially likely to arise. Jules Holroyd and Adam Caulton have included information on implicit bias and stereotype threat in the guidance given to directors of studies at Cambridge University. Dan Egonsson (University of Lund, Sweden) has decided to preferentially call on women students, even if men raise their hands first.[31] Heather Kuiper, a Ph.D. student at McMaster University, has suggested starting exams with a question that happens to refer to a woman philosopher.

Philosophers need to inform themselves about these phenomena and then try out techniques to combat them. And then we need to discuss what works and what doesn't work.[32]

5. Conclusion

We really should not be surprised that women continue to be underrepresented in philosophy. Until very recently, women had very little real chance to engage in philosophy. That legacy of exclusion—combined with a cultural view of women as creatures of emotion rather than reason—helped to generate stereotypes that make it far more difficult for women to succeed in philosophy. The literature on implicit bias and stereotype threat shows us that such stereotypes affect both how women perform and how such performances are evaluated. If what I have argued here is correct, these stereotypes are harming women by denying them fairness and equality of opportunity in philosophy. And they are harming philosophy by causing inaccurate evaluations of philosophical work and philosophers and by impeding women's ability to do the best philosophical work that they can—which causes philosophy as a field to be less good than it otherwise might be. Barring the discovery that philosophers have some rare immunity to the biases and influences that affect others, I think we have

---

[31] Cheshire Calhoun's 2009 paper also suggests some strategies to try.

[32] One thought might be for people to send information about their real-life experiments to the blog: What We're Doing About What it's Like: <http://whatweredoingaboutwhatitslike.wordpress.com/>.

good reason to believe that this is in fact happening. The question now is what to do about it. I have offered some suggestions above. But perhaps the most important point is the simplest: that philosophers need to start discussing this problem.

There is good reason to hope that such efforts will make a difference. One reason for thinking this is that implicit bias and stereotype threat are incredibly important forces that have only recently begun to be understood. It's not the case that we've been trying for decades and failing—we're only just beginning to try, and the literature shows us that small interventions can have large effects. Another reason for hope is that we have already seen this happen: In 1995, C. Wenneras and A. Wold performed a landmark study of Swedish scientific grant awards. It showed that women needed to be 2.5 times as productive as men to get grants. This study got a huge amount of attention in 1995 and even more in 1997 when they published their results in *Nature*. As a result of the 1995 results, procedures were changed, and what is now called "the Wold Effect" occurred: The gender gap vanished. Change is possible.

Acknowledgment

A huge number of people deserve thanks for their help with this chapter (including some I have probably forgotten): Heather Arnold, Albert Atkin, Louise Antony, Helen Beebee, Laura Beeby, Josep Corbi, Ray Drainville, Dan Egonsson, Cathrine Felix, Stavroulas Glezakos, Sally Haslanger, Jules Holroyd, Chris Hookway, Andrew Howat, Katrina Hutchison, Anne Jacobson, Fiona Jenkins, Rosanna Keefe, Daniel Kelly, Peter Kirwan, Rae Langton, Steve Laurence, Carole Lee, Mari Mikkola, Kate Norlock, Angie Pepper, Lina Papadaki, Lindsey Porter, Clea Rees, Komarine Romdenh-Romluc, Frank Saul, Julie Saul, Eric Schwitzgebel, Miriam Solomon, Steve Stich, Virgina Valian, and Alison Wylie. I am also grateful to audiences at Lund University and Cardiff University. I should note that this paper was formerly titled "Unconscious Influences and Women in Philosophy".

References

Antony, L. 2012. "Different Voices or Perfect Storm—Why Are There So Few Women in Philosophy?" *Journal of Social Philosophy* XLIII: 3, 227–255.

Bartky, S. 1990. *Femininity and Domination*, New York: Routledge.

Blair, I. 2002. "The Malleability of Automatic Stereotypes and Prejudice", *Personality and Social Psychology Review* 3: 242–261.

Blanton, H., and Jaccard, J. 2006. "Arbitrary Metrics in Psychology", *American Psychologist* 61: 1, 27–41.

Buckwalter, W., and Stich, S. 2010. "Gender and Philosophical Intuition: Why Are There So Few Women in Philosophy?" talk given at Society for Philosophy and Psychology, Portland, OR.

Budden, A., Tregenza, T., Aarssen, L., Koricheva, J., Leimu, R. and Lortie, C. 2008. "Double-Blind Review Favours Increased Representation of Female Authors", *Trends in Ecology and Evolution* 23:1, 4–6.

Calhoun, C. 2009. "The Undergraduate Pipeline Problem", *Hypatia* 24: 2, 216–223.

Correll, S., and Benard, S. 2007. "Getting a Job: Is There a Motherhood Penalty?" *American Journal of Sociology* 112: 1297–1338.

Fine, C. 2010. *Delusions of Gender*, London: Icon Books.

Goddard, E. 2008. "Improving the Position of Women in the Philosophy Profession", http://aap.org.au/women/reports/index.html#Ausreports.

Goldin, C., and Rouse, C. 2000. "Orchestrating Impartiality: The Impact of 'Blind' Auditions on Female Musicians", *American Economic Review* 90:4, 715–741.

Goodyear, R., Reynolds, P., and Gragg, J. 2010. "University Faculty Experiences of Classroom Incivilities: A Critical Incident Study", paper presented to American Educational Research Association.

Greenwald, A., Rudman, L., Nosek, B., and Zayas, V. 2006. "Why So Little Faith? A Reply to Blanton and Jaccard's (2006) Skeptical View of Testing Pure Multiplicative Theories", *Psychological Review* 113: 1, 170–180.

Hanrahan, R., and Antony, L. 2005. "Because I Said So: Toward a Feminist Theory of Authority", *Hypatia* 20: 4, 59–79.

Haslanger, S. 2008. "Changing the Ideology and Culture of Philosophy: Not By Reason (Alone)", *Hypatia* 23: 2, 210–223.

Johns, M., Schmader, T., and Martens, A. 2005. "Knowing is Half the Battle: Teaching about Stereotype Threat as a Means of Improving Women's Math Performance", *Psychological Science* 16:3, 175–179.

Jordan-Young, R. 2011. *Brain Storm*, Cambridge, MA: Harvard University Press.

Jost, J. T., Rudman, L. A., Blair, I. V., Carney, D., Dasgupta, N., Glaser, J., and Hardin, C. D. 2009. "The existence of implicit bias is beyond reasonable doubt: A refutation of ideological and methodological objections and executive summary of ten studies that no manager should ignore", *Research in Organizational Behavior*

Kang, J., and Banaji, M. 2006. "Fair Measures: A Behavioral Realist Revision of 'Affirmative action'", *California Law Review* 94: 1063–1118.

Kelly, D., and Roedder, E. 2008. "Racial Cognition and the Ethics of Implicit Bias", *Philosophy Compass* 3:3, 522–540,

Lane, K. A., Kang, J., and Banaji, M. 2007. "Implicit Social Cognition and Law", *Annual Review of Law and Social Science* 3: 427–51.

Lee, C., and Schunn, C. 2010. "Philosophy Journal Practices and Opportunities for Bias", *APA Newsletter on Feminism and Philosophy*.

Levy, S., Stroessner, S., and Dweck, C. 1998. "Stereotype Formation and Endorsement: The Role of Implicit Theories", *Journal of Personality and Social Psychology* 74: 6, 1421–1436.

Link, A., Swann, C., and Bozeman, B. 2008. "A Time Allocation Study of University Faculty", *Economics of Education Review* 27: 363–374.

Madera, J., Hebl, M., and Martin, R. 2009. "Gender and Letters of Recommendation for Academia: Agentic and Communal Differences", *Journal of Applied Psychology* 94: 6, 1591–1599.

Misra, J., Lundquist, J. H., Holmes, E., and Agiomavritis, S. "The Ivory Ceiling of Service Work", Academe Online January-February 2011: <http://www.aaup.org/AAUP/pubsres/academe/2011/JF/Feat/misr.htm>.

Miyake, A., Kost-Smith, L., Finkelstein, N., Pollock, S., Cohen, G., and Ito, T. 2010. "Reducing the Gender Achievement Gap in College Science: A Classroom Study of Values Affirmation", *Science* 330: 1234–1237.

Moss-Racusin, C., Dovidio, J., Brescoll, V., Graham, M. and Handelsman, J. 2012. "Science Faculty's Subtle Gender Biases Favor Male Students," *PNAS* 109: 41, 16474–16479.

Nosek, B., Banaji, M., and Greenwald, J. 2002. "Math = male, me = female, therefore math ≠ me", *Journal of Personality and Social Psychology* 83, 44–59.

Rowe, M. 2008. "Micro-Affirmations and Micro-Inequities", *Journal of the International Ombudsman Association* 1:1 (also available at http://web.mit.edu/ombud/publications/micro-affirm-ineq.pdf).

Sadker, D., Sadker, M., and Zittleman, K. 2009. *Still Failing at Fairness: How Gender Bias Cheats Girls and Boys in School and What We Can Do About It*, NY: Scribner.

Sandström, U., and Hällsten, M. 2008. "Persistent nepotism in peer-review", *Scientometricis* 74: 175–189.

Schwitzgebel, E. 2010. "On Being Good at Seeming Smart", http://schwitzsplinters.blogspot.com/2010/03/on-being-good-at-seeming-smart.html.

Solomon, M., and Clarke, J. 2009. "CSW Jobs for Philosophers Employment Study", *APA Newsletter on Feminism and Philosophy* 8: 2, 3–6.

Steele, C. 2010. *Whistling Vivaldi: And Other Clues to How Stereotypes Affect Us*, New York: W. W. Norton.

Steinpreis, R., Anders, K., and Ritzke, D. 1999. "The Impact of Gender on the Review of the Curricula Vitae of Job Applicants and Tenure Candidates: A National Empirical Study", *Sex Roles* 41: 7/8, 509–528.

Stewart, B. D., and Payne, B. K. 2008. "Bringing Automatic Stereotyping Under Control: Implementation Intentions as Efficient Means of Thought Control", *Personality and Social Psychology Bulletin* 34: 1332–1345.

Superson, A. 2002. "Sexism in the Classroom", in Superson, A., and Cudd, A., *Theorizing Backlash: Philosophical Reflections on Resistance to Feminism*, Oxford, UK: Rowman and Littlefield, 201–213.

Uhlmann, E., and Cohen, G. 2007. " 'I think it, therefore it's true': Effects of self-perceived objectivity on hiring discrimination", *Organizational Behavior and Human Decision Processes 104*, 207–223.

Valian, V. 1999. *Why So Slow? The Advancement of Women* Cambridge, MA: MIT Press.

Valian, V. 2005. "Beyond Gender Schemas: Improving the Advancement of Women in Academia", *Hypatia* 20:3, 198–213.

Vedantam, S. 2005. "See No Bias", *Washington Post*, 21 January, accessed at <http://www.washingtonpost.com/wp-dyn/articles/A27067-2005Jan21.html> on 29 July 2010.

Vest, C. 1999. "Introductory Comments", in *A Study on the Status of Women Faculty in Science at MIT*

Wenneras, C., and Wold, A. 1997. "Nepotism and Sexism in Peer Review", *Nature* 387, 341–343.

Women in Science and Engineering Leadership Institute. 2006. "Reviewing Applicants: Research on Bias and Assumptions", <wiseli.engr.wisc.edu/docs/BiasBrochure_2ndEd.pdf>.

3

Women and Deviance in Philosophy
Helen Beebee

1. Typicality, Deviance, and Explanation

The central idea of this chapter is that of deviance: the thought that standards of various sorts in philosophy are determined by what is 'typical' (the 'typical' philosopher being a man), and that, as far as those standards are concerned, women—'atypical' philosophers—are therefore counted as deviant in some way.[1]

One problem with addressing the issue of the lack of female professional philosophers is that it is apt to engender the thought that it is women who are implicitly being told to change their ways, by becoming more like the typical (male) philosopher. This is an instance of a wider phenomenon that is nicely described by the psychologist Deborah Tannen:

> Some women fear, with justification, that any observation of gender differences will be heard as implying that it is women who are different— different from the standard, which is whatever men are. The male is seen as normative, the female as departing from the norm. And it is only a short step—maybe an inevitable one—from 'different' to 'worse'. Furthermore, if women's and men's styles are shown to be different, it is usually women who are told to change. (1990, 14)

The thought that 'the male is seen as normative' in areas where the 'typical' person in a given area is deemed to be male is backed up in a study by Miller, Taylor, and Buck (1991). Their hypothesis was that when explanations are offered for differences between the behaviour of typical and atypical members of a given class, those explanations tend to focus on the behaviour of the

---

[1] Similar dynamics are doubtless at work with other minorities: The 'typical' philosopher, at least in the U.K., is not only male but white and middle class. However I shall restrict my attention to gender in this chapter.

atypical members. A preliminary study ascertained that the 'typical' U.S. voter tends to be thought of as male. Subjects were asked to imagine the characteristics of 'the typical American voter' and either to assign a name or to assign a gender to their imagined typical voter. 82 percent of subjects assigned a male name, and 72 percent described the typical voter as male—and these percentages did not differ significantly between male and female subjects (ibid., 7).[2] In a further study, subjects were asked to explain differences in turnout between male and female voters in U.S. elections.

The results of the study confirmed the hypothesis. Explanations provided by the subjects were coded as 'female'—that is, focused on explaining why women were more/less likely to vote (e.g., 'perhaps women vote less frequently because the electoral system is a less viable means for change for women in society')—or 'male' (e.g., 'men are more concerned about and hence involved with the power structure and economy'). The mean number of female explanations per subject was 1.45, and the mean number of male explanations was 0.4. Moreover, subjects were also asked: 'If the gender gap were to disappear, would it more likely be due to (a) men's turnout rate becoming like that of women's, or (b) women's turnout rate becoming like that of men's?' Eighty-five percent of respondents gave the latter answer, a result reminiscent of Tannen's claim that 'it is usually women who are told to change'.

In a further study, subjects were asked to explain the discrepancy between the number of doctor visits per year between men and women elementary school teachers (where women are regarded as typical) or college professors (where men are regarded as typical). There were more male explanations when the group was identified as elementary school teachers, and fewer female explanations, than there were when the group was identified as college professors. Again, then, it was the behaviour of the atypical members of the group that was generally deemed to require explanation.

What applications does this result have for the issue of the underrepresentation of women in philosophy? In the rest of this chapter, I explore two very different areas in which women might be thought to be the ones who need to change. In §2, I discuss the combative style of informal discussion that is prevalent in philosophy. I argue that there is a clear distinction between style and content when it comes to philosophical discussions, and that an overly combative seminar style serves no philosophical purpose and may be alienating to (some) women. Failure to make this distinction naturally leads to the view that objecting to such a combative atmosphere amounts to holding that women just

---

[2] I ran an unscientific version of this preliminary study in my first-year logic class. In a class of around 100 students, about 50 percent of whom were female, students were asked to imagine the typical student who is good at logic and to either assign a gender to them or give them a name. Ninety-three percent of responses assigned a male name and 76 percent described the typical good-at-logic student as male.

can't cut it in the philosophical battleground: an instance of the view that it is women who are deviant and therefore need to raise their game.

In §3, I discuss empirically discovered differences in philosophical intuitions between men and women in the context of Wesley Buckwalter and Stephen Stich's (2011) hypothesis that these differences play a role in the dwindling proportion of women at successive levels of undergraduate study. I argue that philosophical and pedagogical recommendations for the teaching of areas of philosophy where intuitions play a major role, and where significant gender differences emerge, come together. On the philosophical side, there are no grounds for ignoring significant differences in intuitions across different subpopulations of speakers; and on the pedagogical side, dealing sensitively with such differences (as opposed to, say, telling students who have 'atypical' intuitions that they are wrong) may, if Buckwalter and Stich are right, play a role in stemming the flow of female undergraduates away from philosophy courses. Attempts to lessen the 'selection effect' that Buckwalter and Stich hypothesise would thus be philosophically, as well as pedagogically, legitimate.

2. The Seminar as a Philosophical Battleground

There are easier and harder issues to discuss when trying to make some progress on the question of why the proportion of women in philosophy drops off the way that it does. Easier issues, in a sense to be explained, include those discussed by Jennifer Saul in her contribution to this volume: implicit bias and stereotype threat. These are 'easy' issues in the sense that (a) there is a considerable body of evidence that people in general—and so philosophers in particular—are subject to these phenomena; and, more important, (b) we can accept that implicit bias and stereotype threat exist, and suggest practical ways in which they might be mitigated or overcome, without even having to ask the hard question of whether the relevant stereotype ('women are generally worse at philosophy than men', say) is true.

The question of whether a particular stereotype is true is a hard question for at least two reasons. First, stereotypes tend to be rather vaguely specified (what counts as being 'better' at philosophy?), and second, given the pervasiveness of stereotype threat, it is unclear how the truth of the stereotype could be established in practice, because any evidence that we might take to confirm the stereotype may itself be a result of stereotype threat. To use a familiar example, I don't know whether it's true that whites tend to outperform blacks on IQ tests, but let's suppose for the sake of the argument that it is. This does not constitute evidence that whites are, on average, more intelligent than blacks, partly because it is unclear (to say the least) that IQ tests measure *intelligence* in the ordinary sense of the word (and hence the sense in play in the relevant stereotype), as opposed to the very specific cognitive skills that IQ tests directly

measure; and also because an IQ test is a paradigmatic stereotype-threat situation for blacks, so one would expect a black person with the same level of ability as a white person to get a lower score.

The point here is that, as I say, the 'easy' issues are easy partly because we
can accept the reality of, and consider ways of mitigating, implicit bias and stereotype threat without having to ask the hard question of whether the relevant
stereotype is true. For even if the stereotype *were* true, that would not in any
way justify, for example, judging a particular woman's job application more
harshly than a similarly qualified man's, or failing to attempt to reduce stereotype threat. (Even if girls were generally worse at maths than boys, that would
be no reason not to take steps to ensure that girls perform to the best of their
ability by reducing stereotype threat.)

One question that might seem to fall in the 'hard' rather than the 'easy'
category is whether the culture of philosophical discussion is one that tends
to alienate women. I shall start by discussing what I think should be an obvious distinction between the style and the content of philosophical discussion.
I then turn to discussing a couple of responses that an earlier—very brief—
airing of this issue by me received; this will connect with the discussion of §1
above, as we shall see. Finally, I return to the apparently 'hard' question just
raised and argue that it is, in fact, an 'easy' question, in the sense described
above. Once we grant that combative and aggressive behaviours are culturally
deemed to be masculine behaviours—independently of whether this is really
true—the alienating effects of such behaviours can be seen to be a trigger for
stereotype threat. And stereotype threat, as I have said, is *easy*. We do not have
to ask whether men, or male philosophers, are naturally inclined or culturally
encouraged to be more aggressive or combative than women or than female
philosophers; that question does not need to be answered in order to argue that
a combative seminar style can be alienating for women.

In 2009, *The Philosophers' Magazine* ran a story about the low proportion
of women in U.K. philosophy departments, to which I contributed a couple of
sound bites. Here is a passage from the article:

> Helen Beebee, a University of Birmingham lecturer and director of the
> British Philosophical Association (BPA)…says her impression is that
> there are roughly equal numbers of men and women graduating with
> good bachelor degrees in philosophy and that the numbers of women
> start to drop off at MA level and then again at PhD level. Beebee says
> this tapering off of women may be at least partly caused by a culture of
> aggressive argument that is particular to philosophy and which begins to
> become more prominent at postgraduate level. 'I can remember being a
> PhD student and giving seminar papers and just being absolutely terrified
> that I was going to wind up intellectually beaten to a pulp by the audience,'
> she says. 'I can easily imagine someone thinking, "this is just ridiculous,

why would I want to pursue a career where I open myself up to having my work publicly trashed on a regular basis?"' (Lewis 2009)

These comments provoked a somewhat unfriendly response on a couple of philosophy blogs, to which I shall return shortly. Rather than remove my head from above the parapet, however, I would like to explain just what I had in mind, and why I think there is a legitimate concern here.

There is an extent to which philosophy is, in its nature, an adversarial discipline. By and large, philosophers cannot prove any theorems; nor can we appeal to empirical data to justify our claims. Our arguments typically rely on assumptions that are not beyond reproach, and the arguments themselves often fall short of deductive validity. When we present a paper at a conference or seminar, normally we present such an argument, and our audience is entitled to assume that we believe the argument to start from plausible premises and, given those premises, to be reasonably convincing.

What we tend to find, however—and of course this is a large part of the point of presenting one's work to an audience—is that the argument was less convincing than we realised. It often turns out that our premises are more controversial than we thought, or that we have equivocated at a crucial point, or that there is a counter-example to our conclusion, or that the argument licenses only a weaker conclusion than the one we have drawn, or whatever. And of course we only find these useful things out if people draw our attention to them. Hence the claim that philosophy is, to some extent, adversarial in nature: It is a large, and entirely proper, part of the philosophical enterprise to point out to people where they have gone wrong.

I do not object to any of this. What I want to claim, however, is that seminar discussions frequently enshrine a confrontational attitude that is entirely separable from the philosophical content of those discussions. There is all the difference in the world between, on the one hand, raising an objection in a friendly and constructive manner and, on the other, raising it in a manner (by choice of words, body language, and so on) that suggests that you think the objection is just *obvious*, and hence that the speaker must not be very clever, having failed to spot it for themselves. Similarly, I am certain that most readers will have come across at least one philosopher who—if not kept on a sufficiently short leash by the chair—will continue to harangue the speaker on a particular point long after it is obvious to everyone in the room that the questioner's criticism is a good one and that the speaker is not going to be able to think up a convincing off-the-cuff rejoinder. No philosophical purpose is served by this kind of behaviour.

Or consider how rarely members of the audience make constructive suggestions: 'perhaps you could say this in response to the previous question', or 'actually maybe your argument licenses an even stronger conclusion', or whatever; or how rarely participants preface their question with a compliment about the paper ('I enjoyed that', or 'I thought what you said about X was interest-ing'). Of course, some philosophers take the view that such niceties are social conventions that have no place in the robust pursuit of the truth. (I myself used to take that view, and still find it unnatural to put the speaker at their ease before launching into my objection—so much so that I unfortunately very rarely remember to do it.) But in a seminar setting, social conventions are always in play whether we like it or not: Truth cannot be pursued but through the medium of conversation, and conversation is a social phenomenon. And of course social conventions are not set in stone: In principle, we could choose to make the atmosphere in our seminars more supportive and to regard the pur-suit of truth as a matter of collaboration between speaker and audience rather than conflict.

Indeed, a more collaborative atmosphere may positively aid the pursuit of truth. For example, I would bet that many audience members in seminars that have a combative atmosphere have questions that they would like to ask, but they do not do so because they are not completely confident that they have fully understood the point at issue and are afraid of looking 'dumb' (as opposed to looking 'smart'—see Saul, this volume). This is especially likely to be the case for research students and temporary staff who may assume that their perfor-mance will be taken into account in letters of reference or judgments of suit-ability for future posts in the department. So an atmosphere that encourages rather than discourages people to participate might well turn up some excellent points from audience members who are less confident or who believe (rightly or wrongly) that asking a misguided question will have an adverse effect on their future career that would otherwise remain unheard. And the worst that can happen is that the questioner hasn't understood, and so a couple of minutes are spent setting them straight. This may not aid the collective pursuit of truth, but it certainly benefits the questioner—something that ought to be seen as a good thing and not merely a waste of everyone else's time.

The idea that the philosophy seminar is to be seen as a form of combat is not, thankfully, explicitly embraced very often, as far as I can tell. But it does exist. An example that I gave in the *TPM* article is of a (senior male) member of staff keeping a tally of 'home wins' and 'away wins' on the whiteboard in his office, and initiating discussion in the pub (not in the presence of the speaker, I'm happy to say) of which category the most recent seminar fell under. (I think they were virtually all home wins.) Another example, I think—and a more com-mon one—is the idea that it is a philosophical weakness not to be able to think of an immediate off-the-cuff, decisive response to an objection, and instead to commit to giving the objection further thought later. The ability to think fast on one's feet is doubtless an intellectual virtue of sorts, but I can see no rea-son to think that it is a specifically philosophical virtue. The pursuit of philo-sophical truth is not hindered in any way by its taking someone a few hours, rather than ten seconds, to think of a plausible rejoinder. Similarly, I have been surprised by the extent to which responses that manifestly and deliberately do not answer the question posed, but rather speak to a slightly different, easier one, are favourably regarded, as though they constitute admirable strategic manoeuvres in the face of enemy forces. Again, no philosophical virtue is being exhibited here; quite the reverse, in fact.

The adversarial nature of philosophical discussion has been discussed at some length by feminist philosophers. Trudy Govier, for example, distinguishes between 'minimal' and 'ancillary adversariality', which more or less maps on to the distinction made above between content and style—minimal adversariality being the kind of adversariality I earlier described as part and parcel of the philosophical enterprise, and ancillary adversariality being the kind of aggressive and combative behaviour that is entirely separable from the robust pursuit of truth that philosophical argument is supposed to be aimed at (Govier 1999, especially 244–246).

Phyllis Rooney (2010), while broadly sympathetic to Govier's distinction, argues that even Govier's description of minimal adversariality enshrines an 'argument-as-war' metaphor that misdescribes the dialectical situation by using terms such as 'opponent' and 'conflict', and hence that the minimal/ancillary distinction (and perhaps by extension my content/style distinction) is 'more porous than we might initially think' (2010, 222):

> War-like metaphors (shooting down points, attacking positions and persons, going after fatal flaws, and so on), often enacted more explicitly and problematically with ancillary adversariality, have their less bellicose cousins—but cousins still—in the minimal adversariality informing basic understandings and descriptions of argument and argumentation. They do so to the extent that... we barely recognize them as such, even when they are characterizing argument situations in epistemically erroneous and confusing ways. (Ibid.)

Part of Rooney's point, then, is that the argument-as-war metaphor cuts a lot deeper than is normally recognised.[3] Just one (but by no means the only) aspect of this is that we tend to conceive of face-to-face arguments in philosophy as things to be won and lost: 'I *lose* the argument and you *win*. ... But surely I am the one who has made the epistemic *gain*, however small. I have replaced a probably false belief with a probably true one, and you have made no such gain' (2010, 222). Again, the thought here is that the way in which we often conceive seminar-based philosophical discussion is actually in tension with our own self-image as seekers after the truth: The *epistemic* gain that should be our

---

[3] As may be obvious, I only discovered (a small corner of) the large feminist philosophy literature on this topic after this chapter was substantially written; hence I am doing little more than drawing the reader's attention to it here, rather than discussing it in detail. See Rooney 2010 for many additional references.

goal is supplanted by the aim of winning the battle. Right at the start of my first-year logic course, I tell the students that the sense of 'argument' at work in logic in particular, and in philosophy in general, is different from the more usual sense of 'argument', as in 'having an argument with' someone. They would doubtless find that claim hard to square with the way in which many professional philosophy seminar discussions are actually conducted.

My favourite example of a hostile style—though admittedly not in the context of a seminar—is a blog response that the passage from Lewis 2009 quoted above elicited from a professional philosopher:

> Helen Beebee, though I'm sure you're a wonderful director of the BPA, please think of handing over the reigns [sic]...you don't know the first thing about (a) the fallacious use of anecdotal evidence, (b) the problems of shitty causal inferences that (c) reinforce naturalist assumptions dominant in the culture. And (d) please tell me that you don't think the problem is that women can't cut it. Because men like getting their work trashed?
>
> Or better: maybe if we had more women in place at various universities, you know, getting hired, as Saul suggests, we could find someone to head the BPA (male or female or non-normed gender) who can 'easily imagine' ways to work for different modes of philosophizing, say, as head of something like the BPA....Now instead of asking—from what you can 'easily imagine'— what a PhD student would be thinking, how about asking about a culture that needs to be changed so you can 'easily imagine' this? [4]

The wonderful irony of this response is of course that it exhibits (in admittedly a rather extreme form) precisely the kind of culture of aggressive argument to which I was alluding: the response to the claim that 'this tapering off of women may be at least partly caused by a culture of aggressive argument that is particular to philosophy' is to accuse me of being, in effect, woefully ignorant and professionally incompetent.

Another blog post commenting on the article, this time by Brian Leiter, goes as follows:

> ...some female philosophers in the UK [suggest] that the aggressive, argumentative style of philosophy drives women out. A female philosopher...found this...explanation (quite correctly) demeaning to women....[5]

This passage, it seems to me, fails to make just the distinction between style and content that I have been urging. Philosophy does—in its nature—have an

---

[4] Quoted from philosophyinatimeoferror.wordpress.com/2009/09/07/women-in-philosophy/ (accessed 2 April 2013).

[5] Leiter Reports, leiterreports.typepad.com/blog/2009/10/situation-for-women-in-philosophy-makes-the-ny-times.html (accessed 2 April 2013). The clarification mentioned below also appears at this URL.

'argumentative' style in the sense that philosophical claims are established by means of argument, and seminar questions are normally themselves arguments to the effect that the speaker has made a false or unwarranted or ambiguous claim. But this does not, of course, entail that philosophical discussion is inherently, or ought to be, 'argumentative' in the ordinary sense of the word: pursued in a manner that is belligerent, competitive, nit-picking, or whatever. Nor, obviously, is there anything inherently 'aggressive' about an 'argumentative' style in the first sense: There are nicer and less nice ways of telling someone that she has appealed to an implausible premise, or that her view is subject to a counter-example, or whatever. So to describe 'the' style of philosophy as an 'aggressive, argumentative style' is to fail to distinguish the argumentative substance of philosophical discussion from the aggressive style in which that argumentative substance is often pursued. (I should point out that Leiter later published a clarification of the position I was defending—along the lines described here—at my request. In addition, it may be that the intended meaning of 'the aggressive, argumentative style of philosophy' was in fact something like 'the aggressive, argumentative style of philosophy as it is *in fact* frequently conducted', and not 'the aggressive, argumentative style that is inherent in the nature of philosophy'. Thus interpreted, the quoted passage does not equivocate in the way just suggested. It is nonetheless unclear to me why the suggestion that such an atmosphere 'drives women out' should be considered 'demeaning to women'—see below.)

Both of these responses to the *TPM* article relate to the discussion in §1 of some findings in psychology. Recall that the point there was that explanations for the differences between 'typical' and 'atypical' members of a group (U.S. voters and college professors, for example) tend to focus on features of the atypical group, with the assumption—explicit in the case of the experiment concerning U.S. voters—that it is the members of the atypical group whose behaviour is deviant. (Recall that 85 percent of subjects thought that a change in the gender gap in voting behaviour would be due to the women's turnout rate becoming like that of the men.)

This kind of phenomenon might explain the blog responses described above. The first author took me to be suggesting that 'women can't cut it' in philosophy; the second that women are 'driven out' by 'the aggressive, argumentative style of philosophy'—a claim that is 'demeaning to women'. These interpretations of my words seem to presuppose that an aggressive style is somehow inherent in the philosophical enterprise. I have already argued that that is a mistake; however, the question is, why would someone make that mistake? One answer might be that what is *in fact* a typical feature of philosophical discussion is implicitly assumed to be a *good* thing: the typical feature (namely, an aggressive argument style) is seen as 'normative' (to use Tannen's expression). This being so, my suggestion that that typical feature might be off-putting to women is then read as claiming that women are deviant—they depart from the norm. And, as Tannen says, 'it is only a short step—maybe an inevitable one—from "different" to "worse"', hence the inclination to read my suggestion as 'demeaning' to women—an interpretation that, as should be obvious, was not intended.

I have not yet addressed the question with which I started this section: Whether the somewhat combative atmosphere of (what is in my experience) the typical philosophy seminar is, in fact, one that tends to alienate women. This is of course an empirical question; and it may seem to fall into the 'hard' category identified earlier, since it would appear to be a question about the *truth* of a stereotype (the stereotype in this case being that women are more averse to aggressive styles of argument than men are). But I want to suggest that the first question can be answered affirmatively without addressing the question about the *truth* of the stereotype. So the relationship between the two questions is a little like the relationship between 'do girls tend to perform worse than boys on maths tests?' and 'are girls worse than boys at maths?' The answer to the first question is 'yes' (in stereotype threat-provoking situations at least)—and this is so independently of whether the answer to the second question is 'yes' or 'no'.

As with the maths-test case, we need to set the issue in the context of the kinds of psychological influences to which female students (and staff) are exposed outside of the seminar room. As Saul argues in her contribution to this volume, implicit bias is a pervasive feature of working environments, and there are no grounds for thinking that the philosophy seminar room is an exception. In addition, however, there is evidence that a range of more specific biases are at work within the sciences; and, as a discipline that bears some similarity to the sciences—both (at least in some areas of philosophy) intellectually and (in most areas) in terms of the underrepresentation of women—it is reasonable to assume that similar biases are at work in philosophy. In particular, there is plenty of empirical evidence that in the sciences, women are typically exposed to a vast array of influences that can make them feel uncomfortable, or even unwanted, in their chosen discipline (see Seymour and Hewitt 1997; Margolis and Fisher 2002). These influences start early and can persist through their studies and beyond, and include not only implicit biases of various kinds (women are inherently worse at science; female science students are less attractive than their arts counterparts; women who do well get there through sheer hard work (bad) rather than natural aptitude (good); etc.) but also, in some cases, outright sexism from their peers and teachers.

Of course, the circumstances of philosophy are not identical to those of sciences such as mathematics, engineering, and computer science. For example, as far as I know, philosophy doesn't have the (male) 'geek' image that mathematics, physics, and computer science have; and philosophy is perhaps not seen as an intrinsically solitary, antisocial activity in the way that computer science is seen. So in these respects, philosophy may be less stereotypically 'male' than some of the sciences. On the other hand, the (by now historically uncontroversial) conception of reason as a distinctively male attribute is likely to play more of a role in philosophy than in other disciplines, including the sciences.[6] This is partly because reasoning *simpliciter* (as opposed to, say, mathematical reasoning) is—or is generally regarded as—the cornerstone of philosophical methodology (or at any rate, it is in the areas of philosophy that I am familiar with), and partly also because reason is itself a part of the subject matter of philosophy.

Nor, in my experience, are professional philosophers in general prone to overt sexism; but it does exist. In particular, we need to remember that even if professional philosophers are immune from overt sexism, our students may not be. Two examples spring to mind, both of which I heard from the female students concerned. First, a female Masters student, having presented a paper at a postgraduate conference—indeed she was the only female presenter—was told afterwards by a male student from a prestigious British university that her paper was 'quite good for a girl'. Second, in a postgraduate seminar, a male PhD student made more than one comment—audible to everyone—about the size of a female PhD student's breasts. These comments were met with an uncomfortable silence—but no comment or intervention—from the other students (all male) or the (male) member of staff chairing the seminar. (This is not to say that he condoned the student's behaviour; I suspect he was so shocked that he was literally lost for words. But of course the students may have interpreted his failure to intervene differently.)[7]

At least some female philosophers, then, will have been subject to these kinds of influences to a greater or lesser extent during their studies—on top of the usual implicit biases that appear to exist within the general population. In that context, and given that it is surely uncontroversial that aggression and competitiveness are culturally associated with a masculine environment, exhibiting those traits in philosophical discussions is liable to provoke stereotype threat.

In her contribution to this volume, Saul focuses on the effects that stereotype threat has on performance (see Saul, this volume, for a nice anecdotal description of the experience and effect on performance of stereotype threat in the seminar room). Here, however, I want to focus not on any effect on seminar performance that stereotype threat might engender (failing to give good

---

[6] See, for example, Genevieve Lloyd's *The Man of Reason: 'Male' and 'Female' in Western Philosophy* (1984). See also Sally Haslanger's (2008) application of Virginia Valian's (1998) notion of a 'schema' to the case of philosophy.

[7] Doubtless we would all like to think that cases such as these are rare and unfortunate exceptions to the normally entirely non-sexist behaviour of our colleagues and students. (For more such rare and unfortunate exceptions, see beingawomaninphilosophy.wordpress.com.) We might even believe that such behaviour would never take place in our own institution. However, it's worth asking oneself how likely one would be to find out about it if it *did* happen in one's own institution.

answers to questions, say, or being less fluent in one's presentation), but on its broader psychological effects.

If you are a professional philosopher, consider the number of situations in your professional life in which you have been the only member of an easily identifiable social category. If you are white, able-bodied, and male, the answer is likely to be 'hardly ever'. If you are a woman (or black, or disabled), the answer is likely to be 'more times than I can count'.[8] Such situations might include, for example, being the only female candidate being interviewed for a job, being the only woman in the seminar room, being the only female member of staff in one's department, being the only female speaker at a conference, and being the only woman on a university committee.

Such situations are ones in which stereotype threat is a very real possibility, and it can manifest itself in a number of ways. First, you can feel that you are *representing* women philosophers in general. You might feel that a bad performance in a job interview, say, if you're the only female candidate, will simply reinforce the relevant stereotype, and of course this is probably not something you will want to happen. So—independently of whether your performance is affected—you are under additional pressure relative to your male peers. As Claude Steele notes:

> [W]hen you realise that this stressful experience is probably a chronic feature of the setting for you, it can be difficult for you to stay in the setting, to sustain your motivation to succeed there. Disproving a stereotype is a Sisyphean task; something you have to do over and over again as long as you are in the domain where the stereotype applies. (2010, 111)

Second, stereotype threat can operate in unconscious ways. Steele notes that when black students who underperformed in a stereotype threat situation were asked about how they felt while performing the test, they 'reported no more anxiety than those not under stereotype threat' (2010, 117). But when the standard physiological indicator of stress and anxiety is measured—raised blood pressure—it turns out that those in stereotype threat situations do indeed show raised blood pressure (2010, 118–119). Moreover, there is a correlation between cognitive load and stability of heartbeat: the greater the cognitive load, the more stable the heartbeat. Again, those in stereotype threat situations display a more stable heartbeat than those who are not, indicating that stereotype threat induces an additional cognitive load. As Steele puts it, 'our minds race.... We are defending ourselves and coping with the threat of being stereotyped. We're probably aware of some of this defending and coping. But much of the time we may miss it, unless we try very hard to listen' (2010, 123).

---

[8] Of course there are more relevant social categories than I have listed here. In the U.K., for example, one might add: having a strong working-class or northern English accent.

Let's put all of this together. By and large, given the general lack of women in philosophy from postgraduate level onwards, and given that philosophy itself is an arena within which being female constitutes a negative stereotype, philosophy seminars are already pretty likely to be stereotype threat situations for women. Add in a dose of aggressive—and thus stereotypically male—behaviour (remember, it doesn't matter whether or not the stereotype is *true*), and you make the situation worse for the women in the room by drawing attention to their gender, thereby increasing the threat. (Remember, doing or saying anything that might suggest that you think women are worse at philosophy than men is *not* needed, any more than seven-year-old girls need to be told that girls are worse at maths in order to underperform on the maths test. They just need to be reminded that they are girls.) You may or may not thereby cause them to underperform, or to keep the question they really want to ask to themselves, but you will probably increase their stress levels, whether they are aware of it or not. Add the fact that female graduate students in the room will be imagining themselves being the future target, as a speaker, of this kind of behaviour. Now repeat on a regular basis. Arguably, what you have is a recipe, or at least a part of a recipe, for discouraging women from staying in the profession. As Steele says, 'when you realise that this stressful experience is probably a chronic feature of the setting for you, it can be difficult for you to stay in the setting, to sustain your motivation to succeed there'.[9]

The hard question remains, of course: Do women in fact, in general—or perhaps just more often than their male colleagues—find the aggressive and competitive atmosphere that is often present in the philosophy seminar uncongenial, independently of any effect it may have via stereotype threat? I do not know the answer to that question. I myself do not enjoy being on the receiving end of aggressive and competitive behaviour, and, unlike Brian Leiter's anonymous source, do not think I demean myself by that confession. On the contrary: On my own personal list of thick moral concepts, these both fall under 'vice' rather than 'virtue'. I cannot, of course, speak for others. But my point here has been that there are grounds for thinking that such an atmosphere is alienating for women—and hence good reasons for attempting to change the atmosphere of the seminar room when it is aggressive or competitive—whatever the answer to the hard question; so it is one that we can simply allow to lapse. The role of such an atmosphere in the pursuit of truth is, at best, neutral; at worst, it runs the risk of putting women off philosophy—thereby reinforcing the stereotype that philosophy is a man's world.

---

[9] Of course, it's an empirical question which (if any) situations trigger stereotype threat, and exactly what effects that has (if it exists) on women philosophers. However, the phenomenon has been found in a wide range of social groups (including white males) and stereotypes (from sporting prowess to mathematical ability)—see Steele 2010—so there is every reason to think that it applies to philosophy. I am of course speculating about which specific situations trigger stereotype threat, but the seminar would seem to meet the required conditions.

3. Conceptual Analysis, Experimental Philosophy, and Deviant Intuitions

In this section, I switch attention to the fields of conceptual analysis and experimental philosophy. I summarise some findings in recent studies concerning gender differences in philosophical intuitions when it comes to standard philosophical thought experiments, and briefly discuss the importance of these findings for understanding one possible route to disengagement from philosophy by female undergraduates. I argue that, from both philosophical and pedagogical points of view, the findings suggest that we should be wary of dismissing the intuitions of our students when they differ from our own. We have good reasons not to treat students with differing intuitions as though they are obviously mistaken or wrongheaded or just don't get it. From a philosophical point of view, we should not think of philosophical intuitions as akin to experimental observations, since this (modulo certain assumptions) is incompatible with the finding that there are significant gender differences in intuitions. And, pedagogically, treating students' 'deviant' intuitions in this way is likely to discourage some able students, and perhaps more women than men.

A standard project in analytic philosophy since the early 20th century has been that of conceptual analysis: the project of discovering the meanings of ordinary-language expressions that are philosophically interesting or problematic ('morally wrong', 'free', 'knowledge', 'cause', and so on). A standard part of the methodology for finding a plausible conceptual analysis of a given term is the deployment of 'intuition', often in the context of a thought experiment. Thus, for example, Edmund Gettier (1963) argued that knowledge is not (contrary to received philosophical opinion at the time) a matter of justified true belief on the basis of a thought experiment in which, as every undergraduate knows, Smith has the justified true belief that Jones owns a Ford but, intuitively, does not *know* that Jones owns a Ford. Such intuitions are generally arrived at from the armchair, and their claim to being 'normal' or reliable or widely shared is typically measured by the rather dubious method of stating what, 'intuitively', is the right thing to say, and then sitting back and waiting to see whether anyone objects.

Recently, however, 'experimental philosophy' has become hugely popular. One (though not the only) aspect of experimental philosophy is, precisely, to put standard thought experiments to the test, to ascertain whether, or to what extent, philosophers' armchair claims about what is intuitively correct or plausible (e.g., the claim that Smith does not know that Jones owns a Ford) are, in fact, widely shared in the general population (or rather, typically, in populations of undergraduates taking philosophy classes). The thought here—plausibly enough—is that if a philosopher is making an intuition-based claim about the meaning of an ordinary-language term (such as 'knows'), then that claim will only be plausible if in fact sufficiently many speakers of the language—and not merely a small number of professional philosophers who happen to be publishing papers on the topic—share their intuitions.

Although it is perhaps not surprising that results of actual empirical experiments typically show that the general population (indeed even a group of philosophy undergraduates) rarely delivers a unanimous verdict, one perhaps unexpected result has been that, in a range of cases, there are significant differences between different subpopulations. For example, Machery, Mallen, Nichols, and Stich (2004) found that there are differences in philosophical intuitions between East Asians and Westerners when it comes to the intuitions that underpin standard competing theories of reference.[10] In a recent paper, Wesley Buckwalter and Stephen Stich (2011) survey a large number of empirically tested philosophical thought experiments that reveal significant differences in intuitions between men and women across a wide range of topics, such as knowledge, free will, physicalism, and utilitarianism, including standard cases such as the Trolley Problem, Brains in a Vat, and the Chinese Room.

Buckwalter and Stich advance the hypothesis that this kind of phenomenon is at least partly responsible for the dwindling in women's enrolment in philosophy courses as they progress through their undergraduate programme. (They provide data for one U.S. philosophy department, where the proportion of women drops from 46.2 percent in 100-level introductory courses to 29.3 percent in 400-level courses.) Why might this be so? Well, let's assume for the sake of the argument that female students are more likely than male students to have the non-standard intuitive reaction to the Gettier case: They are more likely, that is, to hold that Smith *does* know that Jones owns a Ford. Then a female student will be more likely than a male student to find herself with a view that is, from the point of view of her teacher, mistaken. Buckwalter and Stich say:

> Different women will, of course, react to a situation like this in different ways. But it is plausible to suppose that some women facing this predicament will be puzzled or uncomfortable or angry or confused or just plain bored. Some women may become convinced that they aren't any good at philosophy, since they do not have the intuitions that their professors and their male classmates insist are correct. If the experience engenders one or more of these alienating effects, a female student may be less likely to take another philosophy course than a male student who...has the 'standard' intuitions that their instructor shares. That male student can actively participate in, and perhaps enjoy, the project of hunting for a theory that captures 'our' intuitions. (2011, 28)

[10] For a critical discussion of what exactly Machery et al.'s experiments show, see Martí 2009.

Buckwalter and Stich thus suggest that 'part of the gender gap in academic philosophy can be explained as a *selection effect*' (2011, 30). Given that the majority of a female undergraduate's teachers will be men, her intuitions have a higher chance than do those of her male peers of conflicting with her teacher's intuitions; and of course the more philosophy courses she takes, the more frequently she is likely to encounter this phenomenon.

Although the investigation of both the relative extent and the effects of 'intuition clashes' between female students and their teachers has a long way to go yet, for the purposes of the rest of this chapter, I assume both that such intuition clashes are more prevalent among female students than among their male peers,[11] and that Buckwalter and Stich are right in claiming that this plays a role in explaining the drop-off of female students as they progress through their undergraduate careers.[12] My interest in the rest of this chapter is in the philosophical consequences and pedagogical recommendations that arise from this assumption.

Let's begin with the philosophical consequences. Intuitions that have different rates of prevalence among different subpopulations (whether distinguished according to gender, ethnic background, or whatever) are philosophically problematic.[13] On the one hand, intuitions are often taken to be analogous to scientific observation; as Ernest Sosa puts it, 'the way intuition is supposed to function in epistemology and in philosophy more generally...is by analogy with the way observation is supposed to function in empirical science' (2007, 106; quoted in Buckwalter and Stich 2011, 28). This conception of the role of philosophical intuition encourages the view that one's own considered intuitions, or perhaps those of the majority, are the right ones to have, and so anyone who disagrees is making a mistake; perhaps they have, as Ned Block nicely puts it, a 'tin ear' (see Buckwalter and Stich 2011, n.36). On the other hand, one would not want to respond to variation between subpopulations by adopting an 'anything-goes' view, according to which all intuitions are equally valid.

---

[11] I have been persuaded by Louise Antony that this assumption is a lot more contentious than I had previously thought; nonetheless, I think it is worth exploring its consequences, even if, ultimately, it turns out to be mistaken.

[12] Of course, this only applies in cases where (unlike, say, most English universities) undergraduates can choose between philosophy and non-philosophy courses. However, if Buckwalter and Stich are right about such cases, then presumably at universities where students are locked into their philosophy degree programme at an early stage, the selection effect will be present but will have a delayed practical effect: Women students cannot vote with their feet until they graduate and decide whether to continue to graduate study in philosophy. In the U.K., there is a markedly lower proportion of women studying philosophy at Masters level than at undergraduate level.

[13] Indeed, the mere fact that intuitions vary among the general population is itself philosophically problematic: Ignoring gender differences, if only about half of philosophy undergraduates think that Smith doesn't know that Jones owns a Ford, where does that leave the claim that it is intuitively compelling that knowledge isn't justified true belief?

One compelling reason for wanting to avoid the latter response—the 'any-thing-goes' view—as a general principle is that some 'folk' intuitions are simply not apt for accommodation in any remotely plausible philosophical theory. One example—presented but not discussed in Buckwalter and Stich's paper—comes from a study by Zamzow and Nichols (2009) involving the Trolley Problem. Subjects are presented with a vignette in which five people can be saved by flipping a switch, thereby diverting a runaway train onto a side track, which would unfortunately result in the death of one person who is standing on the side track and would not have time to get out of the way. Should you sacrifice the one for the sake of the five? In one version of the case, subjects were asked to imagine that the person standing on the side track was their brother or sister. The results showed a gender difference: When responding to the claim 'it is morally acceptable for me to pull the switch' on a scale from 1 ('strongly dis-agree') to 7 ('strongly agree'), men's ratings were on average lower in the brother case than were women's, and vice versa in the sister case. Of course, no sensible moral theory will endorse the claim that if you're a woman it is better to save your sister than your brother, but if you're a man the reverse holds. Whatever the psychological explanation for the difference displayed by Zamzow and Nichols's subjects, the resulting intuitions are unsuited for taking as data on the basis of which to formulate a philosophical theory.

A second reason for resisting the 'anything-goes' view—or rather, a motiva-tion for resisting it—is that it leaves the whole project of conceptual analysis in a very difficult position. If we take seriously the differences in intuition between men and women (or Westerners and East Asians, or whoever) concerning, say, knowledge, it seems that we are forced to conclude that there is no univocal concept of knowledge, such that *it* is susceptible to conceptual analysis.

Whether that is indeed the conclusion we should draw—and whether, or to what extent, a very standard ingredient of the method of analytic philosophy therefore needs to be revised or abandoned—is not a question I intend to try and resolve here. I myself remain optimistic that conceptual analysis still has a legitimate and important role to play in philosophical method. On the other hand, given the apparently pervasive gender differences in intuitions, it seems that it would be unwise, philosophically speaking, to take for granted the view that philosophical intuition is, as Sosa suggests, akin to scientific observation. For that would seem to lead us either to a kind of relativism that most analytic philosophers would not want to endorse—basically, in the current context, the view that men and women literally speak different languages (e.g., they mean different things by 'know')—or else to the view that either male or female stu-dents are more susceptible to having a tin ear. And of course it's hard to see how this latter view might be justified on either philosophical or empirical grounds. In particular, there is no independent way of establishing *which* of the rival intuitions is the 'wrong' one: One cannot, unfortunately, make an appointment with the intuition equivalent of an audiologist and take a tin-ear test.

If the claim that intuitions should not be conceived as akin to scientific observation is right, then—fortunately—it motivates a pedagogical approach to thought experiments and intuitions that might help to mitigate the 'selection effect' hypothesized by Buckwalter and Stich. We can take care to make it clear to students that minority intuitions, or ones that conflict with our own, are not thereby automatically mistaken or indicative of a tin ear, for example by not saying 'obviously...', or 'you'd be crazy to deny that...'. We can take the time to explore the philosophical implications of their intuitions rather than dismissing them and moving on. Or, at least, we can point them in the direction of respectable philosophical literature that sides with them rather than us.

These are small adjustments to class discussion, curricula, and reading lists that anyone can implement without too much difficulty. To the extent that students are likely to become alienated or confused by the implication that their intuitions are off-key, they are adjustments that will benefit a sizable proportion of students, whatever their gender or ethnicity. If they also help to reduce the sense that women in philosophy are 'deviant'—in this case by having the wrong intuitions—then that is surely a good thing.

4. Conclusion

This chapter has made two really quite small recommendations, which may be summed up as 'no aggressive behaviour in the seminar room, please' and 'don't casually dismiss the intuitions of your students when they disagree with you'. In the first case, the aggressive, competitive, and occasionally downright hostile atmosphere in professional philosophy seminars is, I have argued, a contingent feature of (some) philosophical discussions: It is entirely separable from robust philosophical criticism and plays no useful role in the pursuit of truth. Failure to grasp this fact, I think, is—at least in some cases—due to an illicit slide between the normal and the normative: The discomfort that such an atmosphere can create in a speaker or audience member may not be statistically normal, but it is not thereby deviant in the normative sense that it is the discomfited person who is at fault for being inappropriately thin-skinned. And it is women who are the most likely to be discomfited, because it is women who, when situated in a culturally masculine environment, are liable to be subject to stereotype threat.

In the second case, I have urged that nonstandard intuitive responses to thought experiments should not automatically be regarded as deviant. To treat students' intuitions in the classroom as mistaken or a sign of philosophical bad judgment (or taste) is philosophically unjustified and pedagogically unwise in that it risks alienating promising students from philosophy. Again, the danger of alienating women students may be greater than that of alienating male students, if the intuitions that are statistically more likely to be shared by male students are also the standard intuitions that are presupposed by the bulk of the philosophical literature. In other words, it may be women who are more likely to have 'deviant' intuitions: intuitions that differ from their teachers'.

What connects the two issues is the notion of deviance, and in particular the idea that it is 'women who need to change'. Of course, women *do* need to change, inasmuch as female, as well as male, philosophers are capable of contributing to an aggressive seminar atmosphere and dismissing their students' intuitions as tin-eared. But women who are on the receiving end of these phenomena do *not* need to change. There may be a powerful psychological connection between atypicality and deviance, but psychological connections need not correspond to objective connections; and where they do not, it is our thinking that needs to change.

Acknowledgment

Many thanks to Michelle Bastian, Wesley Buckwalter, Melinda Fagan, Katrina Hutchison, Fiona Jenkins, Phyllis Rooney, and Jenny Saul, all of whom provided very helpful comments on earlier drafts of this chapter.

References

Buckwalter, W., and Stich, S. (2011) 'Gender and philosophical intuition'. *Social Science Research Network*, Accepted Paper Series, available online: http://ssrn.com/abstract=1966324, accessed 2/4/13. To appear in J. Knobe and S. Nichols (eds.), *Experimental Philosophy*, vol. 2. Oxford, UK: Oxford University Press, forthcoming.

Gettier, E. L. (1963) 'Is justified true belief knowledge?' *Analysis* 23: 121–123.

Govier, T. (1999) *The Philosophy of Argument.* Newport News, VA: Vale.

Haslanger, S. (2008) 'Changing the ideology and culture of philosophy: not by reason (alone)', *Hypatia* 23: 210–223.

Lewis, B. (2009) 'Where are all the women?' *The Philosophers' Magazine* 47. Available online: http://www.philosophypress.co.uk/?p=615, accessed 2/4/13.

Lloyd, G. (1984) *The Man of Reason: 'Male' and 'Female' in Western Philosophy.* London: Methuen.

Machery, E., Mallon, R., Nichols, S., and Stich, S. P. (2004) 'Semantics, cross-cultural style', *Cognition* 92: B1–B12.

Margolis, J., and Fisher, A. (2002) *Unlocking the Clubhouse: Women in Computing.* Cambridge, MA: MIT Press.

Martí, G. (2009) 'Against semantic multi-culturalism', *Analysis* 69: 42–48.

Miller, D. T., Taylor, B., and Buck, M. L. (1991) 'Gender gaps: who needs to be explained?' *Journal of Personality and Social Psychology* 61: 5–12.

Rooney, P. (2010) 'Philosophy, adversarial argumentation, and embattled reason', *Informal Logic* 30: 203–234.

Saul, J. (this volume) 'Implicit bias, stereotype threat, and women in philosophy'.

Seymour, E., and Hewitt, N. M. (1997) *Talking about Leaving: Why Undergraduates Leave the Sciences*. Boulder, CO: Westview.

Sosa, E. (2007) 'Experimental philosophy and philosophical intuition', *Philosophical Studies*, 132: 99–107.

Steele, C. M. (2010) *Whistling Vivaldi and Other Clues to How Stereotypes Affect Us.* New York: W. W. Norton.

Tannen, D. (1990) *You Just Don't Understand: Women and Men in Conversation.* New York: Morrow.

Valian, V. (1998) *Why So Slow? The Advancement of Women* Cambridge, MA: MIT Press.

Zamzow, J., and Nichols, S. (2009). 'Variations in ethical intuitions', *Philosophical Issues* 19: 368–388.

4

Singing the Post-discrimination Blues
NOTES FOR A CRITIQUE OF ACADEMIC MERITOCRACY
Fiona Jenkins

>...There is a natural aristocracy among men. The grounds of this are virtue and talents [. .. while] the artificial aristocracy is founded on wealth and birth.
>
> —Thomas Jefferson

> There is for me an element of laughable exaggeration in the claims often made for the meritocratic purity of existing arrangements.
>
> —Duncan Kennedy

1. Ain't that Peculiar?

There seems to be an obvious puzzle about the supposedly meritocratic systems governing appointments to senior positions in many areas of public life: If merit is the sole cause of achievement, why is it that the preponderance of talent and hard work is to be found among a small class of white males? Faced with such a puzzle, do we continue to believe in the system of meritocracy as generating some modern version of Jefferson's 'natural aristocracy among men', with status and right to govern conferred by virtue and talent? Or do we conversely find an element of laughable exaggeration in meritocratic claims? Meritocracy is supposed to replace inherited privilege as a way of deciding the allocation of rewards, power, and resources to the talented and hardworking, and thus to both establish legitimate hierarchies and ensure the excellence of what is done. In academia, the rigorous application of meritocratic standards ought, one would think, to be entirely in women's interests, as well as in the long-term interests of disciplines. Yet although meritocratic selection should lead to the best being chosen, it has also been argued to support the self-reproduction of elite groups (Brezis, 2010; McNamee and Miller, 2004; Thornton, 2007) and to limit the value of work produced relative to other, more pluralistic standards (Kennedy, 1990). This chapter considers the self-reproduction of the discipline of philosophy in view of the systemic outcomes of its processes of selection and promotion, with a critical eye to how we might detect, or even learn to laugh at, the faith placed in meritocratic mechanisms. Such laughter, I hold, is much called for, in view of the depressing circumstances in which female academics so often continue to find themselves. Despite the elimination of the most 'overt' forms of discrimination there are still what I call here the 'post-discrimination' blues to overcome, a dismay at ongoing poor outcomes, both personal and collective, that can only be compounded by the sense that institutional arrangements are often *imagined* to have become altogether fair.

Among the indicators of merit in philosophy would be publications in top-ranked journals. The reward for merit would include a position at an elite institution and promotion to the professoriate. There is a very low percentage of female professors of philosophy. Data that Sally Haslanger has gathered also show the generally very low representation of women in top-ranked philosophy journals (2008, 220). In philosophy, it is not only the case that the vast majority of senior positions are held by men; in addition, the vast majority of the top-ranked journals publish articles by women at a rate that is considerably lower than the proportion of women working in philosophy at elite universities. Indeed, other data suggest a strong correlation between elite institutional status and the poor representation of women—or, more precisely, what I shall refer to as the '*minor*' position of women, indicating at once minority status in a numerical sense and the exclusion from seniority that seems to mark women's most common fate in this field. Elite universities, for instance the Group of Eight in Australia, overall have the worst gender profiles for academic employment, particularly in terms of seniority.[1] If it is possible to track a negative correlation between numbers of women and the purported 'excellence' of institutions or departments, or between the number of papers by women and the 'excellence' of a journal, then what conclusions can we draw from these systemic outcomes? How should they be connected with women's 'failure' to achieve seniority in equal numbers in the field or even find themselves in the running to do so?

In this context, it is perhaps worth remarking that drawing attention to the correlations between masculine majority and the markers of excellence may be

---

[1] Selected Inter-Institutional Gender Equity Statistics, 2011; see also Haslanger, 2008, 222, with a table listing numbers and percentages of women in the departments that rank highest in Brian Leiter's 'The Philosophical Gourmet Report' for 2007. See http://www.philosophicalgourmet.com/ for a current version of the rankings.

a double-edged strategy for feminists. Indicators of achievement, like publishing in the 'top' journals, might appear to a feminist eye to evidence a masculine bias.[2] Supposing this to be so, however, the problem feminists face in persuading others of it goes deep; for what needs to come into focus is the institutional frame promoting and protecting claims about the validity of judgment itself. It is an article of contemporary *faith* that elite status, whether of an institution or as marked by promotion to the highest tiers of the profession, is conferred by (gender-blind) merit. And yet, if you were to look at the gender profile of the top departments with a purely instrumental eye to predicting success, and according to current criteria, it would not be too hard to conclude that the best strategy for a department would be to continue to hire more men than women.[3] The difficulty this brings out is that if what *counts* as 'success' or 'excellence' is currently generated and inhabited by a predominantly male cohort, then this constitutes a powerful mechanism of *affirmation* of subsisting institutional arrangements; and despite more or less conscious awareness at elite institutions that the gender gap is a problem, the understanding of what *kind* of problem it is in most cases will be insulated from perceptions of what constitutes excellence, and in the worst cases, suggest a zero-sum game. Indeed, it is a common experience to find that any push to improve gender balance or to promote more women is immediately and without further argument construed as a threat to or 'dilution' of quality.

One crucial issue that arises here is how the relationship between goals of equity and goals of excellence is understood. When gender equity is construed as an 'add-on' goal, one divorced from aims of excellence, it readily seems to enter into competition with the selection for qualities that are presumed to be absolutely integral or essential to the discipline. My suggestion is that this idea of what is 'integral' should be viewed, at least in part, in the context of a propensity toward conservatism in the way that disciplines reproduce themselves, such that the hegemonic conception of the discipline, which is itself reflective of the gender composition of those who occupy positions of authority and influence within it, is taken as a given, or as exemplary of what this discipline is properly about. Consider that if the current 'winning team' (the one deemed to produce excellent results) is asked to reflect on its poor gender profile, whether it is not likely to respond that to prioritise gender equity would be to compromise the goal of excellence, a goal believed to be realised under 'gender-blind' selection processes? Likewise, if it is suggested that new

---

[2] See Rini in this volume.

[3] Consider in this light Rini's speculations (this volume) about why in the last few years 20 men and one woman were appointed to philosophy jobs in New Zealand in the context of the intensification of competitive assessments of research quality, like the ERA in Australia or the RAE in the U.K. Rini comments, "Because this PBRF model is used to determine a university's funding, simple accounting makes it clear that young women philosophers are not as a rule a 'good investment' for a department or a university that is focused on maximizing scores".

jobs be advertised in areas where we know there to be more women, the central importance to the discipline of traditionally male-dominated areas will probably be strongly asserted. Analogies for this defensive conservatism can be found in other areas than philosophy, where the lack of women is at once explained and justified by reasserting the central importance of apparently key disciplinary requirements. If engineering, say, is argued to be essentially dependent on maths skills (rather than emphasising skills in negotiating complex social relationships and team-based problem-solving) the poor representation of women will be explained in terms of the finding that 'women are poor at maths'. But this begs the question of whether engineering, considered within its social context and as an arena in which women's participation matters, might itself be *poorly* conceived in terms of a narrow range of skills and values that leave women indifferent to (rather than incapable of) practising it. If one then considers that there is in fact little about why engineering matters that is of a purely technical nature, the issues at stake might begin to be looked at in another light. More generally, gender balance might become an integral rather than add-on concern of disciplines by casting questions about what matters within them—or what they might be, become, or do—as at least somewhat open-ended; that is, as critical questions that ask disciplines to imagine more inclusive futures, or at least seek to offset conservative tendencies within their own self-reproduction, their tacit ways of reflecting the current gendered composition of leadership and membership.

Thus one focus of this chapter concerns the relationship between disciplines and their self-reproduction, or projection of a future, and I argue that this is tied to questions (a) about how these disciplines conceptualize their nature and place in the world, and (b) their negotiation of the distribution of 'what matters' across gender differences that are themselves not 'natural' but reflective of (contestable) constructions of both value and judgment. My aim throughout this chapter is to highlight ways in which we might reverse a picture in which gender is made to appear as a political or moral consideration that is *external* to the neutral and impartial deliberations of academies. On the contrary, meritocratic judgments are made within a field that is profoundly shaped by gendering operations. For instance, if a largely conservative bias determines the form that merit will take, and this in view of the affirmation of the prevailing institutional conditions that are deemed to be themselves *responsible* for generating and validating disciplinary 'excellence', then canons of excellence will *shape* the contemporary disciplinary institution of philosophy to fit the image of such 'validity'. Moreover, such 'fit' will reinforce the idea that this is philosophy's natural form. Here it matters that the 'masculine' coding of philosophy may also be a crucial means to establishing its success within institutions that are increasingly unfriendly to the humanities and that demand evidence of a social value that philosophy is often hard-pressed to provide. In seeking to bring the feedback effects of these institutional vectors into clearer focus,

I want to suggest that analysis needs to shift from problems of bias to consider how decision-making not only functions but is *validated* as right. For instance, I shall argue here that the kind of example presented by the data on how rarely feminist work appears within 'the' leading journals, and the overwhelming propensity of these to publish articles by men, can only partially be read in terms of an unconscious set of 'evaluation biases' (Haslanger; cf. Valian, 1998, 125–144) working to distort individual judgments of merit. Instead of thinking about 'distortions', I want instead to bring into view the 'productivity' of judgment and what might be described as 'meta-justificatory' frameworks for validating disciplinary achievement; that is, ways in which standards of evaluation secure broad, indeed typically *unquestionable* purchase, and are confirmed and reconfirmed by the practises and processes they authorise. I thereby aim to further the "growing recognition that merit, as it has been defined and measured in academe, intertwines aspects of gender and privileges males" (Krefting, 2003, 272).

This chapter, then, is a response to the prima facie peculiarity of the results that meritocratic regimes in philosophy deliver, and especially to the ways in which the issues this raises seem to become excluded from properly academic concerns, as if the problem of women's minority had a purely social or political status, and thus would be strictly *external* to the discipline itself, or no real business of philosophers to address and resolve. In section 2, I consider how philosophy may be shaped by its position in the 'gendered academy' (Bailyn, 2003). In section 3, I look at how the problem of the minority of women can be constructed in a way that implies it is neither a problem for philosophy as a discipline nor, indeed, even a particularly important problem for women, thus foreclosing any seriously investigative question about how gender may inflect achievement within a discipline. In section 4, I argue that gendered relations of power are effective in making prevailing meritocratic arrangements appear equitable in principle, when in fact there are powerfully conservative tendencies at work in the field, operating through stereotypes to tacitly legitimate the prevailing pattern of outcomes. In section 5, I argue that forms of evaluation currently prevalent in academia tend to intensify rather than ameliorate the problems faced by women in disciplines like philosophy, and that feminists need strategies of response that do not simply presume the perfectibility of meritocratic arrangements, but rather demand responsibility be taken for ensuring less conservative futures for the discipline.

2. Philosophy and the Gendered Academy

In thinking about the specific relation between philosophy and the gender gap in professional academia more broadly, it is worth remembering that the philosophy we are discussing is the version of 'philosophy' that has developed and been supported within institutions. The gendering of this philosophy and the 'gendered academy' thus deserve to be considered together. The gender gap in philosophy might be viewed as in part an effect of a specific colonisation of the resources and plural strands of philosophy's own traditions, that is, of privileging certain aspects of the discipline over others, in view of a range of priorities that *include* philosophy's pragmatic ways of establishing the conditions of its institutional survival and success. If there is ongoing evidence of the dominance of what Haslanger describes as a hyper-rational/masculine coding of philosophy (2008, 217) and especially as expressed in aspects of the discipline associated with elite status,[4] one question that should concern us is how and why this disciplinary emphasis has been maintained and fostered. Perhaps this is at least in part for reasons to do with patterns of vindication of knowledge and achievement in academia more broadly, and thus with cross-disciplinary competition for resources, as much as anything intrinsic to philosophy as such.[5]

There is, after all, very much in the history and 'nature' of philosophy that exceeds or troubles this hyper-rational norm; philosophy is no monolith, but historically riven by competing conceptions of its mission, terms of judgment, and rationality. Could it be, however, that disciplinary philosophy, and those who hold the majority of leading positions within it, have profited professionally by favouring aspects of the subject that align with an elite and masculine coding of the forms of knowledge? And does the way in which this has taken place illustrate how the gendering of philosophy has gone hand in hand with the marginalization of certain orders of critical questions, including those of feminist theory, within the discipline (cf. Gatens, 1991)? In what follows, I shall take it that it would be a mistake to allow it to seem that we have, on the one hand, 'philosophy', pure and unsullied by its institutional forms, and on the other hand, meritocratic forms of judgment that would objectively track either its own high achievements or the achievements of individuals working in the field. There are mutual forms of adaptation between what *can* establish a claim to distinction and where efforts are made in a field. We therefore need to look with a sceptical eye at how disciplinary success correlates with a profound gender gap, especially at the most elite institutions, and where success is judged in the conventional terms of meritocracy, established in discipline-specific ways by philosophy, but nonetheless within the competitive space of the academy.

One important factor to consider here is how a discipline, or the individuals working within it, benefit from being able to present qualities that are readily recognized and assessed as being valuable or of solid and convincing merit. Can these qualities themselves be gendered? We are familiar from the work of

---

[4] Again, consider the data Haslanger draws from the Leiter Report.

[5] Compare Alison Wylie's argument (2011) that we should not seek to insulate the idealised 'epistemic integrity' of a discipline from its evident gender biases as these show up in institutional patterns of hiring, promotion, and so forth.

Genevieve Lloyd and other feminists with the powerful role historically played in philosophy by the figure of the 'man of reason', the embodiment of objectivity, good sense, and neutrality (Lloyd, 1984). The minority position of women may well suggest that this is neither a figure that can be consigned to the past nor one that we can separate from the organization of power within disciplines that perpetuate themselves in highly gendered forms. If impartiality and sober and legitimate judgment are throughout this history associated with the 'man of reason', and emotion, bias, and unruly thought with the feminine, then the schema Lloyd is identifying is deeply entrenched within the very systems of judgment that establish what counts as excellent work, that is, the 'measurable' kind of thing elite status is likely to be built on.

This sort of argument extends well beyond the realm of philosophy alone. Margaret Thornton (2007), for instance, has been able to make use of this order of analysis to examine how meritocracy favours men when it comes to appointments to the judicial bench, in part because of the greater ease with which men 'embody' the impartial mode of reasoning that is called for by the role. Just as importantly, however, one of the things that Lloyd is identifying within the figure of the 'man of reason' is how systems for legitimating knowledge denigrate rival claims and, by the same token, establish hegemonic status. The gendering of philosophy, in this dimension (and comparably with other areas where authority appears in masculine guise), is not simply about the alignment of men and women (considered as individuals) with certain qualities of reason or their lack. Rather, these attributions play a more systemic role and may appear in more concealed forms. Thus feminine stereotypes, of the sort we are familiar with from the pages of all the canonically 'great' philosophers, do not merely posit a set of characteristic attributes of women, such as being emotional; rather, the *attribution* of 'emotion' is a way of positioning women outside reason and thus of *legitimating* their subordination, establishing their minority, in other words, reconfirming a relation of domination and subordination. Such stereotypes are exaggerations of difference that *stabilize* and *naturalize* prevailing social relations. Although taken to reflect natural differences, they in fact function to normalize hierarchical distributions of value and comprise part of a meta-justificatory framework that powerfully reasserts the results a selective system produces. I have more to say about how this works in section 4 below.

Contemporary institutionally successful philosophy operates within a hyper-rational frame that seeks to align the 'best' aspects of the discipline with the status of science, for example, in terms of ideals of neutrality and objectivity. Analytic epistemology and metaphysics are thus heavily overrepresented in the 'top' journals. Simultaneously, achievement in the discipline is coded in ways that skew its emphasis toward highly individualized performance, rather than tangible outcomes. Thus in philosophy, in its present disciplinary incarnation, what matters for the 'rising stars' of the profession is often that they are, or seem to be, 'cleverer than the next man', as established within the arenas of dispute (top journals, important seminars, etc.) that provide the opportunity for demonstrating one's distinction. Outcomes that can be evaluated in terms of the *content* of knowledge are rarely important. Rather, to be good at philosophy is to be good at argument, which is very close to being a *display* of the sheer intelligence that is taken to be the measure of merit. This claim about philosophy is, no doubt, at risk of seeming simply reductive (compare Hutchison, this volume, for a more nuanced reading). What it seeks to capture, however, is the need to pay attention to the form that 'judgments of excellence' can take in a field that has urgent needs to establish merit on the grounds of something like its sheer *elite* status, given the difficulty of establishing, say, the social usefulness that other disciplines might claim. In the case of philosophy, this is on grounds that are very often inward-looking, attaching high value to individual distinction, and although aligned with scientific objectivity, divorced from the more obvious assessments of the social value of outcomes we might associate with science (as a driver of technological progress, for instance).[6]

Indeed, in philosophy, a pressing imperative for the demonstration of value may give impetus to a particular construction of excellence that, in aristocratic fashion, surpasses and *negates* merely practical considerations. We might think of this as something like the 'surplus value' of merit that attaches to those elite disciplines, journals, and institutions that are, to some extent, able to withstand the pressures on academic endeavours and on universities to demonstrate their social usefulness. Although there are aspects of 'merit' that can be associated with pragmatic concerns of efficiency and effectiveness in pursuit of given goals, what is of particular relevance in philosophy is a surplus virtuous quality, something like 'demonstrating being 'excellent' or 'best' in non-instrumental ways'. And although clearly it is important to be able to mark forms of value that exceed instrumentality and to acknowledge the intrinsic value of academic pursuits, my question concerns how that is achieved in the contemporary academy and what its gender implications may be. The hierarchical ranking of journals (including, in the recent Excellence in Research exercise in Australia, that notable and absurd superlative, A*) is one aspect of the contemporary gendered academy that is arguably party to putting an *exaggerated* version of 'demonstrable' excellence and a corresponding hierarchy (the 'natural aristocracy of men') in the place of the plural pathways and means of thought evident throughout the history of philosophy. Not only then does philosophy continue to privilege the figure of the 'man of reason', but critical or simply alternate

---

[6] Armstrong (2011) argues that disciplines such as philosophy do have social usefulness, but that it lies in the opposite direction to the objective and science-like orientation of these disciplines in their current form. It would also be useful to think about the place of 'applied ethics' within the above analysis, which I take it does claim a social usefulness that has attracted significant research funding, but which correlates with its generally low status as an area within the discipline (that is, among philosophers who take themselves to be more paradigmatic of the discipline's true nature and terms of 'excellence'). Unsurprisingly, applied ethics is also 'feminised'.

paths in the discipline are, in a classically gendering operation, exposed to denigration or to marginal status.

Accordingly, one might say that the problem with the way such a category of 'excellence' is posited and established is not only that it forecloses plurality, but also that it forecloses *criticism* by over-determining the *kinds* of questions that can be presumed to have 'merit'. If feminist work is rarely published in top journals, we might read this as a sign of narrowness, or even worse, as a sign that the serious questions feminist work raises about prevailing norms of authority, and the contributions this work makes to contesting entrenched bias and distortion, are blocked from speaking *by* being refused merit. Not only do we then have something that looks like the bad old form of aristocracy, but the meritocratic regime of the gendered academy may thus be responsible for failures on some relatively well-established academic grounds. An overburdened normative frame for establishing what the excellence of the discipline 'is' gives rise to a serious tendency to narrowness and dogmatism. In criticism of such canons, and in particular in view of the gendered patterns of disciplinarity they present, one might then point out that their grip on judgment involves at least the following vectors: (i) concealing the contingency of the prevailing profile of the discipline, by reference to (ii) the 'indisputable' merit of current disciplinary priorities and norms and thus *tacitly* (iii) assuming the acceptability *for the discipline* of a gender gap. The important implication of this, explored further in section 3, is that the gender gap is conceived as a 'problem' that matters (if it does) on grounds that are separate from philosophy 'itself'; it might matter on grounds of general gender equity, but it does not matter 'for philosophy'.

3. The Problem of Women and the Construction of Philosophy

In order to gain a better sense of how the meta-justificatory framework identified above forecloses questions of gender from arising as questions internal to disciplinary excellence, in this section I want to return to the question: What *kind* of problem is the underrepresentation of women in philosophy? For whom or in view of what is it a problem?

In the course of working on this project, the very straightforward question—why should we care about equal numbers of men and women in philosophy?—was put to me by a professor of philosophy, sympathetic to the concern about women's underrepresentation, but genuinely puzzled as to why it should matter much. He framed the issue first in terms of a question about the value of philosophy as a career. What do women themselves lose by not being able to participate in equal numbers here (its not, he pointed out, like missing out on opportunities such as those represented by really lucrative careers, say in banking, or the capacity to exercise significant power, say as a judge)? But second, what is the importance of equal representation in this field; what goals of equity are being missed out on if *not* ones to do with individual satisfaction? Why would equal representation matter here in the way that it clearly does seem to in the context of political life, where there is the idea of the importance of some kind of direct identity-based representation informing the impetus to change? If law schools practice forms of affirmative action on the basis of the kinds of social goods that are at stake in having an inclusive membership of the legal profession, what is the correlative of this in philosophy? Why does it matter if philosophy is mainly done by men?

The difficulty I found in immediately answering is, I think, bound up with a powerful construction of the significance of the discipline and the nature of achievement within it. On the one hand, it seems, access to philosophy is not so important or so valuable as to be coveted; on the other hand, whatever importance it has is removed from the social and political spheres where gender equality might be internally related to the merit of certain practices. I want to focus first on the picture of philosophy this suggests as a practice that is largely indifferent to the issue of specific qualities of any person who engages in it, *other than* 'talent' of whatever kind is appropriate in the particular field. On this picture, once again, gender equality is construed as an agenda that is extrinsic to properly disciplinary goals, the character of which is purportedly gender-neutral. The correlative of 'why should women care to join philosophy?' is, to put it bluntly, 'why should philosophy care about women?' One issue that clearly does *not* appear in this rendering is the value for the discipline of philosophy itself of improving women's representation or remedying their minority. The assumption of irrelevance seems linked to a presumed disjunction between the nature of knowledge and those who produce it, one that is readily aligned with a fundamental meritocratic tenet that "in judging the value of a product, the race, sex, class and indeed all other personal attributes of the producer are irrelevant" (Kennedy, 1990, 709). Duncan Kennedy, to whose critique of academic meritocracy I am much indebted here, points out that this assumption works closely in tandem with the idea that the "value of work is a function of the quality of the individual talent that produced it rather than of the inert matter of experience out of which the individual formed it" (ibid.). The assumptions conjoin to produce a narrow understanding of a special quality, talent, to which merit attaches. Such academic talent, in turn, is the basis for production of a form of knowledge the value of which floats free of the impediment of subordination to any form of social end. As such, the product may pose as neutral.

According to Kennedy, this construction of the value of knowledge involves an aspiration to 'neutrality' that will entail that knowledge producers themselves must embody this virtue. By reference to capacities for neutrality, what is crucially established is the "integrity of the general system of unbiased judgment" itself (1990, 710). This corresponds with aspects of the meta-justificatory framework described in the previous section. In the discipline of philosophy, neutrality that is indexed to indifference as to who makes knowledge claims (barring the possession of 'talent') is linked at an *institutional* level to a higher valuation of such claims, in ways presuming that such unbiased judgment constitutes the proper 'form' of academic work. Quite aside from the questionable nature of this assumption, it has some unfortunate corollaries. One of these is the class and gender-inflected bias that attaches to such work whose value is also held to altogether transcend social ends, generating its 'aristocratic' or elite form. Philosophy is a rarefied form of work that seems to debar it from being so much as an *acceptable* occupation for a single mother,[7] while it can be, conversely, a marker of *prestige* for any member of an established elite. Another corollary is the differential value attached to diverse disciplinary contributions. Here plural ways of thinking are subordinated to overarching disciplinary norms that may be wholly inappropriate to their specific critical objectives (one thinks, for instance, of the way in which continental philosophy is judged by certain analytic philosophers).

Consider also the example Jennifer Saul has given of the different way in which her work is treated when it falls within the field of philosophy of language, versus what happens when she sends her feminist work to the leading journals, which are supposed to represent the discipline as a whole. Whereas the former is sent out to reviewers, the latter is most often declined (see Haslanger, 2008, 215). Assuming that the quality of work from the same author is uniform, what explains this difference? Perhaps something like a bias against avowedly *situated* work is in play, in ways that could be interpreted with reference to the framework for establishing value. In areas of philosophy where the image of 'neutrality' becomes questionable and the 'value' of academic claims correspondingly drops, we will likely find that the idea of the importance of the knower as having a situated position, or particular point of view, has achieved more purchase. There is not, then, an unequivocal indifference within philosophy to the question of the relevance of who produces knowledge, but rather a *differential allocation* of value that will distinguish between different areas of the subject, according to where the question of 'who' does it (in a way that exceeds merely abstract 'talent') becomes more or less salient.

In some areas of moral, social, and political philosophy or, paradigmatically, in feminist theory itself, it is broadly accepted that it may indeed matter that the findings of knowledge are not reached exclusively by a cohort of elite, white males. Importantly, then, it is precisely in these areas in which perspective and interpretation are acknowledged as irreducible, and thus the limitations of situated inquiry appear as inevitable, that we find what are deemed the 'soft' areas of philosophy, these being rigorously contrasted with the 'hard' areas

---

[7] As Kyleigh Langrick pointed out in an eloquent talk about her experiences as a single mother and student of philosophy at Women in Philosophy: A Reflective Symposium, ANU, 10 August 2009.

that do not bow to such conditions.[8] The gendered dimensions of this division to some degree correspond to actual distributions of men and women across the fields of philosophy (there do seem to be far fewer women in the field of logic, say, than in ethics); but more important, perhaps, it corresponds to a normative distribution (Knights and Richards, 2003, 222–223). The 'hard' end of philosophy—logic, epistemology, metaphysics—as well as specific fields of ethical and sociopolitical inquiry that do not merely draw upon but to a large degree *defend* the norms of neutrality, pose as more estimable in their achievements. When journals are ranked as most significant in the field, what is perhaps being privileged is the aspect of the discipline more able to establish its credentials under particular conditions, for instance, to inflect its achievements with a quasi-scientific status that has done much to ensure philosophy's success in an academic world that very often values science over the humanities.

Let me return from this to address the professor's question. Implicit in it is the assumption that the concern with gender is limited to a specific issue of equally representing persons of both sexes, and that this aim, on the whole, cannot be of concern for the disciplinary goals of philosophy. But the matter, I am suggesting, is more complex. The way in which gender 'matters' in this field has to do with the ways in which authority is constructed and sustained within the discipline, as much as the ways in which it is of concern for the fates and potential of individuals. As such, it has wider repercussions than for the discipline of philosophy, or indeed for the question of whether women in particular find themselves excluded from what the professor was inclined to present as a narrow and not particularly enviable space of expertise, itself the product one might think of exceptionally rare and abstract 'talent'. Issues intrinsic to philosophy to do with means of establishing the authority, nature, and the value of knowledge are overlooked here. But further, many questions that are not only of importance to philosophy (such as how the situation of production of knowledge should be taken into account, or what the standing of interpretative work may be) also shape parallel hierarchies between 'hard' and 'soft' ends of other disciplines, perhaps most strikingly where there are comparable gender gaps to that exhibited by philosophy.[9] This gives an indication of one way at least in which allegedly meta-philosophical questions have a profound bearing on the gendering of any discipline that invokes and preserves the 'integrity of the general system of judgment' by reference to transcendence of situation that *a priori* rules out the very *relevance* of gender in the production of knowledge.[10]

---

[8] Compare Dodds and Goddard, this volume, citing Gatens, 1991.

[9] The parallel case of political science with respect to this particular division between the scientific and the merely evaluative is vividly described in Kantola, 2008.

[10] It would be an interesting question, which I cannot however pursue here, to examine how far the mainstreaming of feminist scholarship, or simply the acceptance of the equal validity of perspectival, situated, and interpretative work in disciplinary areas, correlates to an improvement in their gender gap (but see Sawer, 2004; Curthoys, 1998).

Finally, the professor's questions belong to what we might readily think of as a post-discrimination view of sustained inequality. In this view, overt discrimination has supposedly been countered by well-regulated systems of meritocratic appointment and promotion within the academy. We have seen how, within this picture, there is a presumed disjunction between gender concerns and properly disciplinary concerns; equity measures might address the former, but they fold in under the overarching concern for rigorous meritocratic selection of those qualified to belong to the profession. Such selection determines an order of rank among those who belong to and can be said to speak for the discipline. To the extent that this appears to have been legitimately achieved, imbalances that remain must be supposed to bear some *extrinsic* explanation that allows us to consider that they do not matter too much. Whatever residual issues for women there appear to be are to be explained away in terms that in no way question the *discipline* as it is currently practised: Perhaps women simply do not love philosophy as much as men; perhaps men really are better at the logical reasoning so integral to it; perhaps women are 'too practical' to care for its abstractions; perhaps women simply do not get far because they have children (as if men did not!). Through all these patterns of reasoning, the prevailing norms of disciplinary excellence and of achievement under their terms can be protected from further scrutiny. No doubt there are contexts in which any or all of these claims might receive due consideration. What is interesting here, however, is how readily they spring up as ways of explaining women's minority in philosophy without any further investigation proving necessary. As remarked earlier of engineering, it is not at all uncommon that a discipline identifies its very prowess with the factors that allegedly explain the absence of women. Hyper-rationality, logic, indifference to situation or application all mark not only the high end of this discipline but shape introductions to the subject, as Marilyn Friedman argues in this volume; and all can be and are evoked to explain why women do not choose to pursue it, without this often enough leading to questions as to why these aspects are deemed to be philosophy's core business, or indeed, whether these valuations derive their force from dogmatic or at least un-self-critical tendencies.

4. The Myth of Meritocracy

These brief considerations lead me to offer some thoughts on a critique of meritocracy that would challenge not only what appears to a feminist eye as its current flawed operations, but, just as importantly, examine at several levels the modes of investment or 'faith' in the basic, remediable fairness of this system. At the most obvious level, faith in the sound performance of existing systems presents a serious challenge to anyone wishing to question their fairness, because there is a profound presumption in favour of the rightness of the results produced by processes that select for and confirm excellence according to established criteria. Success may breed but also prove success. Although, as feminists we can perhaps clearly see that the gendered 'inputs' and 'outputs' of the meritocratic system are in need of redress, this perception is far from being universally shared. There are thus likely to be very different degrees of conviction about how well meritocratic allocation of opportunity, reward, and so forth is working. The feminist case for change may be especially hampered where, according to the relatively objective measures of success supposedly conferred by rankings of departments and institutions, excellence is being achieved by a largely male cohort. Despite this, it is possible to have a large degree of suspicion about how well the system is working and still be convinced by its capacity *in principle* to deliver fair outcomes.

Yet while it is surely the case that feminists can make some inroads into improving the fairness of formation of judgment within existing frames, for instance by looking at how peer review is conducted and so forth, there is another level of critique of 'faith' in meritocracy that I take to be called for and to be suggested by the preceding discussion. Here we might usefully distinguish between two senses that can be given to the phrase 'the myth of meritocracy', on the one hand, raising questions about whether meritocracy delivers the results that it ought by its own lights (which assumes the in-principle perfectibility of meritocratic mechanisms), and on the other hand, challenging the kind of *belief* the meritocratic system commands, and this not merely as a mode of delivery of certain results, but by virtue of being a productive field of social meaning.

By speaking of 'productive' aspects of meritocracy, what I have in mind is the importance of giving attention within this system to the reiterative dimensions of social meaning and performativity that are so central to Judith Butler's understanding of the institutional forms of gendering (1990). Here I am especially concerned with the way in which forms of evaluative judgment are tasked not only with *applying* norms within a given field but (a) with *constituting* that field and (b) *generating* and *protecting* the very terms on which they exercise authority. The social productivity of meritocracy would thus include ways of creating hierarchies and validating the right to make judgments of excellence; ways of demonstrating neutrality, both in narrowly disciplinary terms and within the terms of 'gender-blind' selection; and ways of explaining away apparent imbalances in the systemic production of results on terms that *reinforce* normative presuppositions. The critique of meritocracy sketched here aims to show that these dimensions of judgment can become objects of suspicion in view of what look to be systemically distorted results, even when those results do not readily show up as inequitable in case-by-case judgments of merit. To illustrate briefly, in view of this aspect of the critique of meritocracy, some questions that might arise are: How does this system for allocating entitlement, discerning merit, and distributing power 'protect' itself as an authority beyond question, as incontestable (despite what we know to be its flawed operations)? How does it attribute agency and responsibility to individuals (as cases to be dealt with) in ways that conceal the agency and responsibility of a 'naturalized' system of judgment? And how does the system in fact *produce* the gendered differences that are normally imagined as raw 'inputs' into a given operation?

Such questions might lead us to reconsider the ways in which inequity becomes evident or is concealed in 'post-discrimination' times. It is worth noting that the other side of the meaning of meritocracy as a system for establishing legitimate hierarchy is that it is, by the same token, a system or an ideology for legitimating inequality (McNamee and Miller, 2). This way of putting things will quickly run into the objection that what meritocracy establishes, and particularly in academia, is a ranking of those who can count as 'equals' according to well-defined criteria. There is then no inequality that cannot be justified by reference to the comparison of merit in individual cases, and thus equal and unequal status is distributed appropriately. According to this defense, there may be inequality, but it is not inequitable. One strategy of response to this claim is to argue over the application and definition of criteria of judgment, questioning what evident gender inequality, for instance, tells us about the equity of current practices. Another strategy, however, and the one I am pursuing here, is to foreground the way in which the system of meritocracy not only defends its particular results as fair, but produces, at a meta-level of justification, a frame of reference in which its results will appear as unquestionably and exclusively *valid*. Moreover, if we are prepared to consider meritocracy as a system of power (albeit in a qualified sense; it is certainly not a 'naked' system of power, nor one that lacks powerful legitimating forms and content), then we need to take the measure of how power is not only distributed, but becomes operative and productive, internalized and self-confirming, differentially enabling and disabling. Whereas inequities may be concealed at the level of individual judgments of merit, they may become more apparent in view of some of the recursive dimensions of securing validity, or in terms of the ways in which the meritocratic system shapes the identities and experience of those who participate within it.

Thus to develop the critique I am sketching here, it would be necessary to look at how the *systemic* effect of decisions is both concealed and protected within a framework that, significantly, focuses narrowly on the individual case and not the general field of operative power. Viewed in this light, a gender differential might appear not as an 'input' but as one of the *effects* of the system of distribution that we see writ large in the profile of disciplines like philosophy (cf. Thomas, 1996). For instance, this differential gives *normative* form to ways of evaluating outcomes for individuals according to a sense of the 'typical' relationship gender bears to the norm, where the deviation to be explained is invariably feminine.[11] Consider here the use of such asymmetrical

---

[11] Cf. Beebee's discussion of the gendered relation of norm and deviance, this volume.

phrases as 'the brilliant young man' and the 'exceptional woman', or the differences in accounts given of career failure—the account of a stalled career
given for the brilliant young man, 'there are simply not enough jobs', versus
the professorial opinion that Haslanger cites in her essay, 'I have never seen a
first-rate woman philosopher' (2008, 211). If we suspend the assumption that
these phrases express attitudes—what we tend to refer to as prejudice, stereotyping, or bias—these ways of thinking might be regarded as expressions vital
to the preservation of conservative normative regimes, and as key elements
in regulating not simply outcomes but the *meaning* of outcomes within the
system, that is, their fairness, correctness, or justice, particularly in contexts
where one group evidently is doing better than another. The man's failure is
explained in terms of context, the woman's as her own failing, but indicative
of her sex; the man is 'brilliant', as one outstanding among peers, the woman
is 'exceptional' in the sense of being unusual - again, for her sex. Inequality is
legitimated and normalised in this way; but the *inequity* attaching to *how* the
outcomes of judgment are normalised risks being missed entirely, especially
if the focus lies only with examining or challenging how decisions are being
reached in individual cases.

Regardless of what we might take to be the disposition toward 'fairness'
internal to its separate instances of decision-making, every time meritocracy
works to reinstitute the gender norm for a discipline or institution, it does *more*
than decide a particular case; it also works to shape the entire field of meaning
of gender in that area, including the way in which gender is experienced, or
counted, as mattering. To speak of meritocracy as a productive field of social
meaning, then, is to draw attention to how *generating* and *reconfirming* a sense
of the validity of its outcomes is constantly at stake within its legitimating
practices, and in ways that reflect the terms of a self-reproduction of hierarchy over time. To establish a degree of self-evidence about judgments of merit
constitutes a moment of closure or non-contestability in the system that is, in
general, crucial for the conservative operation of norms. Or, to put this another
way, conservatism, including the gendered dimension of this, can be the result
of overly constrained or demanding understandings of the kinds of closure
needed to justify decision. To this, for instance, we might attribute the tendency
in philosophy to favour the masculine 'hardness' of a discipline that is highly
vulnerable to questioning over its usefulness, relevance, or value.[12]

Placing emphasis on the productivity of the meritocratic regime also challenges the assumption that individuals enter such systems 'as they are', bearers

---

[12] To bring out the stakes here, a good question to pose might be how far decisions about the
value of work are marked as contestable, versus how far they are taken to be self-evident judgments of excellence. Indeed, this might offer another approach to thinking about the 'hard' versus
'soft' ends of disciplines; within this gendered distinction, the 'hard' is not simply aligned with scientific values but has stronger forms of argumentative *closure* embedded in its self-understanding,
while the 'soft' is inherently contestable.

of talents and capacities, and that they fare as they do within the system in ways that are attributable to performance and identity construed in a strictly individual sense. For meritocracy is not only a system for legitimating social hierarchies, which involves the distribution of equality and inequality, but is also a system that distributes rewards and benefits, alongside reproofs and disappointments, and in these ways operates intensively to shape at once the performance and the social identities of its participants. The 'system', on this critical view, is not external to those who inhabit it, but rather, and in a sense that Foucault did much to elaborate in his account of disciplinary power, individuals are *constituted* through their participation in and subjection within disciplinary systems, and are lent a sense of interiority precisely as the sphere in which merit, or its lack, and thus individual responsibility and distinction, may be found (Foucault, 1991, 181–183). This entails a form of vulnerability to the judgments passed upon one's performance that requires us to consider how these draw upon the wider gendering of accounts of success or failure within the discipline, or interest and disinterest in a career pursuing it.[13]

The essential claim I am making here is that every mechanism in the meritocratic system is 'overloaded' with a productive aspect. It does not merely judge, but seeks to present that judgment as fully grounded and unequivocal; it does not simply accord merit to individuals on the basis of achievement, but shapes the social identities of subjects and adjusts accounts of success and failure, cause and effect, in ways that reinforce a broad pattern of judgment, generally held to be that of 'gender-blind' justice in a 'post-discrimination' environment. I am also claiming that the production and reproduction of *meaningful* gendered differences that might appear either as *given*, or as *unconscious* prejudices, instead have a systemic form that is not adequately explained by treating them as at once attitudinal and somehow concealed from reflection.[14] It is not that I wish to say these attitudes are, instead, conscious and deliberate; rather the important question is what *compels* these attitudes, what *energizes* them, what authority do they *exercise*? On my account, they seem indeed to become exaggerated by the feedback effects of the meritocratic system, in part by attributions of meaning that stabilize the 'ideal' operation of the system according to a perception of fairness, and in part then by the way that the framework of meritocracy—its meta-justificatory dimension—is reconfirmed as binding. Thus I have argued that majority status is linked to the self-confirmation that is operative within this evaluative system, in ways that might be thought of as a recursive form of legitimation effect, establishing the rightness of success within the system by reference to prior outcomes. Minority status, conversely, is

---

[13] Indeed, I would hazard that focusing on this particular sense of vulnerability might offer a fruitful approach to explaining the nature of the experience of 'threat' in 'stereotype threat'. Cf. Saul's discussion, this volume.

[14] As in the view of 'unconscious biases' in Saul, this volume.

linked to a recursive process of disconfirmation, or establishment of the rightness of failure, again by reference to prior outcomes.

I have also argued that disciplinary and academic power is authorized and
rendered unchallengeable by reference to an ideal operation of the meritocratic system, one that organizes a certain version of what the 'inputs' and
the 'outputs' of the system look like, and thus explains success and failure in
ways that systemically *produce* and *reproduce* gendered positions, by treating
gender as if its form were wholly external to the shape of a discipline such as
philosophy. But it is of the greatest importance to note that within academia,
we *inhabit* these systems; criticism cannot proceed from a position wholly outside the places of belonging, respect, and entitlement that academics enjoy,
or the power of judgment that is wielded, albeit in delimited ways, at every
level. Thus those who would be meritocracy's critics in the deeper sense I have
outlined risk undergoing the loss of a faith that, despite all its difficulties, also
sustains one's own sense of one's rights, position, and entitlement within a
hierarchy. This is not an easy option; perhaps it is even an impossible position
to maintain (cf. Butler, 2009, 771). Moreover, as Linda Krefting notes, "those
who seek to alter 'merit' processes are cast as complainers, unable to compete" (Krefting, 2003, 261–262). This position is intensified for women whose
presumptive inability to compete is itself one of the explanatory elements in
'balancing' the gendered nature of meritocratic distribution. My final section,
then, turns to the question of how we might imagine, and survive, the demand
for change.

5. Counter-discourse, Exaggeration, and Laughter

If meritocracy remains unavoidable in contemporary settings, despite all its
limitations, it is to some degree because of its tautological character. How
can we deny that we want to appoint and promote the best people, or that the
quality of work, and the success and prestige of the institution will thereby
be enhanced? When we judge work, do we not necessarily seek to determine
what is 'best'? This self-evidence grounds a ready sense of outrage at any question placed over such judgments, which seem to cast doubt on the integrity
of the individual making them, rather than the integrity of the judgment system in operation. The tautological status of a proposition, however, should be
seen as a clear limitation on its substance, and not simply as a sign of strength
premised on the undeniable. One risk of focusing on the unrealized ideal of
true meritocracy, rather than its inherent limits, is that tautology itself appears
as merit, and the integrity of the general system of judgment, idealized and
presupposed, appears completely unassailable. Another is that we assume that
the content of the idea of what is 'best' or what counts as quality and success
is relatively fixed and uncontroversial, in ways that tend to bypass not only

current questions about the 'fairness' of these standards, but relatively open-ended questions about what the discipline we inhabit might become and how responsibility is taken or power assumed for shaping that. It is to provide a counterweight to these tendencies, I suggest, that feminist critique needs to take on another form than accepting slow progress toward the perfectibility of the meritocratic ideal. It is also, perhaps, not enough to expect that philosophy will change itself. Institutional sites of pressure and accountability need to be devised that will challenge narrow criteria of achievement. Yet equally, I have claimed that forms of evaluation of excellence currently prevalent in academia may work to intensify, rather than to ameliorate, the problem. The academy needs to work at supporting sites where prevailing practices can be questioned and new strategies experimented with, without recourse to full reliance on the authority of its massively dominant masculine elite. Feminism might contribute here not only to asserting the goal of equity, but in articulating an excellence that is bound up with it; that is, by reviving concerns proper to the ends of knowledge, as achieved through open-ended reflection and criticism. It should be noted that it is *never* the claim of my argument here that equity goals should drive out academic considerations; rather it is that even our 'post-discrimination' era may fall short on both counts.

To be clear, the point of such critique is not to imagine that meritocratic evaluation can be completely overthrown, or even to claim that it ought to be. The point, rather, is to better understand and expose to question its logic, mode of sustenance, and effects, and to develop sites of institutional power where such *questions* have some purchase, some legitimacy of their own, capable of challenging the *unquestionable* power that whatever practices of meritocratic evaluation are current tend to wield.[15] These might be the sites of feminist theory, though the issue of mainstreaming such scholarship becomes, on this analysis, all the more urgent. Feminist work is not only 'about' women in a sense that exposes it to all the charges of bias, by reference to some imaginary gender-neutral ideal of philosophy; rather, it is as much about overturning entrenched forms of authority that are severe restrictions on knowledge. As such, feminist work should appear not only in journals devoted to this special topic, but in a plurality of journals, posing robust challenges to uncritical disciplinary norms and boundaries. Some advantage might also be gained by insisting that norms of meritocratic evaluation be pluralized, acknowledging that it is impossible to judge everyone by identical standards, indeed that there is more than one type of person, more than one type of project that we could find very reasonable grounds for supporting. Thus to stock universities with individuals with highly comparable CVs and forms of 'excellence' (only *incidentally* finding, by the way, that when we get to the top, at least 80 percent of these are men) may not,

---

[15] Cf. Butler's discussion of how disciplines can challenge their own norms, 2009.

in the end, be academically justifiable despite the apparent concern for equity demonstrated by the means of appointment.

A further step to change perhaps involves refusing the naturalization of gender differences that figure in explanations of the gender gap. A particular issue to pay attention to are the *exaggerations* of gender difference that emerge out of disciplinary fields, for instance in the polarization of 'hard' and 'soft' aspects of the discipline and their role in stabilizing the intelligibility of a complex interplay of cause and effect. I have argued that meritocratic legitimacy, in its most unequivocal form, turns on establishing a normative field in which it supposedly becomes possible to clearly discern where individual talent and merit lie, in a domain of interaction that, looked at more critically, is at once uncertain in direction and characterized by both feedback mechanisms and the problematic place of human agency within wider assemblages. The need to attend precisely to *exaggeration* in such a context is a point Judith Butler powerfully makes in her groundbreaking analysis of systemic gendering operations, *Gender Trouble* (1990). For Butler, exaggerated differences of the sort that beset the dichotomy of masculine 'reason' and feminine 'unreason' give evidence of the pressing need to *establish* them, that is, to stabilize through exaggerated demonstrations a dichotomous and complementary set of terms that will distribute gender differences unequivocally. This gives reason to be wary about equating stereotypes straightforwardly with the identities they invent, for that risks missing how stereotypes are ideological and prescriptive rather than primarily propositional and descriptive (Krefting, 2003, 262). It is the *articulation of relations* between groups, patterns of dominance and subordination conceived as natural and legitimate, that the stereotype is working exaggeratedly to sustain.

In view of this, I have argued that some loss of faith in the perfectibility of meritocratic systems might be called for from a feminist point of view. Likewise, or at least in a similar spirit, it is at the *exaggeration* of the purity of existing meritocratic arrangements that Kennedy, in the epigraph to this chapter, suggests we might laugh; and one idea for change I am elaborating here proposes an extension of this critical, even satirical spirit: We should mock the pretension that women can only come to the discipline either with lamentable slowness or at dire risk to excellence. We should laugh (for otherwise we might cry!) at the idea that questioning subsisting institutional arrangements leads to the collapse of all standards, the end of any capacity for discriminating judgment whatsoever. This anxiety might be read as a tell-tale sign that an order of meta-justification is growing uncomfortable, just as Butler attributes homophobic violence to a desperate bid to maintain a naturalized order of sexual difference (1990, 2004). Describing the atmosphere of many a philosophy department, contributors to this volume have noted aggression as one of their unfortunate yet common characteristics. Rather than attribute this to an inherently masculine cause, I suggest that we might consider ourselves witness to a benighted aristocratic regime holding onto the vestiges of inherited privilege, and justifying a problematic determination of talent through such arcane rituals as the mortal combat of the philosophy seminar.

Yet this takes place in lieu of a more constructive project—that of giving attention to the subtle process of devising more equitable, less antagonistic approaches to conceiving of the plural and critical futures of the discipline. My proposals for change, then, concern how, within an institutional frame that goes wider than the discipline of philosophy and must involve the gendered academy, means might be found to reinvigorate a responsibility that draws energy from the democratic and academic values of plurality and critical contestation, and holds inherited or recursively legitimated authority to account. The feminist challenge here is aimed at how meritocracy aligns with established constituencies or elites to foreclose vital academic freedoms. The risk in posing critical questions to the mechanism for distributing value (i.e., that one is considered to be engaged in destroying all standards of evaluation) is itself telling. The institution or discipline that is so 'threatened' by dilution of standards can often be seen to be sustaining its own authority by threatening and discrediting others, determinedly concentrating a power that can never be ultimately vindicated and can in no way guarantee that it bears the only claim to value and rightness. The critique I am elaborating thus takes us in the direction of heresy, of a refusal of faith that bears the form of counter-discourse, and will require along the way some empowering laughter, notably at the exaggerated fears that mask and enable exaggerations of power.

References

Armstrong, J. 2011. 'Reformation and Renaissance', *Griffith Review*, Edition 31, 13–51.

Bailyn, L. 2003. 'Academic Careers and Gender Equity: Lessons Learned from MIT', *Gender, Work & Organization*, Vol. 10, Issue 2, 138–153.

Brezis, E. S. 2010. 'Globalization and the Emergence of a Transnational Oligarchy', copyright © UNU-WIDER 2010, http://www.wider.unu.edu/publications/working-papers/2010/en_GB/wp2010-05/_files/82910699597922332/default/2010-05.pdf, accessed 10/1/2011.

Butler, J. 1990. *Gender Trouble.* London and New York: Routledge.

——. 2004. *Undoing Gender.* London and New York: Routledge.

——. 2009. 'Critique, Dissent, Disciplinarity', *Critical Inquiry*, 35, special issue: 'The Fate of Disciplines'.

Curthoys, A. 1998. 'Gender in the Social Sciences in Australia', *Challenges for the Social Sciences and Australia*, Vol. 2, Academy of Social Sciences in Australia.

Foucault, M. 1991. *Discipline and Punish: The Birth of the Prison* London: Penguin.

Gatens, M. 1991. *Feminism and Philosophy: Perspectives on Difference and Equality.* Cambridge, UK: Polity.

Haslanger, S. 2008. 'Changing the Ideology and Culture of Philosophy: Not by Reason (Alone)', *Hypatia*, Spring, 210–223.

Leiter, B. 'The Philosophical Gourmet Report', http://www.philosophicalgourmet.com/.

Lloyd, G. 1984. *The Man of Reason: "Male" and "Female" in Western Philosophy.* London: Methuen.

Kantola, J. 2008. ' "Why do all the women disappear?" Gendering Processes in a Political Science Department', *Gender, Work & Organization*, Vol. 15, Issue 2, 203–223.

Kennedy, D. 1990. 'A Cultural Pluralist Case for Affirmative Action in Legal Academia', *Duke Law Journal*, 4, 705–757.

Knights, D., and Richards, W. 2003. 'Sex Discrimination in UK academia', *Gender, Work & Organization*, Vol. 10, Issue 2, 214–238.

Krefting, L. A. 2003. 'Intertwined Discourses of Merit and Gender: Evidence from Academic Employment in the USA', *Gender, Work & Organization*, Vol. 10, Issue 2, 260–278.

McNamee, S. J., and Miller, R. K., Jr. 2004. *The Meritocracy Myth.* Lanham, MD: Rowman & Littlefield.

Sawer, M. 2004. 'The Impact of Feminist Scholarship on Australian Political Science', *Australian Journal of Political Science*, Vol. 39, No. 3, 553–566.

Selected Inter-Institutional Gender Equity Statistics. 2011. Equity Services, Queensland University of Technology (http://www.deakin.edu.au/equity-diversity/assets/resources/selected-inter-institutional-gender-stats-2010.pdf).

Thomas, R. 1996. 'Gendered Cultures and Performance Appraisal: The Experience of Women Academics', *Gender, Work & Organization*, Vol. 3, Issue 3, 143–155.

Thornton, M. 2007. ' "Otherness" on the Bench: How Merit is Gendered', *Sydney Law Review*, Vol. 29, 391–413.

Valian, V., 1998. *Why So Slow.* Cambridge, MA: MIT Press.

Wylie, A. 2011. 'What Knowers Know Well: Women, Work and the Academy', in Heidi E. Grasswick, ed., *Feminist Epistemology and Philosophy of Science: Power in Knowledge.* Dordrecht, NL: Springer, 157–179.

5

Sages and Cranks

THE DIFFICULTY OF IDENTIFYING FIRST-RATE PHILOSOPHERS

Katrina Hutchison

1. Introduction

Two remarks give the impetus for discussion in this chapter. W. V. O. Quine comments that

> [p]hilosophy has long suffered, as hard sciences have not, from a wavering consensus on questions of professional competence. Students of the heavens are separable into astronomers and astrologers as readily as are the minor domestic ruminants into sheep and goats, but separation of philosophers into sages and cranks seems to be more sensitive to frames of reference. (Quine, 1981:192)

Sally Haslanger, on the other hand, suggests that others have more confidence in the possibility of identifying at least those who are *not* first-rate philosophers:

> In graduate school I was told by one of my teachers that he had "never seen a first-rate woman philosopher and never expected to because women were incapable of having seminal ideas." (Haslanger, 2008:211)

Statistics from around the Anglophone world tell us that women are not represented in philosophy in proportion to their numbers in the wider population (Bishop, this volume). Attempts to explain this must negotiate difficult questions, including questions about whether there is discrimination at work and, if so, how it operates; questions about why *women* are underrepresented (including fraught questions about what women are like, how they reason, and so on); and questions about why *philosophy* in particular has the gender profile that it does. Here my focus lies with the question of what philosophy is like in contemporary institutional incarnations of the subject. Considering what philosophy is like might also reveal ways in which its characteristics could work to exclude others—non-whites, the disabled, or some men, for example, as well as suggesting strategies for change.

The two citations at the beginning of this chapter are both concerned with how credibility is established in philosophy. Quine refers to the difficulty of identifying who is credible, while Haslanger's anecdote highlights the risk that some people will be denied credibility for the wrong reasons. My more narrow focus here is on whether women are at a disadvantage in terms of establishing credibility (and thus authority) in contemporary analytic philosophy.

The structure of the chapter is as follows: In section 2, I give a general account of authority. This draws on both literature on 'practical authority' (political and legal authority) and on 'theoretical authority' (for example, on the authority of experts) and aims to identify what the two have in common. I then discuss theoretical authority in more detail, as I take it to be the form of authority that philosophers sometimes have qua philosophers.

In section 3, I argue that there are at least *some* situations in which we treat some philosophers as authoritative—for example, in the classroom and seminar room. I explore what is unique about such authority in comparison with the authority of academics in other disciplines. Specifically, because analytic philosophy does not engage with (only) independently accessible data like the empirical data of the sciences, but deals with (primarily) more slippery data, such as 'intuitions', there are limits to the possibility of independently establishing one's theoretical authority within philosophy that do not exist in other fields. (But this might seem a controversial claim—more on it later). In particular, I argue that there is a risk that some individuals or groups will be marginalized within the discipline for illegitimate reasons, and I focus particularly on how this might be a risk for women.

In section 4, I offer a suggestion for combating this kind of marginalization within philosophy. My suggestion is that we should be doing more to explore and articulate the methods characteristic of philosophy. I argue that it is important to both *articulate* our methods and also highlight and encourage methodological pluralism. Individuals from marginalised groups can benefit from being able to demonstrate their mastery of established philosophical methods, and they will be better able to do so if we articulate what all our methods are (not only the obvious ones like formal logic) and teach them explicitly. The idea of explicitly identifying the multifarious methods of philosophy is not an entirely novel idea—I take it that Alan Hájek's work on philosophical heuristics is just such an enterprise (Hájek, forthcoming). However, Hájek's focus is quite narrow, capturing mainly the methods and strategies employed by philosophers who practice contemporary analytic philosophy in a particular way, whereas I have something much broader in mind.

In addition to the suggestion that the methods of philosophy should be collected, discussed, recognized, and debated, I also think that our attitude toward teaching philosophical skills should be re-examined. In my view, the methods of philosophy—both those that are widely established such as formal logic and critical thinking and others we articulate through our research efforts—should be taught much more explicitly and thoroughly at the undergraduate level within philosophy programmes. I argue that doing so will provide students (not only women but all students) with the resources to establish their authority as *skilled practitioners* of philosophy, and perhaps more significantly, to see themselves as credible philosophers even when others do not immediately recognize them as such.

Finally, I note that there is a tension between treating philosophers as authoritative and philosophy's role as a discipline that questions claims to authority or expertise. Philosophers are at least as comfortable questioning the assumptions that underpin the authority of 'experts' in various fields as they are claiming authority themselves. In the final section of the chapter, I explore ways in which philosophy can remain true to its critical role, given the existence of structures of authority within the discipline. In particular, I argue that it is of great importance to retain an expansive conception of philosophy and the methods that are viewed as legitimate within it. Such methodological pluralism ensures that philosophy remains able to turn a critical eye upon itself.

2. An Account of Theoretical Authority and Credibility

A distinction is sometimes made between 'practical authority' and 'theoretical authority' (e.g., Waluchow, 1989:48). The former refers to the kind of authority possessed by political leaders and judges—they are individuals whose authoritative commands provide reasons for action. In contrast, the views of those with theoretical authority typically provide reasons for belief, rather than reasons for action.[1] Yet there is one feature that practical and theoretical authority share. The directives of an individual who has authority give others (those subject to their authority) *reasons* for either action or belief that are independent of any first-order considerations. That is, authorities give those subject to them second-order reasons for action or belief.

However, it is essential to this that the directives given by authorities—whether they are practical or theoretical—*do* answer to first-order reasons, or in other words that these directives are justified. For example, in his account of legal authority, Raz says:

The normal and primary way to establish that a person should be acknowledged to have authority over another person involves showing

---

[1] Of course, in some instances, beliefs will give rise to reasons for action, but this is indirect. My belief that running the clothes dryer contributes to climate change will only give rise to an action—hanging the clothes on the line to dry—if it is coupled with a desire to reduce my contribution to climate change.

that the alleged subject is likely better to comply with reasons which apply to him (other than the alleged authoritative directives) if he accepts the directives of the alleged authority as authoritatively binding and tries to follow them, than if he tries to follow the reasons which apply to him directly. (Raz, 1985:299)

Here the key point is that an authority is really only an authority if their analysis of the relevant first-order reasons is likely to be better than that of people who treat them as an authority.

Similarly, the judgment of someone with theoretical authority is usually based on theoretical considerations relevant to the judgment. So, for example, the views of a historian on the causes of a conflict have been formed on the basis of the primary materials they consulted, such as news reports of the day, letters and diaries of parties involved, minutes of parliament, and details of visits and negotiations between parties. Their extensive familiarity with this relevant material is one reason why they are considered an authority on the topic. When I treat the historian as an authority on the causes of a conflict, I take it that my beliefs on the matter are more likely to be correct if I believe what the historian tells me to believe than they would be if I attempted to make up my own mind. This is because I know that the historian has better knowledge of the first-order considerations and has more finely honed skills of historical interpretation than I do.

I take it that this account of theoretical authority is neither novel nor radical. When Stephen Turner, for example, says: "The underlying thought is that the 'authority' has at first hand something that others—subjects or listeners—get at second hand" (Turner, 2006:165), I take him to be expressing the same shared feature of political authority and theoretical authority that I have identified.

One way to challenge someone's theoretical authority is to independently evaluate the justificatory reasons for their authoritative opinions. For example, I can challenge the historian's account of the causes of the war by becoming familiar with the relevant primary historical sources. If I can systematically demonstrate that based on these sources (or all relevant sources), the historian's account of the causes of the war appears implausible, I will have undermined the historian's claim to authority on the issue. In addition, I will have gone some way toward establishing myself as an authority.

It is possible to distinguish three different aspects of theoretical authority— the subject matter, the discipline-specific skill set, and the ability to produce appropriate results on the basis of these. In an enterprise that aims at simple knowledge, these three aspects might be filled out as follows: (1) The authority *knows* the relevant facts or data, or they can collect, identify, or generate them; (2) the authority is able to *interpret* the facts or data, using interpretive practices characteristic of the discipline; and (3) the authority is able to proceed by logical inference to conclusions based on their interpretations of the facts or data. However, not all disciplines aim solely—or even primarily—at knowledge (consider the work of disciplines such as English, critical studies, and the creative arts, for example), and I am interested in a notion of expertise broad enough to apply to those disciplines too. In order to maintain something like this three-way distinction in disciplines that do interpretive or creative work, each of the three prongs must be expanded. For the first, rather than referring to a shared set of 'facts' or 'data,' we could refer more broadly to a shared subject matter. For the second, it must be recognised that interpretive processes and skills are discipline-specific. For the third, it must be recognised that the kinds of ends sought might be different in different disciplines too, and that whereas knowledge might be the goal of some work in some disciplines, in others, the goal is to achieve understanding, in others, it is conceptual enrichment, and in still others, it might be to produce work that is aesthetically pleasing. I intend, then, to draw a three-way distinction between (1) familiarity with a body of subject matter, (2) discipline-specific interpretive or productive skills, and (3) using the skills and the subject matter to reach appropriate endpoints.

We can distinguish three different sorts of first-order criticism that might apply to an authority corresponding to these three aspects of exercising theoretical authority. It is worth noting that whereas we can challenge someone's authority by demonstrating a weakness in any one of these three areas, in order to *establish* authority on some matter, all three must be demonstrated. We do, however, often treat the possession of one of these (in the absence of clear failure with respect to the others) as evidence that the individual has authority in the area. I set the issue of establishing authority aside for now, but it will be significant later when I discuss authority within philosophy.

Corresponding to the first kind of skill, then, I can challenge someone's authority by demonstrating that the data they have ended up with are incomplete, inaccurate, or irrelevant to the current question. In the above example, I could argue that the historian had failed to collect complete data (for example, had ignored sources that pointed toward a different account of the causes of the conflict); had collected inaccurate data (for example, had treated as legitimate a set of forged documents); or had collected irrelevant data (for example, had consulted material concerning parties who did not play a significant role).

Corresponding to the second kind of skill, I can challenge someone's authority by criticizing their interpretive methods. Perhaps a medical researcher has set their threshold for significance too low, so that inconclusive data are interpreted as showing significant trends. Or, to return to the above example, I might criticize the historian for giving more weight to official documents than to diaries and letters. It is worth noting that the interpretive methods a theorist selects may ultimately be a matter of intuition or 'feel'. For example, there may be no objectively right answer about which kinds of sources the historian should accord more weight to in identifying the causes of the conflict. Nevertheless, there will be *some* interpretive methods that are out of the running. Perhaps more important, there is space to discuss and defend those methods used even in the absence of any criteria against which the 'right' methods can ultimately be identified.

Corresponding to the third kind of skill, I can challenge someone's authority by pointing to invalid steps of reasoning that they have taken. Sometimes I might be able to demonstrate such invalidity formally by using (as philosophers sometimes do) the apparatus of formal logic. More often, however, I will rely on informal means of identifying such invalid steps. Suppose the historian's sources reveal that a highly offensive personal letter was sent from one party to another immediately before the latter initiated the conflict. On the basis of the timeline alone, I cannot validly claim that the letter played a *causal* role in the beginning of the conflict. All I can establish is that the letter did indeed arrive immediately prior to the first strike. Further evidence will be needed to support the stronger claim.

Someone who is unfamiliar with a particular field will not be able to evaluate the claims of an authority in that field based on an appeal to first-order considerations of these kinds. However, non-experts *do* need to be able to evaluate the *claims to authority* of those with whose subjects they are unfamiliar. For example, when consulting an authority on climate change, bushfires, cyclones, or mining safety, the media or government must decide who is an authority in the field. When they do so, they appeal to indicator properties. In the example we have been considering, such indicator properties might include the following: The individual is a notable historian at a good university; they have published books on the topic that are highly regarded by their peers; and they are able to answer questions on the topic in a way that suggests they have done more than memorise a script. Some indicator properties, such as those I have just listed, will be treated by almost everyone as indicative of theoretical authority in a field. Others will be more tenuous. But it is important to note that non-experts are bound to trust indicator properties when identifying those who have theoretical authority, because they do not possess the relevant knowledge and/or skills to evaluate their claims directly. Someone is *credible* when they are treated by others as an authority on the subject, due to possessing the relevant indicator properties for theoretical authority in that domain.

Everything I have said about theoretical authority thus far assumes that someone—the authority—has access to first-order considerations that justify the claims they make. The preceding discussion assumes a kind of nexus involving (1) subject matter, as generated, collected, or identified by an individual with theoretical authority; (2) an observer or interpreter with theoretical authority; and (3) indicator properties that allow a non-expert to identify who has theoretical authority or who is credible. Now here is an important point: Someone who has skills and knowledge in a particular field *but is not recognized as such* by others inside or outside of the field, does *not* have authority, because others will not treat their opinions as reasons for belief. That means that having authority involves more than simply being skilled and knowledgeable in the field. It also involves being treated as credible by your peers and by others outside of the field.

Miranda Fricker identifies two ways in which being credible can come apart from being a good interpreter of the facts or evidence:

> 1. An agent who is knowledgeable about and a good interpreter of the data may not be recognized as such, and will thus lack credibility.
> 2. An agent who has credibility may in fact not be knowledgeable about, or a good interpreter of, the data, and will thus have *mere credibility*.
> (Fricker, 1998:167)

When knowledge and credibility come apart in either of these ways, we can ask what the indicator properties are actually tracking (because where the two come apart, they are not tracking what they are supposed to track, i.e., knowledge and trustworthiness). Fricker investigates the relationship between indicator properties and power. In simple social situations—think for example of a small group of people who are living in a state of nature—indicators of whether or not someone knows key information such as the location of food and water are likely to track what they are supposed to. However, Fricker argues that in complex societies, there is potential for indicator properties to become distant from the abilities that they are indicative of. For example, wealth is required to attend a top private school, and to the extent that the mere fact of having attended a top private school is treated as an indicator property for credibility (in some domain), there is potential for a mismatch between the indicator property and competence:

> In a significant range of contexts, the position of powerlessness may place one under general suspicion of being motivated to deceive, in a way in which the position of powerfulness does not. Further, powerlessness diminishes one's ability to protest one's trustworthiness—especially if it would be at the expense of the reputation of someone more powerful.
> (Fricker, 1998:169)

Fricker does not, however, think that credibility tracks power all the way down. She offers a genealogical account of the role of the good informer: At some basic level, good informing is a vital social activity that allows humans (as social creatures) to share knowledge about where essentials are to be found, where danger lies, and so on. At this basic level, it is essential that indicator properties track competence and trustworthiness; when they don't, there will be direct consequences (for example, if someone tells you where to find water and they are wrong or have deliberately misled you, this will quickly become obvious). However, as the sorts of things humans know become more complex and abstract, it is much more difficult to ensure that credibility tracks competence and trustworthiness. So the more complex the subject matter (think of the complexity of medicine or law, for example) or the more abstract the subject matter (think of philosophy), the more chance there is that indicator properties will fail to track competence and trustworthiness, and might instead come to track power or other epistemologically irrelevant differences between individuals.

In the present context, it is pertinent to ask whether indicator properties might systematically track gender. In a recent book, *Epistemic Injustice*, Fricker has argued that they might in contexts in which prejudicial stereotypes of women are operative. Specifically, she argues that we make use of stereotypes as indicator properties when judging the reliability of others' testimony, and when such stereotypes are prejudicial, they can lead us to unfairly deny credibility to the testimony. Sometimes these stereotypes are non-prejudicial and, indeed, useful because there is a systematic association between the group and the attribute in question. The example Fricker offers here is the stereotype of the family doctor as dependable: "[I]t is epistemically desirable that the stereotype should help shape the credibility judgements we make when such doctors give us general medical advice" (Fricker, 2007:32). This example is in keeping with the account of theoretical authority offered above—the indicator property of being a qualified, practicing doctor is relevant to the role of giving medical advice, because the trained doctor is more likely to offer good medical advice than someone without medical training. In contrast, prejudicial stereotypes involve false associations between groups and attributes. Fricker notes that such false associations are commonly held of marginalised or powerless groups:

> Many of the stereotypes of historically powerless groups such as women, black people, or working-class people variously involve an association with some attribute inversely related to competence or sincerity or both: over-emotionality, illogicality, inferior intelligence, evolutionary inferiority, incontinence, lack of 'breeding', lack of moral fibre, being on the make, etc. (Fricker, 2007:32)

The best evidence that there are indeed such prejudicial stereotypes operating against women comes predominantly from psychology. Some of the characteristics that psychologists have found to be gender-stereotyped as male include being emotionally stable, objective, and well informed (Schein, 1973). In an analysis of a decade of work on gender, Kay Deaux found that although there are significant differences in stereotypes of men and women—specifically men are stereotypically viewed as possessing traits associated with high levels of competence, whereas women are stereotypically viewed as possessing traits associated with high levels of warmth—there is little evidence of actual differences between men and women (Deaux, 1984). In a recent survey article, Kite et al. observe the same association between men and competence and women and warmth, noting that there is also a relationship between perceived compe-tence and command of respect (Kite et al., 2008:210).

Given that men are prejudicially stereotyped as more competent, emotion-ally stable, objective, and well informed than women, it is likely that their tes-timony—insofar as such stereotypes are active as indicator properties in the assessment of it—will be judged to be more reliable than women's. In the next two sections, I discuss the nature of philosophy and argue that it is a disci-pline in which indicator properties are particularly likely to be relied upon, and where prejudiced judgments are more difficult for the wronged party to rebut. As such, I argue that women in philosophy are particularly susceptible to hav-ing their credibility underestimated, and thus being denied authority for the wrong reasons.

3. Theoretical Authority and Credibility within Philosophy

In the previous section, I gave an account of theoretical authority. According to this account, someone is a theoretical authority when their beliefs give oth-ers (those subject to their authority) reasons for belief that are second-order reasons in the sense that they do not look to, but replace, first-order consider-ations based on (for example) relevant evidence. In this section, I look at how philosophy fits this account: Can philosophers be authoritative qua philoso-phers? I argue that they can, and that we do treat at least some philosophers as authoritative in their capacity as philosophers in at least some contexts. But I point out that exercising theoretical authority in philosophy is different than doing so in other disciplines, largely because it is not obvious that philosophy is anchored by an independently accessible body of subject matter similar to that which grounds work in other disciplines. I suggest that the relative absence of an independently accessible body of subject matter creates a greater reliance on indicator properties. In turn, this increases the likelihood that prejudicial gender stereotypes will operate as indicator properties and result in lower cred-ibility being attributed to women.

There are at least two contexts in which philosophers appear to exercise theoretical authority in their capacity as philosophers. The first is in the class-room. Students treat their lecturers as authoritative, as both knowers and crit-ics. Usually, students defer to the lecturer on questions of who said what and on questions of interpretation. They expect the lecturer to have better knowledge of both the material covered in the course and the wider context within which this material sits. Students will also usually take critical questions raised by the lecturer more seriously than those raised by other students (see also Hanrahan and Antony, 2005, for a discussion of authority in the philosophy classroom).

These same forms of authority operate among philosophers within the profession. We typically know who in our department is an authority on recent work in philosophy of mind, or epistemology, or Kant. Likewise, we can all think of someone whose questions in seminars we are inclined to take more seriously than those of others, because they have a fearsome reputation for identifying the weak point in an argument. When we treat the fact that Christine Korsgaard has offered a particular interpretation of Kant as a reason for accepting this interpretation, we treat her as an authoritative knower. When we treat the fact that a particular individual has asked a question as a reason to take it seriously—quite apart from its content—we treat that individual as an authoritative critic.

In the previous section, I noted that theoretical authority in a field is typically anchored by the shared subject matter of the discipline; and that the person with theoretical authority exercises a set of abilities in relation to this subject matter. In this section, I apply this account of theoretical authority to philosophy. I argue that philosophy is not anchored as firmly by its subject matter as other disciplines. It is therefore not abilities associated with familiarity with the subject matter, or identifying, collecting, or generating data that are of central importance in philosophy.

Two implications of this, I suggest, are (1) that it is particularly difficult to challenge the authority of an established philosopher or to establish oneself as an authoritative philosopher, because any attempt to do so is not firmly anchored by shared subject matter in the way it is in other disciplines; and (2) that authority in philosophy is much more firmly attached to the ability to argue rationally and persuasively than it is to identifying the 'right' answer.

It is widely accepted (at least within analytic philosophy) that the raw data of the subject are intuitions. By way of offering some kind of evidence supporting this, I briefly discuss some literature on intuitions in philosophy. It is worth noting first, however, that there are two quite different views on the role of philosophers in generating, collecting, or identifying such intuitions. According to one view, intuitions are the kind of commonsense things that non-philosophers, as well as philosophers, have ready access to. According to this view, first-rate philosophers do not have special access to facts or data that anchor philosophical viewpoints; indeed anyone has access to this body of commonsense facts or intuitions and can generate them with no more than a few moments of reflection. The other view, in contrast, sees philosophers as skilled at identifying which intuitions are the 'right' ones. According to this view, non-philosophers are more likely to have faulty or corrupt intuitions. For example, they might have incoherent sets of intuitions, or their intuitions might be subservient to other objectives they have (such as their own desire for material goods, power, and so on).

Rawls's theory of reflective equilibrium offers an account of how intuitions and theory in philosophy can be balanced in a manner analogous to the balancing of evidence and theory in the sciences (Rawls, 1951, 1999). Focusing on the role of intuitions in ethics, Singer has criticized Rawls's approach on the basis that one important role of philosophy is to challenge accepted wisdom, and that this means challenging (rather than accepting) at least some of the intuitions people hold (Singer, 2005). Yet Singer himself acknowledges that intuitions are difficult to escape:

> Whenever it is suggested that normative ethics should disregard our common moral intuitions, the objection is made that without intuitions, we can go nowhere. There have been many attempts, over the centuries, to find proofs of first principles in ethics, but most philosophers consider that they have all failed. Even a radical ethical theory like utilitarianism must rest on a fundamental intuition about what is good. So we appear to be left with our intuitions and nothing more. If we reject them all, we must become ethical skeptics or nihilists. (Singer, 2005:349)

And some of Singer's own work makes use of one set of intuitions to cast doubt on another. Consider the structure of "Famine, Affluence and Morality": In this paper, Singer's own argument depends upon our intuitive acceptance of the claim that "if it is in our power to prevent something bad from happening, without thereby sacrificing anything of comparable moral importance, we ought, morally, to do it" (Singer, 1972:231). Singer attempts to show that our intuitive acceptance of this principle should lead us to reject a number of other intuitions, including intuitions about where the distinction between charity and duty ought to be drawn.

It is notable that those who are critical of the role of intuitions in philosophy do not necessarily claim that they are not the raw data of the discipline. Consider Alvin Goldman's critique of the role of intuitions in revisionary metaphysics. Goldman does not argue that intuitions play no legitimate role in philosophy, far from it. He argues in a number of different places that the idea that intuitions give good evidence for claims about the structure of reality is misguided (see, for example, Goldman and Pust, 2002). But he has pursued the project of describing our intuitions in both metaphysics and particularly in epistemology, and offering psychological explanations of how we come to have them.

Taking the data of philosophy to be intuitions, we can consider how they are generated, collected, or identified. Philosophers use a range of techniques to generate intuitions in those reading or hearing their arguments. One is the use of examples that are likely to bring about the same intuition in the audience as they do in the author. Such examples, often fictional 'thought experiments', are sometimes referred to as 'intuition pumps' (Dennett, 1995). Some philosophers, including Dennett, have been critical of the use of such 'intuition pumps'. However, their criticisms are not universally shared. One argument for accepting the practice of 'pumping' intuitions is that it doesn't matter whether some intuition is artificially generated or not; the important thing is that it is a widely shared intuition in the given case. As such, it is appropriate to expect its occurrence to be explained by a satisfactory theory of the phenomenon in question.

Recently, experimental philosophers have undertaken the process of collecting intuitions by surveying members of the general population (or, more often, members of the undergraduate population at their universities). The 'experiments' conducted by these philosophers seek to collect and analyse the intuitions of a wide range of different individuals, to avoid the risk of relying on the intuitions of professional philosophers, which may, for example, have become distorted after many years of bearing the weight of the philosophical theories they are supposed to support. Perhaps experimental philosophy can equip us with a set of broadly accepted data on intuitions. 'Accepted', at any rate, if we view the process of philosophy as analogous to the process of linguistics; as describing and explaining (but not critically evaluating or revising) a set of beliefs or practices; in the case of linguistics, practices of language use; in the case of philosophy, perhaps, our commonsense beliefs about concepts such as truth, freedom, justice, beauty, time, causation, and so on. Some philosophers, such as P. F. Strawson, have indeed defended something like this conception of philosophy (see the introduction to Strawson, 1959). But this is by no means unanimously accepted, and is, I think, highly controversial. It is at odds, for example, with Rawls's account of the character of philosophical process as a quest for reflective equilibrium. Therefore, even if experimental philosophy can provide a robust set of data on commonsense intuitions, we would still need to explore and discuss what sort of intuitions philosophy looks to *and* what role these intuitions play (for example, whether reaching a reflective equilibrium ought to be the goal of our philosophical investigations).

Finally, it is difficult to see how the philosopher's process of identifying intuitions might be successfully challenged, especially when the idea is to consider a particular example and examine one's own intuitions in response to it. Of course it seems possible in principle that I could either deliberately misidentify my own intuitions (for example, because the ones I really have do not fit the theory I advocate), or that I inadvertently misidentify my intuitions. The latter might occur, for example, if I have thought so hard about some particular philosophical situation that I am no longer capable of having clear, uncorrupted intuitions about it. In such cases, it is not clear that someone else would be able to establish that I have erred in identifying my own intuitions. There is no possibility of challenging my authority by pointing to the data. Likewise, it is not possible for me to *establish* that I have correctly identified my own intuitions, because they are not independently verifiable. In this respect, philosophy appears to differ from other disciplines, the data of which are independently accessible.

Insofar as philosophy does differ from other disciplines in this way, it is more difficult for a philosopher who has been denied credibility by his or her peers to re-establish that credibility. The philosopher lacks one of the key means by which participants in other fields might demonstrate their competence to others—reference to independently accessible subject matter. In English literature, it is possible to pick up a copy of a text and point to the passages that are indicative of a particular interpretation, and in science it is possible to replicate an experiment or share data (although in some cases there might be practical difficulties). If, as I suggested at the end of the previous section, women are more likely to be denied credibility than men, then they will find it particularly difficult in philosophy to re-establish themselves as philosophers with theoretical authority.

It is worth saying something briefly about another kind of subject matter that features in philosophical investigation, especially as it was suggested by the examples that I gave at the beginning of this section. That is, the works of authoritative philosophers, or (approximately) the relevant tomes in the philosophical canon. While it is typically assumed that 'first-rate' philosophers do more than interpret the work of other philosophers and repeat familiar objections, certainly one aspect of being a credible philosopher is familiarity with the canon, or at least some part of it. Many excellent philosophers stand on the shoulders of other great philosophers, contributing to the debate by developing or extending their ideas. Yet the best work of this kind is surprising and creative—making interpretations that are both unexpected and plausible, or extending an existing idea in an unlikely but fruitful way. It is the demand that philosophers be creative—that they produce 'original' philosophical ideas—that is at the centre of evaluations of individuals' contributions to the discipline. When Haslanger's professor stated that "women were incapable of having seminal ideas", he not only implied by his choice of word that maleness (i.e., having semen) was associated with being a first-rate philosopher. He also said (and clearly intended to say) something that most philosophers—including women—agree with: that having original ideas, and especially having original ideas that are interesting enough to be taken up by other philosophers, is characteristic of first-rate philosophers. Of course the professor is wrong: Women philosophers do have original ideas. However, if women are less able to establish their authority—less able to establish themselves as 'sages', rather than 'cranks', in Quine's terms—then they will struggle to have their ideas taken seriously, and built upon by other philosophers.

4. Suggestions for Combating the Marginalisation of Women

Given that philosophers do not appeal to raw data that are objectively accessible to others (in the way that historical sources or the empirical evidence of science are) but rather to (personal) intuitions, their ability to challenge the authority of those currently deemed to be first-rate (credible) philosophers is limited. So too is their capacity to establish themselves as first-rate philosophers.

However, there is more than one way to challenge someone's theoretical authority—it is possible to challenge their authority by challenging their interpretive methods or the validity of their inferences. Often our criticisms of others' philosophical work do look either to their interpretive methods or (perhaps even more often) to the logic of their argument. Whenever we challenge the validity of someone's move in an argument by demonstrating that it is inconsistent with the rules of formal reasoning, we are doing this. And it is very powerful when we can do so. In this section, I suggest that a partial solution to the problems I have drawn attention to might be to expand our ability—and our students' ability—to demonstrate competence in philosophical methods. Incidentally, if women are stereotyped as less competent than men, this strategy will also give individual women a means of demonstrating competence, and show that the stereotype is not true of them.

Even within analytic philosophy there are competing conceptions of what philosophy is, what it is for, and how it should be practiced.[2] It is not my aim to adjudicate between these conceptions of philosophy. On the contrary, I think that such diversity is good for the discipline and should be encouraged rather than resolved. Here, I look at two different conceptions of analytic philosophy—an interpretive conception and a combative conception—endorsed by Bernard Williams and Alan Hájek respectively. These different approaches are characterised by different methods, and illustrate, I think, an important point—that any two philosophers (even two white, male, analytic philosophers) might routinely use different methods, and that if they do not understand one another's methods, they risk misunderstanding or underestimating one another.

Bernard Williams has characterized philosophy as

> part of a more general attempt to make the best sense of our life, and so of our intellectual activities, in the situation in which we find ourselves. (Williams, 2000:182)

According to such a characterization, philosophy aims at understanding—'making the best sense' of our lives—and is presented as a process that is undertaken by individuals who are situated both physically and temporally, and thereby have only a limited capacity to transcend their own perspectives. Interpreting, explaining, and understanding our intuitions and practices will, on this view, be central to the process of philosophy.

Although Williams was not alone in holding this conception of philosophy, it does not seem to be very widely shared in contemporary analytic philosophy. In a seminar at the ANU recently, the consensus of the audience was that philosophy is a search for *truth*,[3] rather than *understanding*. There

---

[2] Marilyn Friedman also discusses different conceptions of analytic philosophy. See Friedman, this volume.

[3] The paper that these comments responded to apparently supposed that philosophy qua philosophy aimed at *nothing*, but instead involved the exploration of logical space through argument.

are good reasons to think that philosophy as a search for truth will always fall short. One reason is that philosophy is sometimes taken to comprise a set of residual hard problems, problems to do with the nature of such things as time, causation, existence, and knowledge, insofar as these pose questions that have not been commandeered by the sciences. Another reason is that questions of value (in ethics and aesthetics, for instance) are not agreed by all philosophers to aim at truth (especially not by anyone who is not the relevant kind of realist—a moral realist, for example). If philosophy will always fall short in its search for truth, then perhaps as philosophers we ought to pay more attention to our interpretive methods and the role of interpreting, understanding, and explaining in philosophy. Furthermore, if the philosophers who think that philosophy is a search for truth come to understand the methods of those who think it is a matter of interpretation, and vice versa, they will be in a much better position to debate about their meta-philosophical differences, as well as to engage on other philosophical issues, rather than just talking past each other.

A characterization of philosophy that differs from Williams's is offered by Hájek in his discussion of philosophical heuristics. He says that doing philosophy involves

> trying to come up with an original philosophical position, or an original argument, or a counterexample to someone else's philosophical position, or trouble for an argument of theirs, or solving a puzzle, or resolving a paradox. (Hájek, forthcoming)

Whereas Williams's characterization aligns philosophy centrally with skills of interpretation, Hájek's characterization aligns it centrally with skills of argument—both in the logical and in the combative senses. Viewed as such, philosophy differs from other disciplines that are firmly anchored by a body of subject matter—some set of facts, literature, or body of data, and in which data generation, collection, or identification, along with interpretive skills, are the primary skills associated with exercising theoretical authority.

We have some well-established methods in philosophy for constructing such arguments. The most obvious is the formal apparatus of logic, although relatively little interesting philosophy is presented in formal logic. Indeed, even those papers that do make use of formal logic usually also employ other methods. Many of these other methods are, or are supposed to be, true to principles of informal reasoning—they are supposed to proceed validly from premises to conclusion, to avoid a range of fallacies (the sort students are sometimes introduced to in undergraduate critical thinking classes) and so on. However, the strategies that philosophers use—even those who conceive of philosophy as an activity focused on argument and reason aiming at truth—extend well beyond what is covered in the textbooks on formal and informal logic, as Hájek's own project recognises (Hájek, forthcoming).

All these methods, as well as the interpretive skills required to practice philosophy as Williams characterises it, are much less scrupulously described and taught in philosophy than the formal methods of logic. In this respect too, philosophy differs from other disciplines. Disciplines such as mathematics and science explicitly teach methods. A mathematics class is typically a class in the methods relevant for solving particular classes of mathematical problems. Similarly in the sciences: Laboratory classes focus on teaching a range of experimental methods, while theory classes teach, among other things, interpretive methods including statistical analysis. This is typical of teaching in a range of academic disciplines, as well as the teaching of non-academic pursuits. As Hájek has observed:

> ...[C]onsider some other skill—say, skiing. A skiing instructor does not just say: "You've seen people ski well; now do it yourself! Go on: SKI!" Rather, the instructor gives you *skiing heuristics*, breaking down skiing into manageable bits: "shift your weight to the downhill ski", "keep your hands forward", and so on. Yet in philosophy we typically just show our students finished pieces of philosophy—the classics, the recent literature— and then effectively say: "You've seen people philosophize well; now do it yourselves! Go on: PHILOSOPHIZE!" (Hájek, forthcoming)

And he makes this point more striking by reference to science, noting that it would be strange if scientists were not introduced to the scientific method.

Of course there is a significant literature on matters of philosophical method. The material on intuitions that I referred to earlier is one example. The literature on formal logic is another. But very often we go on as though our less formal methods are well established and understood. It is worth noting, in particular, that the literature on philosophical methods tends to be focused fairly narrowly. There are papers on intuitions and their role; there are papers on formal logic, its status and role (and competing forms of logic). I imagine that in other traditions there are also papers on, for example, deconstruction (although I am not familiar with this material). Philosophy employs an extensive range of methods—perhaps more than other disciplines. This is no doubt partly due to its unparalleled scope in comparison with other disciplines. Hájek claims to have identified hundreds of different philosophical heuristics, for example.

To press this point further: If philosophical methodology is something we are familiar with mainly through having encountered good philosophy, we are likely only to be familiar with the methods employed within our own sometimes narrow areas of specialization. But this means that we are often very badly placed to judge the quality not only of the *contents* but also of the *techniques* employed in other areas of philosophy. A more open and robust discussion about methodology would give all of us the opportunity to become familiar with (and when relevant, to question) the techniques we use as philosophers, including the ones that have legitimacy outside of our own narrow areas of specialization. Fiona Jenkins has drawn attention to the fact that "there is [...] more than one type of project that we could find very reasonable grounds for supporting" (this volume), and she argues that having one set of standards of excellence might miss this point, ranking as 'better' or 'worse' projects with aims so different as to make such comparison laughable. So too, our peer evaluations become ridiculous when we make false presuppositions about the methods being employed, or the way in which the 'products' might be valued. This is a real problem, given that in some contexts (hiring and promotions panels, for example), it is not specialists in some narrow area who are entrusted to make decisions, but typically the most senior philosophers in the institution, irrespective of their areas of specialization. There are two risks: (1) that in general, we tend to undervalue work produced using methods we do not understand; but also (2) that in specific cases, we may overvalue such work, failing to recognize it as a poor example of its kind.

It is worth saying just a little more about the first of these risks—the risk of undervaluing in general work produced using methods we do not understand. There is a view held by some analytic philosophers that analytic philosophy is superior to continental philosophy because it proceeds by rigorous argument, rather than questionable rhetoric. Neil Levy cites this as a common distinction:

> It is often said that what distinguishes analytic from Continental philosophy is the greater place and respect for argument in the former. Dagfinn Føllesdal, for example, characterizes the difference between analytic and nonanalytic philosophy as essentially a difference in the place given to arguments, rather than rhetoric. (Levy, 2003: 286)

To the extent that this is a widespread view, it surely fails to acknowledge the role that rhetoric plays in all forms of philosophical argument, including the arguments of analytic philosophers. Hájek's heuristics, for example, include devices aimed at *persuading* one's opponent or audience. One such is his set of heuristics for answering problems associated with extreme, self-referential, or weird cases. These include a range of side-stepping manoeuvres such as asserting that "the case is too far-fetched for us to trust our intuitions about it" (Hájek, forthcoming). Further evidence for the role of rhetoric in analytic philosophy includes the regularity with which criticisms like "that's implausible", "that's just crazy", and "I don't understand what you're saying" figure in the question-and-answer sessions after seminars. Even when an argument is presented in formal logic, the use of logic itself plays a rhetorical role. For example, it seems to be a presupposition of some philosophical exchanges that arguments presented in purportedly valid formal logic demand an answer, whereas those that are not presented in this form do not. One reason to view this as a partly *rhetorical* device, rather than a purely rational one, is that the contents of logic are hotly disputed by some philosophers. To treat an argument presented in formal logic as holding a special claim presupposes that the logic it is presented in leads safely from premises to conclusions, a claim that those who dispute the content of (given forms of) logic will not necessarily accept. Part of the problem with the above characterisation of the difference between analytic and continental philosophy seems to be the overly narrow conception of 'argument' that it turns on. If argument in general is identified with what passes for argument in analytic philosophy (or possibly with something even narrower than this!), then it will not be possible to appreciate the range of ways that argument might be constructed elsewhere when the aims and motivations of the discourse are different. As I have already indicated, I think that methodological pluralism is important, and that coming to understand the methods of those philosophers whose aims and motivations are different from one's own is also important. Undervaluing such work by refusing it the label of 'argument' works against such pluralism, and, as I later indicate (see section 5), against the critical spirit of philosophy.

The position I have been developing—that we should examine and articulate the methods of philosophy more thoroughly and exhaustively—has, in my view, a very important application to undergraduate teaching. Undergraduate programs often offer critical thinking and logic courses, both of which give students some explicit grounding in philosophical methodology. However, not even this happens across the board. Significantly, limits to our understanding of the methods we use as philosophers, and limited resources articulating what these methods are and how they can be used constrain our ability to teach these methods to undergraduate students.

There are a lot of good reasons for developing a rich understanding of the methods we employ as philosophers, and for viewing the teaching of these methods as an important aspect of undergraduate philosophy programmes. As I mentioned at the beginning, one potential benefit of doing so may be to give all students who come through our undergraduate programmes the means to establish their authority within the discipline. I think this takes two forms. First, in the absence of the kind of data that can be banged down on the table accompanied by "You look at the data—they bear out what I'm saying!", the ability to say, "I've done this carefully and rigorously—I'm a skilled practitioner" and to be able to point at least to the method that has been used is very powerful. Second, and perhaps more important, is the confidence derived from being able to identify and articulate one's own skills. If students know what some of the various methods of philosophy are, and they have completed courses in them with success, then they will be able to see themselves as skilled practitioners. Having a grounding in the methods and techniques of philosophy offers a way of establishing oneself as authoritative in philosophy, whether or not one has access to its (informal) power networks.

5. Reflections on the Role of Philosophers as Critics

The preceding discussion has taken for granted that philosophers can be authoritative qua philosophers. But there are reasons for thinking that the notion of theoretical authority might *only* apply to those fields of inquiry where the raw data are readily accessible. Philosophers might not be properly viewed as possessing theoretical authority, precisely because the discipline is not firmly anchored by a body of facts or data. In a paper on epistemic dependence, John Hardwig indicates that his claims about expertise (a notion that I take to be intimately related to theoretical authority, if not synonymous) are restricted "to belief in and knowledge or propositions for which there is evidence."(Hardwig, 2006:329). If, as I have already argued, philosophical propositions are propositions for which the evidence—intuitions—is more slippery than that of other fields, then the theoretical authority that philosophers have as philosophers may turn out to be a very marginal form of theoretical authority. Steve Fuller offers a salient distinction here between the 'expert' and the 'intellectual'. According to Fuller:

> An intellectual takes the entire world as fair game for his judgments, but at the same time he opens himself to scrutiny from all quarters. Indeed, the intellectual's natural habitat is controversy, and often he seems to spend more time on defending and attacking positions than on developing and applying them. In contrast the expert's judgments are restricted to his area of training. The credibility of those judgments are measured in terms of the freedom from contravention that his colleagues accord him. (Fuller, 2006:342–343)

Perhaps, according to this distinction, philosophers are intellectuals rather than experts, and as such, their claims invite controversy rather than giving non-philosophers reasons for belief. The central role that critical engagement plays in philosophy is apparent throughout the discipline. It influences the way we run our tutorial classes, the way seminar and conference presentations are structured (and the nature of the discussion after them). It is also apparent in the role philosophers play in public life. From Socrates to Peter Singer, philosophers appear in public as critics of (some of) our pervasive assumptions and unreflective habits.

Speaking of philosophers' role as critics of our pervasive assumptions and unreflective habits, however, leads me to make a final comment about the quoted passage above. Although it might seem a cheap shot, it is worth noting Fuller's use of male gendered personal pronouns in describing both 'intellectuals' and 'experts'. It is worth noting, because the prejudicial gender stereotypes that psychologists have measured, and which Fricker suggests feed into judgments of credibility, do not come out of nothing. To the extent that philosophers thus reinforce rather than unsettle existing gender stereotypes in their work (by the use of the male pronoun for occupations associated with competence, objectivity, and being well informed, for example), they fail to challenge a pervasive assumption and show themselves to be susceptible to unreflective habits.

I think most philosophers would agree that philosophy must accommodate the critical content that is characteristic of much of the best and most influential philosophy, *as well as* the possibility of establishing one's authority as a philosopher—of demonstrating one's 'professional competence' as Quine puts it in the opening quote, or of making judgments about whose work is 'first-rate'. Yet if treating someone as an authority means taking their opinions on some subject as reasons for belief independent of the first-order considerations relevant to that subject, then this is clearly at odds with the idea of being critical of pervasive assumptions and unreflective habits. Taking another person's word for it because they're widely regarded as an authority is just the sort of unreflective habit that some philosophers counsel against. And it is surely just as important within philosophy that we remain open to the critical challenges of others (and the possibility that these challenges can come from unexpected directions and can strike at the founding assumptions of our thought) as it is in the world outside the discipline.

Briefly, then, I suggest two strategies that I think will allow us to retain both of these aspects of philosophy, while diffusing what is most worrisome in the tension between them.

First, I want to return to the earlier discussion of philosophical methodology. During that discussion, I stressed the importance of understanding and explicitly discussing the various methods of philosophy. I argued that it was a problem that discussions of philosophical methodology are often narrow and speak only to practitioners of certain forms of philosophy. One reason for my emphasis on this was a concern that philosophers from different traditions or different sub-specialities are increasingly unable to engage in meaningful dialogue, even when such dialogue might yield valuable insight. By failing to familiarize ourselves explicitly with our own methods, we also fail to articulate them in ways that can make them accessible to other philosophers who use other methods. By failing to teach a range of different philosophical techniques to our students, we effectively force them to choose specializations not only by subject matter but also (by default) by method. At the same time, we rob ourselves of the tools we need to engage critically with one another in terms that will be understood by all members of the discipline. The first strategy I suggest, then, is the same one I suggested above: that we undertake more research, and more expansive research, into philosophical methodology, both so we better understand the different (legitimate) forms it can take ourselves, and so we can teach it more explicitly and broadly at the undergraduate level. This will allow philosophy to fulfil its critical function more effectively.

The second strategy is to recognise and question ways in which, in practice, we exclude one another from our own areas of specialisation, and thus stifle important forms of critical engagement. Our tendency to do this is evident in the existence of many philosophy journals that are sub-discipline-specific, as well as many conferences that are sub-discipline-specific, and the streaming of general conferences (such as annual conferences organised by national philosophical associations) into sub-discipline-specific streams. In the face of changing measures of research output, there also seems to be a trend toward specialisation of departments, so that departments foster 'centres of excellence' around particular research topics, at the expense of breadth. There are obvious advantages to this in terms of securing competitive external funding, but its implications for the shape of the discipline, the effect it has on our opportunities for engagement outside of our own narrow areas of research focus, and the way philosophy appears to students who take courses at such universities as undergraduates cannot be ignored.

Of course, specialised journals and conferences provide important opportunities for philosophers working on the same topics to come together and share work at the cutting edge. This, however, presupposes that most of us spend most of our time working at some (physical) distance from others in our areas of specialisation, and that getting together is thus an occasional *exception* to the status quo. Current arrangements seem to risk making it the norm.

Haslanger's research into journal publication rates offers a useful example of the risks specialist journals pose to critical engagement. Haslanger's data show, among other things, that the mainstream general philosophy journals publish hardly any work on feminist philosophy (Haslanger, 2008:220). Yet the insights of feminist philosophy are almost always primarily aimed at those doing mainstream philosophy rather than other feminist philosophers. So publishing these papers in, say, *Hypatia* (a well-respected specialist feminist philosophy journal) implies that they are papers in 'feminist philosophy' rather than papers in, say, epistemology or ethics. It is not entirely clear what we should do in response to this, given that it is clearly appropriate for the discipline to retain a mixture of specialist and general journals. Perhaps recommendations are best aimed at those journals that purport to be for all forms of philosophy. The *Australasian Journal of Philosophy*, for example, includes the following on its website:

> The *Australasian Journal of Philosophy* (*AJP*) is one of the world's leading philosophy journals. It is recognized as publishing the very best work in the analytic tradition, but is not narrow in what it regards as worthy of acceptance. (*AJP* website, http://www.ajp.aap.org.au/)

The *AJP* wasn't included in Haslanger's data, and I don't have any data of my own on the basis of which to make claims about what it does and doesn't publish. But it seems that journals like this, under the auspices of national philosophical associations, are the ones that we should expect to genuinely consider a wide range of material for publication.

6. Conclusion

In this chapter, I argued that it is more difficult to challenge those with authority in philosophy than it is to challenge those with authority in (at least some) other disciplines. And I argued that it is—for the same reasons—more difficult to establish oneself as an authority in philosophy. The reasons for this are that the raw data of philosophy—taken to be intuitions—are not objective or independently accessible in the way that the raw data of (at least some) other disciplines are. In addition, the methods of philosophy are more varied than those of other disciplines, but they are often learned only implicitly. Philosophical methods are not articulated and examined as widely by philosophers as they could be; nor are they taught as rigorously in undergraduate programmes as they could be. I suggest that more research and explication of the multifarious methods of philosophy could mediate these difficulties. I furthermore argue that ensuring that a wide range of methods are recognized as valid within philosophy (and understood by as many philosophers and philosophy students as possible) will help to mediate the tension between authoritative structures within philosophy and the role that philosophy plays as a critical discipline. Drawing on Miranda Fricker's work on epistemic injustice, and findings about gender stereotypes from social psychology, I have argued that the difficulty of establishing oneself as an authority in philosophy is likely to be a greater problem for women than for men, because women are more likely than men to be unfairly denied credibility.

I began this chapter by quoting Quine, who stated that philosophy suffers, as other disciplines do not, from a wavering consensus on questions of professional competence, and that identifying who are the sages, or first-rate philosophers, and who are the cranks is particularly difficult within philosophy. I have attempted to offer an account of why this might be the case, and why it might particularly disadvantage women. According to my argument, Sally Haslanger's graduate school professor's claim that women are not capable of being first-rate philosophers because they are not capable of having influential ideas contains a kernel of truth. It is likely that the important and original ideas of some women in philosophy have not been influential because it has not been possible for them to establish their authority within the discipline.

References

Deaux, Kay (1984) "From individual differences to social categories: Analysis of a decade's research on gender", *American Psychologist*, Vol. 39, No. 2, 105–116.

Dennett, Daniel (1995) "Intuition Pumps" in Brockman, ed., *The Third Culture: Scientists on the Edge*, New York: Simon and Schuster, 181–197.

Frankfurt, Harry (1969) "Alternate Possibilities and Moral Responsibility", *The Journal of Philosophy*, Vol. 66, No. 23, 829–839.

Fricker, Miranda (2007) *Epistemic Injustice: Power and the Ethics of Knowing*, Oxford, UK, and New York: Oxford University Press.

Fricker, Miranda (1998) "Rational Authority and Social Power: Towards a Truly Social Epistemology", *Proceedings of the Aristotelian Society*, Vol. 98, 159–177.

Fuller, Steve (2006) "The Constitutively Social Character of Expertise" in Selinger and Crease, eds., *The Philosophy of Expertise*, New York: Columbia University Press, 342–357.

Goldman, A., and Pust, J. (2002) "Philosophical Theory and Intuitional Evidence" in *Pathways to Knowledge*, New York: Oxford University Press, 73–94.

Hájek, Alan (forthcoming) "Philosophical Heuristics and Philosophical Creativity" in Paul and Kaufman, eds., *The Philosophy of Creativity*, New York: Oxford University Press.

Hanrahan, Rebecca Roman, and Antony, Louise (2005) "Because I Said So: Toward a Feminist Theory of Authority", *Hypatia*, Vol. 20, No. 4, 59–79.

Hardwig, John (2006) "Epistemic Dependence" in Selinger and Crease, eds., *The Philosophy of Expertise*, New York: Columbia University Press, 328–341.

Haslanger, Sally (2008) "Changing the Ideology and Culture of Philosophy: Not by Reason (Alone)", *Hypatia*, Vol. 23, No. 10, 210–223.

Kite, Mary E., Deaux, Kay, and Haines, Elizabeth L. (2008) "Gender Stereotypes" in Denmark and Paludi, eds., *Psychology of Women: A Handbook of Issues and Theories*, 2nd edition, Westport, CT: Praeger.

Levy, Neil (2003) "Analytic and Continental Philosophy: Explaining the Differences", *Metaphilosophy*, Vol. 34, No. 3, 284–304.

Locke, John (1689) *An Essay Concerning Human Understanding*, Nidditch, ed., Oxford, UK: Clarendon, 1975.

Quine, W. V. O. (1981) "Has Philosophy Lost Contact with People?" in *Theories and Things*, Cambridge, MA, and London: Harvard University Press, 190–193.

Rawls, J. (1951) "Outline of a Decision Procedure for Ethics", *Philosophical Review*, Vol. 60, No. 2, 177–197.

Rawls, J. (1999) *A Theory of Justice*, 2nd edition, Cambridge, MA: Harvard University Press.

Raz, Joseph (1985) "Authority, Law and Morality", *Monist*, Vol. 68, 295–315.

Schein, Virginia Ellen (1973) "The Relationship between Sex Role Stereotypes and Requisite Management Characteristics", *Journal of Applied Psychology*, Vol. 57, No. 2, 95–100.

Singer, Peter (1972) "Famine, Affluence and Morality", *Philosophy and Public Affairs*, Vol. 1, No. 1, 229–243.

Singer, Peter (2005) "Ethics and Intuitions", *Journal of Ethics*, Vol. 9, No. 3–4, 331–352.

Strawson, P. F. (1959) *Individuals*, London: Methuen.

Turner, Stephen (2006) "What is the Problem with Experts" in Selinger and Crease, eds., *The Philosophy of Expertise*, New York: Columbia University Press, 159–186.

Waluchow, Wilfred (1989) "The Weak Social Thesis", *Oxford Journal of Legal Studies*, Vol. 9, 23–55.

Williams, Bernard (2000) "Philosophy as a Humanistic Discipline", reprinted in Moore, ed., *Philosophy as a Humanistic Discipline*, Princeton, NJ: Princeton University Press (2006), 180–199.

{ 6 }

Models and Values

WHY DID NEW ZEALAND PHILOSOPHY DEPARTMENTS STOP HIRING WOMEN PHILOSOPHERS?

Adriane Rini

Since July 2005, New Zealand philosophy departments appointed 20 men but only one woman.[1] To date there has been little discussion about the matter, and little discussion about whether this hiring ratio is acceptable or unacceptable to New Zealanders. Some people might ask whether hiring women *matters* in philosophy, and of course that is a real question and deserves an answer. But in order to answer, we need first to get clear about what exactly is being asked, because there are different questions here: Is it important to hire women? Is it important to hire women in philosophy? To simply say 'no' to the first is to express a sexist opinion. But what about the second question? Is there a reasonable argument against hiring, even inadvertently, only men in philosophy? As a referee for this chapter explained, some people do say, for example, that philosophy is about 'universal truths', and because the gender of the philosophical practitioner is simply irrelevant to this, hiring women in philosophy doesn't matter to the outputs of the discipline. It is not clear that it matters to the content whether you have a man or woman teaching logic, or Locke, or possible-worlds metaphysics, and so on. What surely does matter, however, is that the 20:1 hiring ratio makes it look like women are being shut out of

---

[1] In 2009, I began collecting data on the appointment of women to philosophy positions in New Zealand. Some of those data are included in appendix 1 (Bishop et al.). I have continued to track appointments since Bishop's analysis was completed, and the figures in the present chapter are based on information available to me for the period from July 2005 to April 2013. The woman was appointed to a 0.5FTE permanent lectureship in 2011. (In New Zealand, a permanent lectureship is a tenured position, and 1FTE is a full-time position and 0.5FTE is half-time.) As far as I have been able to find, four of these recent appointments have been to part-time positions. The 20:1 hiring ratio does not include people hired as postdoctoral fellows, or tutors (whether permanent or temporary), or entry-level temporary lecturers.

philosophy, and that the discipline in New Zealand is once again becoming more exclusively male.

My interest in this chapter is how well-intentioned philosophy departments, in spite of an interest in supporting women in philosophy, have ended up with a 20:1 hiring ratio in just over six years. The chapter explores various factors that contribute to and perpetuate our hiring practices. In particular, it is I think important to look at some of the changes that have confronted New Zealand universities during the past two decades, for we have seen major changes in the funding models, governance, and management of our universities, and I highlight these because I think that they could help to explain why our departments have (whether consciously or not) been more attuned to hiring male philosophers and why the gender imbalance within philosophy has not been addressed. I should emphasize that I am looking at the subject in the very specific context of New Zealand philosophy. Although that might seem an especially narrow focus because New Zealand is a small country and has only a small number of philosophers, the situation here should have wider interest not least because of the fact that we have a long tradition of gender equality. This is a source of pride to most New Zealanders. But it may be that our egalitarian tradition has allowed us to become complacent. Most New Zealand philosophers are not comfortable with anything that smacks of sexism and so won't want to say that hiring women never matters. Yet just as certainly, we are *not* hiring women in philosophy, and New Zealand philosophers need to be aware of this and begin to take account of it.

The first part of this chapter argues that it is possible to identify various factors that have made the 20:1 hiring ratio possible. The second part of the chapter sets out some of the kinds of arguments I have heard given about whether it matters to hire women in philosophy, and then looks at how to evaluate these arguments. I think it is important to look at these arguments about hiring women, because they give good insight not just into how women are missing out, but also illustrate how people attempt to justify the fact. If the 20:1 ratio is a problem for us, then such 'justifications' need to be more closely examined. In the third part of the chapter, I take a different approach from several other authors in this volume who focus on what might best be described as factors 'external' to philosophy—by which I mean factors that are perhaps not specific to philosophy. My focus in the third part is factors that are 'internal' to the discipline, factors central to the discipline that directly concern the health, breadth, and direction of philosophy in New Zealand. I think it is important to consider internal factors because of the significant role they play in determining the real shape of our discipline. This can be seen in the way that, among other things, they influence what we do teach and what we don't teach. Moreover, these internal factors often guide our hiring, and—a point I want to look at in some detail—they affect our judgments about what counts as success in philosophy.

1. Performance-Based Research Funding and a Model of a Good Scholar

Since 2003, New Zealand has operated a system of 'Performance-Based Research Funding' (PBRF). The Tertiary Education Commission selects a mechanism for measuring academics' publication rates and for measuring the prestige of our journals and publishers. Journals are rated A*, A, B, or C, with A* the highest.[2] PBRF also tries to measure and assess one's scholarly reputation and level of active participation in the scholarly community. Each member of academic staff who is on a 'research' or a 'research and teaching' contract submits a personal research 'portfolio', which is fed into the system so that each individual scholar can be assigned a 'score' of A, B, C, or R.[3] Ultimately, the share of government funding allocated to a university is linked to the scores of its individual researchers. A-rated researchers are 'worth more' to a university than B-rated researchers, and so on. As a result, publishing a certain quantity of work and publishing in highly ranked journals have become important objectives for philosophers working in New Zealand universities. Taken at face value, that might sound like a reasonable and even a good scheme. Let's assume—for the moment at least and for the sake of argument—that it is a reasonably good system.[4] Even so, it is a system that works to the disadvantage of women in philosophy.

A colleague recently sent me a link to an online discussion that I think provides a useful framework for looking at this, because it serves as a point of reference when considering women's participation in philosophy. In the discussion, a woman whom I will call X expressed frustration at her inability to progress in the academy, and she turned to the online forum to ask for advice. A well-meaning scholar whom I will call Y responded and explained to X that she should do as Y does, and this includes publishing four articles in A*-rated journals a year. Y was concerned enough to respond, and so clearly acted with goodwill and was trying to be helpful. But Y's advice is not really helpful. I want to look at why. Rephrasing Y's advice brings to light separate themes within it. Perhaps the following rephrasing will do:

(A1) If you do as Y does, then you are contributing something of value.

---

[2] The ranking system used is in fact one devised by the Australian Research Council (ARC), but in 2011, Australia abandoned it. New Zealand persists with it still. Some of our universities operate a research database system whereby when you type in the bibliographical details of your publications, the system will automatically generate the ARC ranking of the journal or publisher.

[3] Some but not all 'fractional' or part-time contracts require participation in PBRF. And recent years have seen a trend toward permanent positions for 'senior tutors', whose job description does not include a research component, and so does not require participation in PBRF, which measures research.

[4] Most academics I know think that in practice it is a terrible scheme. Bureaucrats, accountants, and managers don't see it as so terrible because it makes calculating the value of scholarship easy for them to do quickly, and without any specialist knowledge.

(A2) If you publish as much as Y does, then you are publishing sufficiently.

(A3) If you publish where Y does, then you are publishing in the best journals.

Let's consider the practical difficulties about (A1)–(A3). First, there is the matter of 'trendiness'. If the key to success is to 'do what Y does' and publish four articles a year in A* journals, and if we are talking about philosophy, then by and large, a philosopher has to commit to publishing in certain areas (i.e., those areas that are more highly represented in A* journals). There are some philosophical specialties where Y's advice is simply impractical, specialties in which a philosopher cannot really expect to publish four articles per year in A* journals. Y's advice ignores this fact, and so is not well equipped to assign value to scholarly work in *all* areas. Examples of what is easily undervalued in this scheme might include, say, a definitive study that is the fruit of decades of careful scholarship, or work in interdisciplinary research areas that falls outside the mainstream. To work in some specialist areas is to face a system in which one's research is from the outset likely to be assigned a lesser value than work in a more popular area. There is some evidence from the 2006 PBRF round that research publications in the area of continental philosophy were not judged of comparable value with research publications in the area of contemporary analytical philosophy. And without a doubt, our current rankings do privilege some groups. Some might argue that rankings and scores are artificial and perhaps shouldn't worry us so much. However, this is cold comfort if they are nevertheless contributing to a general narrowing of the discipline, or if they are contributing to the exclusion of women. One point that future studies about women's participation should consider is whether our hiring is mainly in trendy areas. We need to know whether trendiness is innocuous or if it is a factor in the 20:1 hiring ratio. If it is a factor, then a department that is genuinely interested in hiring women might do well to advertise positions as 'open' with respect to research area.

Part of the appeal of a model like (A1)–(A3) is that it appears to provide a practical assessment measure and does not require time-consuming scholarly judgments about individual pieces of research. When PBRF was introduced in New Zealand, I remember being told it would replace the "old boys' opinions" with something much more "transparent" and "egalitarian". The effect, however, is that the people in the Human Resources Office, for example, can use a model like (A1)–(A3) to make judgments about philosophical 'quality' without having to actually read any philosophical research and without having to consult any specialists. This can be used to completely replace scholarly evaluation so that even a non-philosopher can judge the 'quality' of philosophy. We know that the old system was not entirely sympathetic to women, and no one is advocating going back to the days of exclusively male philosophers.

But it seems that one problem with PBRF is the way it can systematize and reinforce existing biases in philosophy. Since the 20:1 hiring ratio between 2005 and 2013 closely coincides with the shift to PBRF in 2003, it would seem that if we want to improve the gender balance in philosophy, then we might begin by reconsidering how PBRF measures success and what it counts as a research exemplar in our discipline.

I think there is a case to be made for saying that PBRF makes judgments *too easy.* I once heard a non-philosopher administrative head describe a candidate for a philosophy chair this way: "I *know* [Z] is an excellent scholar; I know the quality of the journals he publishes in." As a referee for this chapter pointed out, "Bibliometrics such as journal rankings are devised precisely so that people outside the field can make judgments about the quality of a scholar's work quickly and easily." That is no doubt true, but the question is whether that is appropriate.[5] Certainly, knowing some rank ordering of philosophy journals cannot legitimately stand in for actually reading and evaluating philosophical work and, very certainly, it cannot when evaluating job applicants. We do of course expect there to be some genuinely philosophical scholarly judgment operative in the selection processes of journals and in the journal-ranking process. But it is not at all clear that the extent to which *these* judgments are legitimate should lead to *further* judgments about the quality of individual philosophers. Even if the rankings are legitimate, it does not follow that a person is a bad philosopher or a good philosopher because they publish in certain journals. When we are evaluating particular pieces of scholarship, we know that there are good articles in bad journals, and bad articles in good journals. But journal rankings alone cannot distinguish between these two situations. Because the 20:1 hiring ratio coincides with the introduction of PBRF, we need to establish that our system of journal ranking *does not* have the effect of discriminating against women. What the defender of journal rankings needs to prove is that despite the 20:1 ratio, the system is working.

A related point that Y's advice helps to highlight is the fact that Y's model admits a simple mechanical application. Certainly in New Zealand, the process of evaluating research and scholarship has become much more mechanical than it was in the past. There is less opportunity for careful judgments about an individual's scholarly merit or about an individual scholar's particular contributions, because the evaluation processes that universities use are often watered down to a matter of adding up weighted points. One simply gets so many points for work in an A* journal, so many for work in an A journal, and so on. These mechanical assessments are also supposed to be quick—I'm told PBRF assessors usually spend ten minutes on a scholar's file. It's hard to see how ten minutes could be an invitation to form a judgment. Both the timeframe and the method

---

[5] See Valian (1998) and Haslanger (2008), who each raise concerns about what is involved in quick and easy assessments, and about how such assessments can tend to disadvantage women.

suggest that at best it is an invitation to confirm someone else's prejudgment. It is worth noting too that while the peer-review process does involve the judgment of a piece of work by a specialist, the peer reviewer is not charged with responsibility for determining the author's status as a researcher, but only the suitability of a particular piece of work for publication in a particular journal. When these judgments are then used by others to stand in for careful assessment of a scholar's capabilities, they bear a weight they were not intended to carry.

So far my concern has been to highlight unintended sexist consequences of the PBRF system. Some of the reasons why we should want proof that PBRF does not work against women are reasons concerning overt sexism. Haslanger (2008) discusses the fact that some, possibly many, philosophers still do assign work a lesser value when it is known to be by a woman. And that has the effect that when a journal submission is known to be written by a woman, it is, statistically, more likely to be devalued, and is therefore in greater danger of being rejected. There is nothing a female author can do in such a situation except to take the precaution in future of making her journal submissions completely 'blind' in the sense that no part of the article can be easily traced to her.[6] But if women are not already taking such pre-emptive measures, then until these attitudes change, women are not going to have as easy a time getting philosophical work accepted for publication. And so the institutional system again reinforces existing biases.

One *good* thing about our system of PBRF is that it does help to provide a check against overtly sexist denigration of women's published work, because once the research is published, it is assigned a rank on the basis of the rank of the publisher. But that provides only limited protection. If editors and referees unconsciously judge philosophy journal submissions more harshly when they can see that the author is female, then we should expect too that philosophers judge *published* work more harshly when it is written by a female. And that is something that clearly can affect the kinds of judgments made when determining shortlists and when deciding which candidate to hire. Women face a twofold difficulty—first, because they may be contending with the search committee's unconscious devaluing of their work because it is work authored by a female, and second, these women are likely to have fewer publications than their male peers because of the same devaluing by philosophy journal editors and referees. The current funding model does not recognize this. Its focus is on the quantity of one's publications, on the prestige of the publisher, and on the 'esteem' that peers accord one's research. This disadvantages young scholars, whether male

---

[6] At the 2009 ANU Symposium, several women reported that their own efforts to 'blind' their work regularly include such things as (i) omitting altogether any trace of the author's name on anything that will be sent to referees and (ii) making sure that the title cannot be linked to the title of any previous publications or conference talks that might themselves indicate the gender of the author.

or female, and favours senior scholars with established careers and a steady flow of publications.[7] So, again, the way the system is constructed leaves questions about its fairness and makes it difficult to address existing bias.[8]

Because the PBRF model is used to determine a university's funding, simple accounting makes it clear why a department or a university that is focused on maximizing scores might not see young women philosophers as a 'good investment'.[9] Not only are men winning the jobs, but further, a significant proportion of the jobs they are winning are positions that are only advertised at the senior professorial level. It should be clear that I am explicitly *not* claiming that there is conscious or even unconscious bias against women in this regard. That is, it is not that departments are saying "we would love to hire women but they are not good investments". What happens is more subtle. It turns out that the factors that lead to an appointment happen to have the consequence that fewer women get hired. The number of senior appointments would seem to indicate that it is the established male philosophers with research records that measure up well according to our current system who are seen to be 'good investments'.

Ironically, the adoption of the PBRF model roughly coincided with an increase in the numbers of women gaining a Ph.D. in philosophy and entering the job market. New Zealand's first official round of PBRF came in 2003, just around the time when New Zealand philosophy departments were beginning to hire more young women. But by the time of the second round of PBRF in 2006, philosophy departments in New Zealand had stopped hiring women philosophers. (As noted above, the last time a woman was appointed to a permanent full-time appointment was in mid-2005.) One possibility is that it is not the philosophers who are sexist, but that the system we work in is sexist or is compelling us to be sexist in our hiring. So perhaps we might argue that the 20:1 hiring ratio is an unintended consequence of things beyond our control.

Consider two points that make it plausible to suppose that it's the system, not *us*. First, there's little reason to think that New Zealand philosophers did actually intend to exclude women. Departments *were* beginning to hire women

---

[7] The Association for Women in the Sciences (New Zealand) produced a booklet, 'Women in Science: A 2011 Snapshot', which includes data (p. 16) on the 'Percentage of researchers by gender achieving different PBRF grades'. The authors note: 'The PBRF grades are loosely associated with age, with less than 1% of < 35 year researchers obtaining "A" ratings and approximately 80% of researchers < 35 achieving "C", "CNE", "R" or "RNE" grades. However, when comparing achievement within age groups, women tend to be overrepresented in the lower grades and underrepresented in the higher grades' (p. 16).

[8] Writing in 2005, Bruce Curtis and Steve Matthewman put some of the blame for the skewing of appointments on university managers. Writing about PBRF, Curtis and Matthewman note: "The most immediate and likely result is in the area of staff hiring, where senior management and HoDs are extremely reluctant to hire junior staff who may accrue R's."

[9] Much might change if our legislators decided to make some level of gender representation a factor in determining university funding. But to my knowledge, this has not been tried in New Zealand. PBRF is just about research (i.e., the scheme focuses exclusively on 'research outputs', 'peer esteem', and 'contributions to the research environment').

before PBRF came into play—a number of women were appointed between 2001 and 2005. And by 2001, the departments at Auckland, Waikato, Massey, Victoria, Canterbury, and Otago all had at least one woman on the philosophy staff. A second reason for supposing that it's the system that is sexist, not us, is that while academics prize scholarly values like collegiality and scholarship, in the late 1990s, New Zealand universities fell victim to a managerial culture with its own set of values, according to which universities exist in a 'competitive market', and where universities set 'strategic research priorities' to align research expertise with chosen focus areas. This new culture brought sometimes vast changes, but it offers little that's conducive to improving women's participation. Instead, the new style of management gave birth to a divide between New Zealand academics and their managers. Wilf Malcolm and Nicholas Tarling detail this history in their book *Crisis of Identity? The Mission and Management of Universities in New Zealand* (2007). Malcolm and Tarling do not consider whether the managerial model has tended toward more exclusion of women. But it is, perhaps, worth noting that women's participation in New Zealand philosophy closely mirrors women's participation in the New Zealand business sector, where the managerial model is common. In 2008, the New Zealand Human Rights Commission published its Census of Women's Participation, which makes cross-spectrum comparisons possible.[10] According to the 2008 Census, "Women hold 8.65% of board directorships of companies listed on the New Zealand Stock Market" (p. 17). In 2010, philosophy came in slightly worse than this, with women in just 8.3% of professorships in New Zealand philosophy departments, and recent appointments indicate a worsening of this rate rather than an improvement.[11]

2. Reviewing Some of the Justifications Offered

The 20:1 hiring ratio might reflect changes in university culture, but the new managerialism is not solely responsible for the failure to hire women philosophers. We philosophers bear some responsibility for it too. We are involved in drawing up the shortlist for jobs and interviewing candidates. Our record of hiring indicates that hiring women philosophers is not particularly important to us, but then neither is this something we talk about much. In order to motivate some discussion and debate about the importance of hiring women philosophers, in this section, I set out some of the arguments that I have heard

---

[10] The 2008 New Zealand Census of Women's Participation is available online at http://www. hrc.co.nz/hrc_new/hrc/cms/files/documents/28-Mar-2008_12-59-39_2008_Census_of_Womens_ Participation.pdf.

[11] It is not clear whether these figures reveal anything about similarities in the mechanisms of exclusion.

philosophers put forward to explain why a department did not hire a woman. Setting these arguments down might serve to alert young women in the job market to potential traps and alert departments to patterns of reasoning that are at least partly responsible for the low level of women's participation.

One argument that is often used to explain the reason why another man was appointed goes like this: "While the department would very much like to hire a woman, and indeed looked carefully at the women who did apply, nevertheless, in this particular case, for this particular job, the most important concern is to hire someone to fill [So-and-So's] shoes." This explanation trades on an ambiguity, blurring the distinction between needing to hire someone to teach the courses that So-and-So used to teach and wanting to hire a colleague who is like So-and-So. But consider each separately. Often the shoe-filling argument is used to justify the final appointment on the ground that it is the route that is 'least disruptive' of the teaching programme: So-and-So's courses are popular or part of the requirements for the major, etc. This argument is fine for preserving the status quo, but it simply is not an effective method for increasing the participation of women when women traditionally constitute a minority in the field. So, in spite of any reasonableness about wanting someone to teach specific courses, there is a de facto prejudice in this approach to hiring, the impact of which might be that it is men's interests in philosophy that are allowed to define what is important in philosophy. But it is the more general version of shoe-filling that is perhaps the more troublesome—that is, the version according to which a department wants to hire someone who is *like* So-and-So. For when So-and-So is a man, the most obvious replacement is someone who looks and sounds like So-and-So himself, and this makes a woman easier to overlook than to see as a good fit for So-and-So's shoes. This is especially pronounced when the So-and-So is a well-published senior man and the applicant a young woman, because a young woman philosopher *looks* less like a senior male than anyone else. The young man has his maleness in common with him, and the senior woman has her seniority in common with him. The young woman is doubly removed from the perceived model of success. She might easily be appointable, but she is just not what the department is 'looking for'.

Another factor at play in the shoe-filling argument concerns what the loss of a high-ranking senior male philosopher means to a department. Such a loss is something that his colleagues frequently regard as a terrible blow to their own status and the status of their department. A really top-notch senior philosopher lends a prestige to a department and to the individuals in that department. To be in So-and-So's department is to be part of a good thing. As the older generation of (mostly male) So-and-Sos begins to retire, departments looking for high-status philosophers to fill those shoes will have to be especially imaginative in order to see the women in the job market as possible replacements for the large number of retiring men. Otherwise, shoe-filling is not going to do much to increase women's participation in philosophy.

It is worth noting that if shoe-filling is a factor, it doesn't run the same way when the So-and-So is a woman philosopher. Three of six New Zealand departments (Auckland, Massey, and Victoria) have lost women philosophers in recent years but have *not* replaced them by hiring other women. In each case, a woman was replaced by a man, and in at least one of these cases, a sub-professorial woman was replaced by a man at the professorial level. Is it that we place so little value on women's participation in philosophy that we are not working even to preserve very minimal levels of participation?[12] One referee suggested to me that these appointments could be taken as evidence that departments are not engaged in shoe-filling. My answer is simply that I have several times been offered shoe-filling as the explanation of why an appointment went the way it did, which indicates that people at least sometimes do regard shoe-filling as an adequate justification when men are being replaced. Of course, the general point is just that shoe-filling is no way forward: We cannot consistently say that we want to hire more women but that 'in this particular case' we have to 'fill shoes'.

A second argument about why the woman couldn't be hired is that "she's too junior and hasn't finished her Ph.D." I have heard this said when the one woman who was included on a shortlist for a starting lectureship had not yet finished her Ph.D., while all of the men on the shortlist had a degree in hand. There is something inherently dishonest in this response. Not having a degree in hand cannot be a reason against hiring the woman if it was not a prior reason against shortlisting her. There is not a good argument here. Now it might be that the woman looked interesting to the selection committee and that they wanted the opportunity to consider her more closely, and so they shortlisted her. And it might be that on closer examination, she turned out not to be appointable, but at that point in the hiring process, the ground for deciding whether she is appointable cannot be that she has not finished her Ph.D. If, on the other hand, it is the case that she was only included on the shortlist in order to have a woman on it and so avoid appearing sexist and avoid scrutiny from any Equal Opportunity Officer or Human Resources Department, then the ploy speaks for itself.

However good our intentions, our actions, as evidenced by our 20:1 hiring ratio, are excluding women from philosophy. Most New Zealand philosophers when they come to know this are not likely to be comfortable with it, because

---

[12] The web and calendar entries for our departments can sometimes make it difficult to tell how many women are actually working in a department. As several colleagues pointed out to me when I was compiling the statistical data for this volume, it would have appeared to an outside observer that the University of Auckland has four women in the department, but one was a dean, one was retired but continuing in a fractional position, and only two women were on regular full-time research and teaching contracts in philosophy. There is no easy way to come to know this kind of information without 'inside' knowledge of the department. And of course interpreting such information is also tricky.

most are not sexists. And because most of us are not sexists, the most common argument about why we didn't hire a woman goes like this: "There is no real sexism involved in the decision-making, but rather it was a matter of simple happenstance. We would have hired a woman if we could have, but the best candidate just happened to be a man." Of course, it might in fact be more often the case than not that a man is the best candidate. But when it happens to be the case almost all of the time—as in the New Zealand example, 20 times out of 21—then there is reason to suspect that there are some sexist opinions at work. There is also the possibility that men simply are better than women at philosophy, but few (if any) New Zealand philosophers say that women are not well equipped for abstract reasoning. In fact, philosophers here are more often heard boasting about the outstanding philosophical abilities of our female graduate students and boasting about their placement records in top Ph.D. programmes around the world. The problem we face in New Zealand is not one of not supporting outstanding women students in philosophy. It is a problem about allowing them (and welcoming them) into the discipline along-side us as our peers by hiring them. Part 3 of this chapter attempts to explain why that might be.

A look at the Australasian Philosophy Family Tree reveals something else that is worth considering. It is clear that at the Ph.D. level in Australian phi-losophy, women supervisors make a difference: Individual women supervi-sors 'beget' more women philosophers than any individual men supervisors.[13] Dodds and Goddard (this volume) discuss problems with the often touted 'pipeline' solution to allow more women to participate in philosophy. And the evidence from the Australasian Philosophy Family Tree suggests that, rather than the pipeline, the crucial factor may be 'sponsorship' of women. Women supervisors, it appears, are good advocates for women philosophers, seeing them through the degree and into jobs. New Zealand philosophers generally have proven to be good sponsors of women philosophy students qua students, and this surely counts as one of our successes. But there is a need to also extend this to women as colleagues. We cannot keep saying "Yes, we'd love to appoint women, but...".

3. Hiring Factors 'Internal' to Philosophy

In this section, I want to consider what I have called 'internal' factors in New Zealand philosophy that either directly or indirectly limit women's participa-tion. I am treating issues such as the devaluing of women's work, mentioned in

---

[13] See http://consc.net/tree.html, accessed in December 2010. According to the data listed there, Genevieve Lloyd and Moira Gatens each appear to have supervised more women Ph.D.s in philosophy than anyone else in Australasia.

part 1, as external factors because they are shared with other disciplines. (The labels 'internal' and 'external' are, admittedly, clumsy in this context, though I hope they may be some help in at least framing the discussion.) Among internal factors, then, we should include the distribution of women across different sub-disciplines or areas, the concentration of women in areas of philosophical fashion or trendiness, and the implications for gender balance of what we philosophers say counts as a healthy, well-rounded programme. In this discussion, as in part 1, I am considering these factors specifically in the context of New Zealand philosophy, and looking at how they affect our 20:1 hiring ratio. The internal factors in New Zealand might not map onto philosophy in other parts of the world. But internal factors seem to me to exert a very powerful influence on the shape of our discipline, and so they should be considered closely in the particular context of women's participation and status in philosophy. Identifying internal factors might help to indicate respects in which, as philosophers and teachers, we might review our priorities if we do want to begin to address the 20:1 ratio.

There is a view of philosophy according to which it is fundamentally a historical subject, because it is about what great thinkers say about certain topics, and because it is not a discipline in which there is an agreed background of facts from which it begins. (Logic, of course, is a philosophical discipline that does proceed from an agreed background, and in this respect it is like mathematics and many sciences, but less like other humanities subjects.) The pull of the view of philosophy as a historical discipline comes in part from the fact that when you want to begin to study philosophy, you cannot open a textbook to learn the basics. You have to begin by reading what philosophers themselves have said. There is another view of philosophy according to which history of philosophy is something separate and distinct from philosophy itself, and this view treats history of philosophy at best as a kind of specialist area. I have frequently heard people who subscribe to this second view make a distinction between, on the one hand, 'doing philosophy', by which they mean reacting, oneself, to what others have said about a topic, thereby contributing one's own voice to the ongoing discussion, and, on the other hand, 'doing history', by which they mean studying what others have said as an end in itself. Colleagues who make this distinction usually see historical study as characterized by a *passivity*—that is, the historical scholar is not required, and sometimes not even expected, to engage in the argument or discussion, only to report on it. I once heard a philosopher explain to students that philosophy has such a long history and commentators have been reporting on it for at least two millennia, so there is less expectation of finding anything new and interesting to say in historical areas. He went on to point out that this is why philosophers working in historical areas have a lesser imperative to publish. In contrast, 'doing philosophy' would then appear to encourage a lot of publication, because it is supposed to be about contributing one's own reactions, so that each participant is helping to shape the discussion. In part 1 of this chapter, I explained how quantity of publications has become one of the principal measures of success in New Zealand philosophy. The view that distinguishes philosophy from its history embraces this quantitative measure. It also makes it easier to develop the distinction between this style of philosophy and purportedly 'passive' scholarship.

Philosophers do have different views about the discipline,[14] but I worry that, as a result of the PBRF funding model, we have now constructed a feedback loop that is reinforcing one particular view of what it is to be a good philosopher. By these modern measures, a good philosopher is one who is frequently cited by others, who is busily engaged in publishing, and who is responding quickly to of-the-moment developments and shifts in discussions. Reasons to be worried about this include that it represents only one view of our discipline, and it omits accounting for the quality of other approaches to philosophical scholarship. It also leads, I think, to too much being published, often of too low a quality. These are worries about the health and direction of our discipline. In short, I think we have become too narrow and that this is a loss. Not everyone will agree. And at a certain pragmatic level, becoming narrow has what might be seen by some as this advantage: It allows us to restrict the definition of what counts as philosophical excellence to simply exclude what we are not already doing. Most of our current models reinforce a preference for quick reaction and exchange of ideas. And because they do, they do not always communicate much respect for the slower, more contemplative approach to philosophy. And yet this is just the kind of study that many women tend to prefer, particularly when they are beginning philosophy. The kind of mind that flourishes when engaged, say, in a long-term textual study of Locke's *Second Treatise* has an important and legitimate place in philosophy, and it needs to be properly recognized. Mastering a canon takes time, but there is little in our system that takes account of that.

The view of philosophy as separate from its history can slip quite easily from studying great thinkers to studying 'trendy' thinkers. This might not matter much to someone interested in current discussions, who perhaps sees them as representing the state of the art. But the slip from 'great' to 'trendy' can act as a disincentive to anyone interested in longer-term historical or foundational scholarship, and who might not find the trendy discussions as philosophically rewarding. Although this is not gender-specific, it seems that privileging trendiness does sometimes lead to the privileging of a certain kind of (typically, male) student. And in my experience, this also leads philosophers to more easily overlook other kinds of contributions and talents.

Here is an example to illustrate how one philosophical voice can be excluded. Many years ago, I joint-taught a third-year course on metaphysics of time. The

---

[14] One of the places where the debate is fiercest is within history of philosophy itself. See, for example, Rist's 1996 response to Barnes 1990.

class was reading about A and B theories of time. The one other woman in the classroom raised her hand to speak. She said she was worried that she was confused. She could not understand a real difference between A and B time because they seemed to her to be just different ways of explaining the very same thing. Her classmates were all happily plumping for A time over B time, or B over A. And they laughed at her and told her she did not understand, and when she tried to explain her concern, they proceeded to explain to her, all over again, what the A theory says and what B says. The question of whether A and B are the same is not the issue here. The issue is that a student was laughed at for questioning the presuppositions of a discussion. She was made to feel stupid, and she dropped the class.[15]

Are situations like this common in philosophy? Do they generalize across the discipline? Is there anything to suggest that women might more often be the lone voice? (If so, this might help to explain why so often women in a philosophy class or at a philosophy conference prefer to wait to ask their questions or make their points one on one, *after* everyone else has finished and left.) Whatever the answers, in studying the participation of women in philosophy, we should be exploring the possibilities and asking questions like these.

4. Conclusion

The discussion between X and Y, in part 1 of this chapter, provides a useful point to return to here. In New Zealand, from 2005 to 2013, we had a 20:1 hiring ratio of men to women, and there is a question about how to fix it. We might give different answers. One is the kind of answer that Y gives: Women need to learn to play the game, to play the system. But the real problem with Y's advice is that Y does not appear willing to question the nature of the system. And generalizing from Y's advice to X, the assumption is that there is something more that women need to do, or something *wrong* with women, because the system works fine when you know how to play it, as Y does. Another answer to the 'how to fix it' question is that we need to revisit the ways in which we measure quality and ability and contribution to philosophy, to reconsider the system itself. And if that is right, then one thing we need to do is re-evaluate our responses to PBRF.

---

[15] I've seen women students exclude men too, but never with similar consequences. In my teaching experience, the men continue in philosophy. Possibly the worst case I have seen of a man excluded in a philosophy class involved a large group of middle-aged female nurses who together signed up for a class on practical ethics. The only other student was an 18-year-old man. He was a good philosopher, but the women were playing their own games, and they could not hear him. The 'A time/B time woman' and the 'practical ethics man' were lone voices within separate groups of philosophy students, and in each case, the group would not allow that the lone voice could be saying something interesting or worthwhile.

Reflections of the sort in the preceding paragraphs might not carry much weight with Y. Y offers measures that the appointments committee, the promotions committee, the grant committee, or the dean might all insist are tried and true—and all of these measures seem to indicate that Y is a successful scholar. On the face of it, Y has no reason to question such a model. The model works for Y. And so there is a residual problem: How might we show Y that those standards (i.e., the model itself) might be a problem? Plato faced a similar difficulty. In a well-known parable in Book 7 of the *Republic*, Plato imagines humankind as prisoners in a cave, cut off from the world outside. These prisoners develop games and contests among themselves, rewarding themselves for their level of mastery. In terms of Plato's allegory, we might suppose that, perhaps, Y means to advise X about how to succeed in the contests in the cave. This need not involve any serious judgments about the worth of the contests in the cave. It might just be well-meaning and practical advice about getting along in the modern university, about how best to play the game. But if that is so, then Y is like the prisoners in Plato's cave. In Plato's tale, the well-foundedness of the philosopher's knowledge is what marks the crucial separation between him and any pretenders. In the real world, although Y's assessment purports to be based on quality, we don't know whether in fact it is, or whether it is based on tradition, privilege, popular trends, chance, or even sheer luck. The problem remains that the (A1)–(A3) model purports to provide an objective and reliable basis for genuinely qualitative comparative assessment. Y is advising X about *comparative* success. But the model Y uses does not provide an objective and reliable basis for comparison, because it uses standards that themselves fall short.[16]

Let's assume that X is actually quite *good*. We have to assume that what X is asking is *in these circumstances* what she can do to make her way in the profession. There is, as Plato tells it, a journey that is for the individual alone. That is the journey out of the cave. Plato sends the newly minted philosopher back down into the cave, to fix it. But, ultimately, Plato's philosopher is not left to struggle on his own, guided only by his vision of the forms—because of course in Plato's ideal republic the philosophers will be nurtured and supported by the state. The parable of the cave is the preamble to his account of how to fix society's injustices. Plato's solution almost 2,400 years ago was to recommend a system of education that would produce philosophers suited to be society's true guardians. He thought such a society would require a certain number of people doing various jobs. One way of realizing this would be something very like a quota system. Although Plato may not have envisaged a quota of women or other groups included among the guardians—indeed, no one could argue that

---

[16] It is not enough to say that the journal rankings are decided by philosophers—for the rankings reflect judgments about the quality of *past* publications in those journals, and there is enough evidence to raise serious questions about the legitimacy of the current journal rankings. As noted earlier, in 2011, Australia but not New Zealand abandoned the rankings.

the *Republic* advocates a democratic system of government—nevertheless Plato saw that the making of a just society required some level of state intervention in order to guarantee that the right number of the right sort would be educated and supported and encouraged.

So is a quota system a good idea? It might be argued that in fact the current PBRF *is* a quota system—since it has been introduced we have been hiring almost exclusively men in philosophy. At one level, the current system works for New Zealand philosophy. New Zealand has had two separate rounds of PBRF (2003 and 2006). Both times, philosophy came out on top, as the nation's highest-scoring research discipline. But in order to win at this game, have we contrived a system that assigns excessive value to some areas and some styles, while devaluing other areas and other styles? Is this perhaps related to why we stopped hiring women?

It seems to me that there is an obvious step we can take to improve the environment for women and to encourage more women to participate and persist with philosophy. For a start, we can advertise positions as open rank and open specialty in order to catch the widest possible interest. We can then make diversity an explicit priority in our appointments. It may be that at least in the short term, these must be enforced by some sort of quota system. I am aware that some will resent having quotas. Indeed I am myself unhappy that it seems the only solution. But surely everyone must agree that we have a problem. We don't want the hiring ratio to become 25:1, or 30:1, or 35:1, or..., with everyone still agreeing that there is a problem.

References

Australasian Philosophy Family Tree, http://consc.net/tree.html.

Barnes, Jonathan, 1990, "Review of Rist 1989", *Notes and Queries* 37:318–319.

Curtis, Bruce, and Steve Matthewman, 2005, "The Managed University: the PBRF, its impacts and staff attitudes", *New Zealand Journal of Employment Relations* 30(2), 1–18.

Dodds, Susan, and Eliza Goddard, 2013, "Not just a pipeline problem: Improving women's participation in philosophy in Australia", this volume.

Haslanger, Sally, 2008, "Changing the Culture and Ideology of Philosophy: Not by Reason Alone", *Hypatia* 23(2), 210–223.

Malcolm, Wilf, and Nicholas Tarling, 2007, *Crisis of Identity? The Mission and Management of Universities in New Zealand*. Wellington, UK: Dunmore.

New Zealand Human Rights Commission, 2008, New Zealand Census of Women's Participation.

Rist, John. M, 1996, "On Taking Aristotle's Development Seriously", in *Aristotle's Philosophical Development: Problems and Prospects* (ed., William Wians). Boston: Rowman and Littlefield.

Valian, V. 1998, *Why so slow? The advancement of women.*Cambridge, MA: MIT Press.

7

Not Just a Pipeline Problem

IMPROVING WOMEN'S PARTICIPATION IN PHILOSOPHY IN AUSTRALIA

Susan Dodds and Eliza Goddard

Introduction

Why are there so few women philosophers employed in Australian universities? It was earlier assumed that the number of women studying philosophy and pursuing academic philosophy as a career was directly related to the number of women introduced to philosophy at university. From this it would follow that once government policy supporting mass education had reduced economic barriers to tertiary education, and the number of women arts undergraduates approximated the number of men, the imbalance in women's completion of philosophy doctorates and participation in the philosophy profession would be resolved. In this way, women's underrepresentation was assumed to be a "pipeline problem" that would be fixed once the number of women in the academic pipeline increased. This assumption about the nature of the problem has been widely challenged in feminist literature (Allen and Castleman 2001; Schiebinger 1999), but it remains the dominant model guiding institutional responses to the underrepresentation of women in the discipline. In this chapter, we argue that institutional responses must reflect growing evidence that the pipeline model misrepresents the nature of the problem.

In the first section of this chapter, we demonstrate that the pipeline model is an inappropriate characterisation of the problem of women's underrepresentation. We do this by using longitudinal data spanning a 40-year period, collected by the Australasian Association of Philosophy (AAP) and the Australian Commonwealth Department of Education, Employment and Workplace Relations (DEEWR). We show that, despite increases in the number of women students commencing first-year philosophy (so that they are now the majority of students studying undergraduate philosophy), fewer women than men choose to complete a major in philosophy, and women comprise about only a third of Ph.D. students. In addition, women make up only a quarter of full-time and fractional teaching and research positions in philosophy programs. As we reported in 2008 (Goddard 2008), this figure has been almost stagnant for a decade. The pipeline has not just been leaky, requiring fixes and patch-ups here and there: *The pipeline model itself is flawed* because it does not explain the persistence of women's under-participation.

We argue here that this model fails because it misrepresents the academic terrain as gender-neutral. As a result, recommendations adopted by the AAP (and similar bodies elsewhere)[1] concerning women in the philosophy profession have failed to address the reasons for women's lesser participation in philosophy, while at the same time they have obscured the problem of women's participation as one that requires action and led to complacency by many in the philosophical community. The Australian data provide substantial empirical support for the anecdotal assessment by Calhoun and Grant that the pipeline model is flawed (Calhoun 2009; Grant 2002). In the second section, we use material from Australian philosophers Moira Gatens and Genevieve Lloyd to support a shift to investigating the cultural and social factors that impact women's participation and, in turn, how the discipline is understood by those who practice it. Gatens and Lloyd each express their concerns about the "maleness" of philosophy in their contributions to the AAP debate, as well as in their work in feminist philosophy. We argue that attention to feminist theoretical work about women and philosophy may better identify the causes of women's low participation in the discipline. In particular, we wish to take up the question of the place of feminist philosophy in the discipline, in the way in which "philosophy" is understood and "philosophers" are represented, and in the effects of the marginalisation of feminist philosophical concerns in the teaching of philosophy on the participation of women in philosophy programs.

We extend this work and conclude our chapter in the third section, by exploring the potential for the AAP and the philosophical community to take action to effectively improve the participation of women in philosophy. The aim of the AAP is the promotion of the study of philosophy in Australasia and the exchange of ideas among philosophers in Australia, New Zealand, and Singapore. Its membership overwhelmingly comprises current or recently retired academic philosophers and current research higher-degree (M.A. and Ph.D.) candidates. This chapter takes the view that, given their membership base and independence from departmental interests, bodies like the AAP are

---

[1] Samantha Brennan (this volume) shows that in Canada also, there has been a failure of recommendations aimed at ensuring procedural fairness to bring about the desired level of change. However, rather than focusing on culture, as we do in this chapter, Brennan focuses on responding to the harms caused. Although we don't take the same approach as Brennan in our chapter, we acknowledge that Brennan's response might be part of the answer.

well placed to consider strategies and approaches to respond to the current imbalances in the number of women studying philosophy at higher levels, the appointment of women in positions in philosophy programs, and women's career advancement in university philosophy programs. However, they must do so on the basis of more complex models of the obstacles to women's participation than those suggested by the pipeline model.

Recognising that women are a minority in the philosophy profession, the AAP has had a 30-year history of reports on women in the philosophy profession. In Australia, as in Canada and New Zealand, the good intentions signalled by the 30 years of effort by the AAP have failed to change the situation of women as a minority. These include efforts to collect data on appointments and specific recommendations to the profession, philosophy departments, and academic appointment committees aimed at improving women's participation in Australasian philosophy. In the past, the AAP has tended to accept and act on only those recommendations from the reports that fit the pipeline model: monitoring and reporting on appointments and the distribution of men and women in departments. It looks as if those to whom the recommendations are addressed have not been able to implement, accept, or even hear proposals that are based on anything other than the pipeline model. In light of the failure of pipeline models and the apparent invisibility of alternatives, we believe that it is important (if repetitive) to revisit what the alternatives are and why the pipeline model must be discarded.

1. The Failure of the Pipeline Model to Theorise Gender Equity in Australian Philosophy

The pipeline model for improving women's participation in higher education and employment has been prevalent in analyses by researchers and recommendations of policymakers in the Australian higher education sector (Allen and Castleman 2001). The model deploys the imagery of a 'training pipeline' running from entrance to university education through advanced training to the hiring of qualified university professionals. It proposes a simple causal mechanism for increased participation in the sector—increase the numbers of the target group coming into the pipeline and, over time, there will be growth in the relative participation of the target group. In the case of university education, the pipeline model hypothesises that as women attain mass education, the numbers of men and women with a university education and in academic positions will equalise. Yet this has not happened. For more than a decade, women have made up the majority of undergraduates in philosophy in Australia, but they continue to comprise the minority of Ph.D. candidates and those employed as academics.

Allen and Castleman argue that the pipeline metaphor for thinking about women's participation in universities has been the most broadly adopted by researchers and academics in analyses of the higher education sector, informed by the belief that "women's position in higher education is slowly but steadily improving in response to their increased educational achievement, unproblematic change and the decline of gender discrimination in hiring, promotion and tenure" (2001, 152). They identify a number of forms of the pipeline argument in higher education,[2] but all presuppose that an open intake into the pipeline will itself produce gender equality in due time, once the equitable intake works its way through the pipe. Pipeline arguments posit a steady underlying trend toward gender balance and rest on the notion that there is an unavoidable lag between policy change (removing discriminatory access to the pipeline) and organisational change. All that is required to address the gender imbalance is patience. Allen and Castleman challenge the assumptions of the pipeline arguments and contend that despite "years of substantial change and expansion in higher education and a significant labour force turnover, women still constituted the minority" (2001, 153).

The Australian experience in philosophy reinforces this conclusion. The empirical evidence from reports submitted to the AAP (MacColl, Tapper, Lloyd, and Roxon 1982; Tapper and Thompson 1990; Goddard 2008) shows that the significant growth in the proportion of women studying philosophy at undergraduate level in Australasia is not reflected in the much more modest growth in the proportion of women with Ph.D.s or employed as philosophers. These empirical data support, in the Australian context, the anecdotal speculation that feminists in New Zealand (Grant 2002) and the U.S. (Calhoun 2009) have drawn on to argue for a different approach to addressing women's underrepresentation among philosophy majors, Ph.D. students, and academic members of the profession at all levels.[3] Even though the numbers coming in have increased, and women have for the past decade been overrepresented in the undergraduate philosophy classroom, they are not coming out at the end of the

---

[2] Allen and Castleman distinguish models that rely on a job pipeline aimed at increasing the number of women with jobs—prevalent in the 1980s, and on a qualification pipeline that assumes that improving the number of women with higher qualifications will lead to both more women in jobs and improved promotion rates—more prevalent in the 1990s and 2000s (2001).

[3] The most recent report to the AAP on this topic, which uses data from the (Australian) Commonwealth Department of Education, Employment and Workplace Relations (DEEWR), shows that while women make up more than half of all undergraduate philosophy students, they constitute (on average) just over 40 percent of students who complete a major in philosophy and, by research doctorate level, they comprise just over a third of the student population (Goddard 2008 Report C, 6–8). Analysis of enrolment data in philosophy units at bachelor level by number of units, year level, and gender shows that as the level of study increases, from one to four or more years, and the number of units or subjects increases, from one to three or more, the proportion of female enrolment decreases markedly (Goddard 2008, Report C, 12). This trend is not new; it was recognised even in the early 1980s: "The pattern of *at least* equal female enrolment in First Year is often reversed in Second Year, and invariably reversed by Third Year" (MacColl, Tapper et al. 1982, 2). Cf. figure 5, 'Seeing the Trends in the Data', this volume.

Ph.D. in equal numbers, nor are they securing employment as philosophers at levels that reflect their undergraduate participation.[4]

In 2006, women were appointed to continuing (tenurable) teaching and research positions in roughly the same proportion (25–30 percent) as they applied for them (Goddard 2008, Report B, 4). The good news from this is that women do not appear to be disadvantaged in appointment into the profession once they obtain the qualifications needed to compete for positions.[5] If most continuing appointments are obtained within ten years of the successful applicant commencing philosophy study, the equalisation of the number of men and women in undergraduate philosophy should be reflected in the current appointment rates. Yet while about five times the number of women were employed in teaching and research positions in philosophy programs in Australian universities in 2006 (33.8 full-time equivalent positions) than were employed in the mid-1970s (seven positions), the rate at which women hold continuing teaching and research positions in philosophy has leveled out at just under a quarter of the overall positions for nearly a decade (Goddard 2008, Report A, 7).[6] Worryingly, it has also been argued that recent gains in women's participation at higher academic levels can be better explained by more general demographic trends in Australian universities than by the effect of a pipeline (Hugo 2005). The proportional growth in the number of women employed in the philosophy profession and the increasing proportion of women in higher level appointment are largely explained by the retirement in the late 1990s of philosophers (mostly men) who were appointed in the "boom" years of mass education in Australia in the 1980s, and not by substantial growth in the number of women being appointed or promoted.[7]

---

[4] The proportion of women who pursue honours in philosophy (the normal route into postgraduate research candidature) drops sharply relative to women's representation in undergraduate philosophy overall, and this drop has persisted for more than three decades (Goddard 2008).

[5] However, only 13 continuing teaching and research positions were filled in Australia in 2005–6, so it would be imprudent to place great weight on these numbers.

[6] Cf. figure 1, 'Seeing the Trends in the Data', this volume. The AAP report (Goddard 2008) uses data collected from heads of philosophy programs in Australia. While there are some differences, a similar pattern of female participation in the profession is evident in other Anglophone countries—USA, UK, NZ, and Canada. Christina Bellon reports that recent statistical assessments for the United States put the number of women who have jobs as philosophers in the range of 20–23 percent of professional, academically employed philosophers. Bellon notes that "this number has been fairly static. Hovering around 21 percent over the past several years" (Bellon 2009, 1). An appendix at the end of this volume contains some figures on Australia, as well as New Zealand. Although the New Zealand data are incomplete, they suggest similar proportions to Australia of women in philosophy positions.

[7] Between 1996 and 2006, the total number of philosophers in continuing positions fell by more than 60, and the number of women at level C or above dropped by 2.5 full-time equivalent positions (Goddard 2008, Report A, 9). In the most recent years, 2008 and 2009, the number of women in full-time and fractional full-time teaching and research positions has increased proportionally to men; yet the female full-time equivalent participation rate remains nearly the same as in the years prior.

Not only has the number of women entering the philosophical profession plateaued at a much lower proportion than the now majority entering as under-graduates, but they are also not progressing up the academic hierarchy from associate lecturer to professor in proportion to their entry into lower level posi-tions. Despite concerted efforts by universities and philosophy departments to increase women's participation at senior academic levels, women's participation in academic employment at senior levels in philosophy do not even come close to meeting the Australian Vice-Chancellor's Committee targets for women's partici-pation at higher levels, that is, for women to hold 25 percent of level E (professor) positions and 35 percent of level D (associate professor) positions by 2010, and continue to lag behind other disciplines. Women comprised 16 percent of level E (professor) and 24 percent of level D (associate professor) positions in Australian universities in 2005, but only 6 percent and 12 percent of philosophers at levels E and D respectively in 2006 (AVCC 2006). Therefore, any improvement to wom-en's participation in the philosophy profession will require more active strategies.[8]

We have shown that the assumption that the underrepresentation of women in philosophy is the result of a pipeline effect is not borne out by the Australian data. As such, it appears that the pipeline model is conceptually flawed and lacks resources for theorising gender equity. In our view, this is because it falsely assumes that educational and academic environments do not reflect gendered institutional and social structures. The model assumes that the pipeline is neutral, or that flow through the pipeline is unconstrained, in the face of substantial literature to dem-onstrate the gender structure of work and organizations, including universities (Chilly Climate Collective 1995). It fails "to acknowledge the complexities of male advantage, gender power and the gendered nature of organizational dynamics and the implications of organizational change…" (Allen and Castleman 2001, 156). This echoes a point made by Londa Schiebinger in her analysis of the gender imbalance in science: "The pipeline model, built on the liberal assumption that women (and minorities) should assimilate to the current practices in science, does not provide insight into how the structure of institutions or the current practices of science need to change before women can comfortably join the ranks of sci-entists" (1999, 64). Schiebinger argues that in order to address the deeper forms of discrimination that affect women in science, one needs to look at how gender ideologies inform and shape the cultures of science.[9] The pipeline model, further,

---

[8] There is also little evidence that the pipeline model can be applied to higher education more generally, even though other disciplines have more favourable gender ratios than philosophy. Allen and Castleman review data from DEETYA (the precursor to DEEWR) for evidence of a higher education pipeline. Using data from the 1980s and 1990s, they find no evidence of pat-terns that would be expected if the pipeline had started to work. Despite the introduction of affirmative action legislation in the 1980s, women are still underrepresented in the academy and concentrated in lower level, as well as less secure, positions. They conclude that gender inequali-ties continue to be reproduced in Australian universities.

[9] For further discussion of women's participation in science, see Hanson et al. 1996 and Berryman 1983.

oversimplifies organizational change. Allen and Castleman write: "[I]t ignores systemic and structural discrimination....[It is] an inadequate model of social change, one that is explicitly mechanical and neutral rather than political and contingent. The cause-and-effect nature of the pipeline...neglects the unequal and gendered effects of workplace practices..." (2001, 157).

The first of these criticisms attacks the assumption that what we understand by 'student', or 'employee', or 'academic' is gender-neutral. The pipeline model is used to support the proposition that women's continuing concentration in low-level and insecure employment is a legacy of the past, rather than the result of current practices. Allen and Castleman label this claim the 'pipeline fallacy'.[10] The second criticism is aimed at the idea that historical gender disadvantage can be effectively addressed passively, without conscious change to workplace practices to support gender equity. As such, the pipeline model may actually be counterproductive to the task of supporting women's participation.[11] The pipeline model works to encourage complacency and does not encourage a reflection on the gendered characteristics of the profession itself. Given these conceptual failings, the pipeline model should die a "well-deserved death" (Allen and Castleman 2001).

How, then, should we start to think about these problems outside the pipeline approach? In the following section, we look to other ways of thinking about the problem of women's underrepresentation in philosophy, focusing on reports submitted to the AAP, as well as the work of Moira Gatens and Genevieve Lloyd. These contain critical discussions of the representation of the discipline to itself and practitioners and the relationship between philosophy and feminism. From these discussions, in the final section, we frame a set of ways forward that the AAP (and bodies like it) might work from to improve the participation of women in the philosophy profession.

2. The Role and Potential of the AAP in the Shaping of the Philosophical Community and Philosophical Culture

In this section, we review the discursive arguments presented in the 30 years of AAP reports that urge action beyond monitoring of the philosophy pipeline. It is notable that a number of those who authored or contributed to the AAP

---

[10] They call this notion the pipeline fallacy because writers frequently use the metaphor of a pipeline to describe the (delayed) processes of social and organizational change (p. 151).

[11] This goes some way in explaining the longevity of the model—why it has been popular and why it has persisted despite a lack of evidence. Because the assumption of the pipeline model is that the numbers will change, given time, this leads to complacency about practical action by not only national bodies, but also among academics. If all we have to do is wait, then nothing needs to be done in the meantime. Moreover, this gives the impression that the underrepresentation of women in the profession is not a problem, or that while it is a problem, it will change with time.

reports in this area were Australian feminist philosophers whose philosophical writings articulated concern about the maleness of the culture of philosophy and the philosophy profession. We explore these works to consider the possibility for feminist philosophy to contribute directly to shifts in the culture of university philosophy programs and the academic community through a body like the AAP.

There were early indications contained in reports on the profession submitted to the AAP in 1982 and 1990[12] that the "problem" of women's participation in philosophy may be a problem with the discipline of philosophy and not simply a pipeline issue. Although each report included "pipeline" recommendations supporting collection and reporting of data on the number of positions advertised in philosophy and the proportion of those positions that were offered to women, these reports also sought to articulate the causes of women's low participation in terms of the "maleness" of Western philosophy. This includes the historical and cultural association of philosophy with knowledge, reason, and reasoning; and the association of rationality and reasoning with masculinity and virtue, to the exclusion of the feminine.

The 1982 report (MacColl, Tapper et al. 1982) followed a 1981 AAP Annual General Meeting resolution to create a committee to investigate "the special problems concerning women in the philosophy profession", at a time when there were 12 women holding philosophy positions in Australia (out of 155). Although that report found, as did all three reports, that "despite a significant increase in the number of female graduates who might be expected to enter the profession, there has been no significant improvement in the representation of women in tenured posts" (MacColl, Tapper, Lloyd, and Roxon 1982, 1), it also draws attention to the potential significance of the "maleness of philosophy" in explaining the lack of women graduates pursuing the profession. "Philosophical thought has been symbolically associated with maleness; and the very concept of *the feminine* has been in many ways structured by a succession of exclusions from the emerging forms of what was taken to constitute Reason" (MacColl, Tapper et al. 1982, 4–5).

It is no accident that this understanding informs the report, given the involvement of Genevieve Lloyd, author of the *Man of Reason* (1984), who was developing her argument concerning the dichotomous thought pervading Western philosophy at the time she was collaborating on this report. On her view, to the extent that the history of Western philosophical thought is permeated with

---

[12] A further committee was established to update the recommendations of the 1982 report and to revise them in light of the Australian Affirmative Action (EEO for Women) Act (1986) (MacColl and Russell 1991). The AAP reports were San MacColl, Marion Tapper, Genevieve Lloyd, and Barbara Roxon (1982), "To investigate the special problems concerning women in the philosophy profession"; Marion Tapper and Janna Thompson (1990), "Employment of Women 1983-9"; San MacColl and Denise Russell (1991) "To update the recommendations of the 1982 report 'concerning women in the philosophy profession'".

the characterisation of reason as a masculine trait, and to the extent that the study of philosophy is understood to be centred on the activity of reasoning, it is not surprising that those engaged in studying and teaching philosophy come to value the exercise of reason as the highest human virtue, while being blind to gendered exclusions inextricably bound to their understanding of philosophy. The authors of the 1982 report recognise the difficulty of challenging this conception of philosophy and its associations with maleness, but argue that some changes can be made to reduce the more overt gender biases in philosophy departments. The report notes that whilst

> [t]he long-lasting effects of these past alignments between philosophical thought and maleness cannot be removed by any act of the will or [AAP] council resolution…these historical associations are overlaid with a range of rather more specific and more readily changeable gender-related traits and preoccupations. (MacColl, Tapper et al. 1982, 5)

These specific areas include challenging the style of philosophical debate and the impact of that style of debate on women students; questioning the ways in which gender is mapped onto core and periphery subjects in philosophy; and sexism and sexual harassment. As a "first step", the report's authors recommend that it would be helpful if their male colleagues could be self-reflective and "realise that the image of the philosopher which they bring to seminar discussions and teaching situations, as well as to appointments and promotions committees, is by no means as gender-neutral as they think" (MacColl, Tapper et al. 1982, 6). Lloyd herself later stated, "As women begin to develop a presence in Philosophy, it is only to be expected that the maleness of Philosophy's past, and with it the maleness of the ideals of Reason, should begin to come into focus" (Lloyd 1984, 108).

At the same time, the report articulates the concern that developing subjects in the philosophy of feminism could raise new tensions, including that women's philosophy could become marginalised. One submission to the 1982 report, stated,

> The very existence of such courses…can give students the impression that women's involvement in philosophy proceeds in separation from the mainstream; and the fact that this mainstream is frequently left untouched, in style and content, by feminist consciousness means that the end-result is a containment of the impact of feminism on the activities of a department. (MacColl, Tapper et al 1982, 13)

Feminist philosophy challenges dominant assumptions of philosophy and as such can raise antagonism by established philosophers toward those (mostly women) who engage in this area of philosophy. These tensions frequently spill out of the common room and into the classroom, with throwaway comments about the value of feminist thought or feminist philosophers. While many feminist philosophers may intend to change the assumptions and approach of mainstream philosophy, their efforts are often unwelcome, and those students who may have found that feminist concerns resonate with their experience do not find a way of re-imagining their relationship with philosophy. Instead, they may gain a new vocabulary and conceptual framework through which to understand their marginalisation and isolation, but on this very basis, choose to move out of the discipline.

So, while the 1982 AAP report was, indeed, explicitly concerned with progress and blockages in the philosophy pipeline, the report's analysis of these problems suggests a more cultural source of the failures of the pipeline. It identifies the self-understanding of the discipline itself as a possible cause for women's underrepresentation in it, and recognises the difficulty of successfully challenging that understanding. The report identifies four related puzzles concerning women's participation in philosophy that need to be better understood: the career impediments facing women who complete Ph.D.s in philosophy and who do not find jobs in philosophy departments at universities; the problems of overt and less obvious sexism in the teaching of philosophy and in the day to day organizational culture of philosophy departments; the "maleness" of philosophy arising from the overlapping associations of reason with masculinity and of philosophy with rational thought; and the marginalisation of feminism within philosophy. The AAP response to the report, however, by adopting recommendations concerning the monitoring of appointments and reporting on new appointments by gender to the AAP (MacCall, Tapper et al. 1982, 17), focused on the pipeline, not the cultural factors shaping women's engagement with philosophy.

Not surprisingly, given the failures of the pipeline model to address women's under-participation, the problem did not go away, and a few years later another committee was formed to address similar concerns. In 1989, at the Women in Philosophy Annual General Meeting, a follow-up to the 1982 report was commissioned, authored by Marion Tapper and Janna Thompson and presented to the AAP Annual General Meeting in 1990 (Tapper and Thompson 1990). The 1990 report notes an increase in the number and proportion of women filling jobs since the 1982 report (20 women out of 166.5 philosophy positions), yet it sounds a note of caution concerning any optimism here, given the low numbers of women going on into the profession from postgraduate study, despite large numbers of women undergraduates (Tapper and Thompson 1990, 3). The committee recommended that more information should be sought concerning women postgraduates—their aspirations and problems in pursuing a career in the profession, and also that attention should be paid to the special problems facing unemployed and casually employed women philosophers and women philosophers who work as academics outside philosophy departments (1990, 6).

As in the 1982 report, the 1990 Thompson and Tapper report also addresses cultural aspects of the discipline of philosophy in order to understand and help to explain the apparent failure of the philosophy pipeline. The very last page of the report notes the "alienating environment" women face in philosophy departments and the importance of AAP support for conferences for women in philosophy in mitigating these conditions. A separate issue that Tapper and Thompson raise in their report is that the increase in the number of women employed in philosophy departments may only be in limited areas, most specifically in feminist philosophy (ethics and political philosophy are also mentioned), and that these areas may ghettoise women's involvement in the profession. They note "[T]he fear is that departments which hire women to teach feminism may believe that no further women are necessary" (Thompson and Tapper 1990, 4).

A strand of thought influencing this report can be found in Moira Gatens's *Feminism and Philosophy* (1991). Her concerns may give reason to be sceptical that women's inclusion in the profession as *feminist* philosophers reflects an acceptance of women as genuine philosophers. Gatens's writings help to show that the cultural factors shaping women's feelings of alienation or exclusion from participation in philosophy as students or academics may be doubled— inextricably bound up with the "maleness" of philosophy that Lloyd's work identifies (on the one hand) and the marginalisation of women's philosophy when it is explicitly feminist (on the other).

In writing on the apparent tension between philosophy and feminism, Gatens draws attention to the ways in which developing and being able to recognise a "philosophical style" is part of the philosophical education, and that this education involves both learning the indicators of philosophical legitimacy and honing one's skills as identifying and excluding (de-legitimating) non-philosophical arguments and appeals. These indicators, she argues are shaped by a dominant understanding of the normative (and philosophical) values of rationality and objectivity and the indicators of clarity, logical order, and argument:

> Philosophy aims at the universal, the abstract, stressing rationality, the creation of a clear mind, whereby the universal may be apprehended. It is not concerned with the particular, with the contingent. Personal opinion is to be overcome or to be transformed, if possible into public and authorised knowledge. (Gatens 1986, 22–23)

Gatens draws out this point to show that what is accepted as "legitimate" philosophy stands in tension with feminist research, given the *political* aims of explicitly feminist work and the challenges to previously accepted distinctions between what is "private", "subjective", or "personal" and what is "public", "objective", or "political" in feminist theory. She argues that recognition of these tensions can lead to productive development of both feminism and philosophy, and that this development recognises that "philosophy is not neutral in character, that the problem of the relationship between women and philosophy, of how women's subjectivity is put into philosophical discourse, is not merely a problem of content" (Gatens 1986, 24).

Gatens's account of the ways in which the philosophy student is trained to recognise the universal, abstract, and rational as the proper concerns of philosophy may illuminate women's sense of alienation from philosophy, and especially the sense of alienation and discouragement of women who are motivated by feminist concerns to challenge the assumed neutrality and objectivity of masculine perspectives. Students struggle to come to terms with the abstract, conceptual nature of philosophy and very often find that their attempts to draw on their own experience and emotional responses to do so are discredited as personal, experiential, emotive, and contingent ("mere" psychology, faith, or sociology). Such students may lose confidence in their own abilities to reason about what is philosophical and may find it more difficult to challenge philosophical claims to universality when these are in tension with their own experience and understanding. Although philosophy may be challenging, it may also be alienating or seem irrelevant to students whose motivations for study and critical inquiry arise from practical worldly problems and questions.

Gatens's point concerns the marginalisation of feminist theory *as* philosophy. She builds on Lloyd's account of the maleness of the archetypal concepts of Western philosophy. Together, the insights provided by Lloyd and Gatens add conceptual weight to the concerns of the 1982 and 1990 AAP reports on women in philosophy that call upon Australian philosophers, philosophy departments, and the AAP itself to consciously reflect on the ways in which Australian philosophy has constructed itself and its articulation of the Australian philosophical style. Dominant themes in Australian philosophy during the 1980s and 1990s amplified some of the most abstract and universal aspects of late 20th-century Anglo-American philosophy, with an emphasis on theories of mind, cognition, language, and ethics that abstract from any social or firsthand personal experience. To the extent that the past 20 years have seen change in what is understood as philosophical style, it has been to reassess the adequacy of these abstracted approaches, influenced to some degree by feminist work in ethics, moral psychology, and epistemology, as well as by work from psychology and cognitive science. It is possible that this "softening" of some aspects of the philosophical style has reduced the alienation of some women students; however, it is still the case that to a large degree feminist philosophy is presented in the philosophy curriculum as marginal to the proper business of philosophy.

Although the AAP reports of 1982 and 1990 drew on this rich work by feminist thinkers, the AAP did not act on any of the associated recommendations. It is time to ask "Why not?" and to reflect on the barriers to cultural change and how these can be overcome. The cultural critique of philosophy contained within earlier reports and the feminist theory informing it provide clues to alternative approaches for understanding women's underrepresentation in philosophy; we believe these could be taken up by philosophy departments and the AAP. Recognition of the cultural practices of academic philosophy may help explain the tenacity of the gender disparities in Australian philosophy departments. We focus on four of these cultural factors here.

First, there are the ways in which specific philosophy departments welcome and foster women as students or colleagues. While it is unlikely that the level of overt sexism reported in the 1982 AAP report occurs in most Australian philosophy programs, it is evident that unconscious gender stereotyping occurs (Grant 2002); in other words, whether the climate can be "chilly" for women students because of overt or unconscious gender stereotyping ("the image of the philosopher they bring into the seminar room"), sexism, or uses of examples that exclude women (see Chilly Climate Collective 1995).

Second, there is the way in which philosophy is taught, the methods of philosophical training, as Gatens's account articulates it, and the way in which one comes to recognise and adopt the philosophical style (1986). This addresses how philosophy students become habituated as philosophers, trained to legitimate modes of argument and perspectives that reflect the historical association of philosophy with abstract reasoning and the philosopher with the masculine traits of rationality, objectivity, and abstraction.

Third, there is the issue of the effects of the marginalisation of feminist philosophy within philosophy departments, as well as on students' educational and career choices. The marginalisation of feminist philosophy impacts (i) the careers of those women who teach in this area (whose philosophical work that is not specifically feminist may also be overlooked); (ii) the academic and career choices of students who are influenced by their perception of the value and worth of the men and women academics they encounter and the subject matter they study; and (iii) the capacity for feminist challenges to be heard by philosophers *as* philosophy and for these challenges to inform developments in philosophical argument or practice.

Fourth, operating both within and outside academic philosophy is the less tangible cultural influence of the broader social and historical context, the Enlightenment tradition, within which Western philosophy arose (and which philosophy actively contributed to) and the range of dichotomies unconsciously and uncritically sustained within philosophical writing and academic practice. These shape what Valian (1998) refers to as "gender schemas"—a set of unarticulated inter-subjective and cultural hypotheses about sex differences that shape our expectations and evaluations of men and women, and their work and professional performance. We come to absorb these unconscious associations between gender and cultural practices in negotiating the structures and relations of the world around us. We shape and are shaped by our interactions; literary, artistic, and policy manifestations; and social norms concerning both gender and philosophy; they are neither wholly consciously chosen nor completely unconscious. Indeed, they are most evident when our attention is drawn to the clash between our understanding of ourselves and these cultural expectations.

Of the four sets of cultural factors shaping philosophy, gender schemas are the least likely to be significantly shifted through conscious action by individual philosophers, philosophy departments, or the AAP. The issue of what can be done about them is, however, addressed elsewhere in this volume (see Saul; Brennan). In the final section of this chapter, we suggest some avenues for further research that could be supported by organizations like the AAP as concrete steps to address the underlying sources of women's continued underrepresentation.

3. Conclusion: The Role of the AAP in Improving the Culture of Philosophy in Australia

Because the pipeline model is flawed, simply waiting for women to flow through the undergraduate/postgraduate and employment pipeline will not significantly redress the imbalance between men's and women's participation in academic philosophy. We have shown that in addition to the calls in the AAP reports for monitoring the number of women progressing through the philosophy pipeline, there has also been a consistent concern about the philosophical culture and style that alienates many women students, discourages their progress, and marginalises feminist philosophy (which explicitly acknowledges the gendered assumptions of mainstream philosophy). For the past 30 years, these calls for cultural change have apparently fallen on deaf ears. Given that most Australian philosophy programs have fewer than ten full-time equivalent members,[13] it is rare for an Australian philosophy program to have three or more women in continuing positions. It would be unreasonable and unfair to expect those women to take on the bulk of the work of challenging the dominant philosophical culture. It is also unlikely that the experience of staff and students in small philosophy programs can be generalised locally. We argue here that the AAP has a particular role to play in supporting moves to improve the philosophical culture in each university in order to achieve its mission of promoting the study of philosophy and fostering the exchange of ideas among philosophers in Australasia. One advantage of placing the challenge of improving the culture of philosophy in the scope of the AAP is that it can allow for a more generalised understanding of the issues and depersonalise them, which may assist those who wish to contribute

---

[13] Six out of 21 (29 percent) philosophy programs surveyed for the ALTC Forward Thinking Report stated that they had ten or more FTE staff in 2007; four out of 18 reported three or more FTE women academics; these were disproportionately at level A (associate lecturer) and B (lecturer); Goddard 2010, staff report, 5 and 9.

to the critique to speak up (when doing so in a small program would threaten collegiality) and may assist those who are unconscious of their own behaviour to be prepared to reflect on the ways in which their assumed philosophical style affects their students.[14]

The suggestions here are simply first steps to foster improved knowledge of the issues and to support critical reflection on philosophical pedagogy. We believe that in taking these steps, individual philosophy departments and philosophers as teachers, collectively, may start to shift the proportions of women who continue in philosophical study beyond their undergraduate years and into academic employment.

HOW DOES IT LOOK TO THE STUDENTS?—TALKING TO THEM

The Tapper and Thompson AAP report (1990) recommended conducting research to find out about postgraduate students' experience and concerns. A survey of all philosophy postgraduates was conducted by Linda Burns and Nick Agar and reported to the AAP in 1991. It identified factors that echo the anecdotal concerns expressed in the 1982 and 1990 reports and recommended follow-up studies (to our knowledge, these have not been undertaken) (Burns and Agar 1991). Similarly, in the *Improving the Participation of Women in the Philosophy Profession* Report, we made a recommendation for further research involving a qualitative study of 60–80 men and women in honours and Ph.D. programs to ascertain the reasons shaping students' decisions to continue or not continue with philosophy (Goddard 2008, Executive Summary, 14–15). Surely, one source of information about how undergraduate students (both men and women) experience the philosophy classroom, philosophy departments, and philosophers is to engage in well-designed qualitative research involving undergraduates honours and postgraduate students, to analyse what they have to say about what philosophy is, who is a philosopher, how philosophy is done, and what makes for good philosophy. Gender schemas are not fixed entities; they change and develop over time in relation to the cultures in which they develop, so it cannot be assumed that undergraduate students today experience the philosophy classroom, philosophy, and philosophers in the same way that a similar cohort would have 30 years ago. Finding out what students think, especially just before the crucial "cliff" points when women students opt out of philosophy (after doing one or two units, but before completing the major or starting honours), is likely to provide important clues to why women are more likely than men to stop studying philosophy.

To do this properly, the AAP would need to invest some of its accumulated funds in the skills of social science researchers (we should be aware of our

---

[14] See also Haslanger (2008) for further comments on the need for cultural change in philosophy.

own disciplinary limitations and biases when it comes to conducting empirical research). Given the recent Universities Australia research on women in research (Bell and Bentley 2005) and continuing research on the bachelor of arts through ALTC (Gannaway and Trent 2008), it is now possible to develop studies that can effectively compare the experience of philosophy students with those in related disciplines. In the past, the AAP has been reluctant to commit substantial resources outside the discipline, but it is likely that as there is increasing pressure on Australasian philosophy programs to maintain core philosophy load, the AAP will recognise that by supporting able women students to participate fully in the discipline, it will promote the study of philosophy in Australasia, given the dramatic demographic changes that will affect the academic workforce and the student body over the next 10 to 20 years (Hugo 2005).

AAP CONFERENCE STREAM ON PHILOSOPHICAL PEDAGOGY

In the past, the AAP has tended to focus its conferences on "doing" excellent philosophy and engaging in philosophical debate. There has been little attention to philosophical pedagogy as a disciplinary concern, despite the active involvement of a number of philosophy academics in developing innovative curricula (and obtaining national awards for their contributions to learning and teaching through the Australian Learning and Teaching Council [ALTC], now Office of Learning and Teaching [OLT]). When there has been attention to teaching, it has tended to be allied with interest in the Philosophy in Schools program and the idea of harnessing pre-tertiary students' passion for ideas before they get to university. With the growing attention given to quality of teaching at university level, it may be timely for the AAP to support critical reflection on how to teach philosophy well; one step would be to encourage discussion and debate about the philosophical works that are used in undergraduate teaching; a second is to encourage reflection on *how* to introduce concepts in a manner that makes the issues real to students and overcomes some of the alienating characteristics of philosophy. There is room for not only sharing of successful teaching strategies, but also for conducting careful research into philosophical teaching methods (compare Beebee; Hutchison, this volume).

INTRODUCING MORE WOMEN'S WORKS IN THE CURRICULUM

Few of the AAP reports have attended to the content of the curriculum, beyond acknowledging that the contemporary philosophy curriculum may be alienating to women. One way of challenging the gender schemas that juxtapose our sense of who can be a philosopher with what it means to be a woman is to bring the works of more women into the reading lists of all philosophy subjects. Women have written important articles and books relating to all areas of philosophy. Many of the so-called masculine topics in philosophy (e.g., epistemology, philosophy of mind, and philosophy of language) can be addressed very well by a lecturer who consciously decides to predominantly select relevant works by women—they do not need to make a fuss about it; they just need to remember to spell out authors' first names and use the correct gender pronoun in referring to the relevant author. A collaboration between the AAP and Macquarie University is collecting works by women philosophers for this purpose, and the references are available online.[15] Pursuing this approach can reduce the risk that women philosophers (as students or academics) will be ghettoised in feminist philosophy or other areas thought to be more appealing to women (supposedly "soft" areas including ethics, applied ethics, continental philosophy, and political philosophy). Indeed, by consciously drawing on more works by women, the contestability of the division of "hard" and "soft" areas of philosophy can be seen more readily and explored. The aim of this approach is to challenge two latent ideas that foster these oppositional schemas: that women are not able to write serious philosophy and that serious philosophy addresses material that is inherently masculine.

MAKING PHILOSOPHY LESS ABSTRACT AND ALIEN

Similarly, previous reports have noted the ways in which the teaching of philosophy may create a "chilly" climate for women students, but they have not considered possible steps to redress this effect. Universities have increased their attention to academic pedagogy—often requiring new academics to take courses in how to teach better. This creates an opportunity for critical reflection on how philosophy is taught to make it more inclusive. For example, we might consider adapting the approaches to inclusiveness in the classroom that were originally intended to assist in bridging the differences between domestic (Australian) and international students to address the differences between women and men as philosophy students. These may include using less abstract examples; using names in examples rather than abstract letters ("Sonia believes that it is Tuesday", rather than "X believes that p"); and using a wider array of examples that reflect ordinary life. It is worth critically assessing whether the stock examples of philosophy genuinely aid contemporary students. Are the conceptual issues associated with understanding personal identity really best captured by examples involving standard-bearers in battle or Martian teletransportation? Philosophical examples have often been invented on the assumption that new students have had a relatively rigorous and "old-school" secondary education, an assumption that

---

[15] See http://women.aap.org.au/WomensWorks, accessed 3/4/2012.

clearly disadvantages or alienates many students in the current era of mass education. Good lecturers and tutors know that they need to translate (repeatedly if necessary) non-English terms (π, "*Londres est joli*", *akrasia*) and to explain which aspects of the example are relevant ("Hesperus is phosphorus"), and so on. Philosophy departments are more likely to retain students (both men and women) if they take the time consciously to consider the gaps between their own experience and prior education and that of their students when framing lectures and tutorial discussions. It is very likely that better attention to *how* philosophy is taught will have additional benefits; not only will women be less likely to feel alienated, students from a range of backgrounds are more likely to comprehend what is going on in the classroom and to be intrigued by philosophical thinking (compare Mackenzie and Townley, this volume).

TACKLING ASSUMPTIONS ABOUT THE RELEVANCE OF PHILOSOPHY

The title of Barbara Grant's paper "I thought philosophy was a girl thing" raises a question about the perception of philosophy as a discipline of study and as a qualification for future employment. Students frequently face incredulous comments regarding the value of studying arts degrees generally and philosophy more specifically. Australia's tendency to view education primarily in terms of its utility in securing employment (or supporting growth in the economy) makes the philosophy student ripe for ridicule. These comments point to a lack of understanding about what the study of philosophy entails and the types of skills students of the discipline typically attain. It also indicates an assumption that the discipline is irrelevant, a kind of intellectual needlework for "idle" ladies, as suggested by the title of Grant's paper. Providing well-targeted and attractive information and testimonials to students and employers that demonstrate learning outcomes and future employment possibilities would go some way to alleviating these issues. In the professional report *Forward Thinking—Learning and Teaching Philosophy in Australian Universities*, submitted to the ALTC, we noted that there is evidence that graduates with philosophical skills are in greater demand by employers, both in Australia and overseas (Goddard, Significance of the Discipline, 6–7, 2010, 7). We did not argue that the study of philosophy should be advocated simply as a means of attaining "generic skills" applicable to a number of professions. Rather, our report argued that the substantive study of philosophy, although valuable in itself, demonstrates the importance of being able to deploy a range of intellectual attributes to difficult, enduring, complex, and conceptual issues, and that through addressing substantive conceptual issues, philosophy hones these skills. What was of interest to us in the ALTC report was that a wide array of employers has come to value and employ students of philosophy because they wish to draw on that intellectual training. Further, the AAP could support research that explores in which areas philosophy students undertake employment, why employers seek out philosophy graduates (if they do), and which abilities philosophy students typically attain that are valued by employers (Goddard et al. 2010, 25).

CONCLUSION

At present, the AAP conducts an annual census of the number of women studying philosophy and those employed in philosophy at each level; this allows us to monitor women's participation in philosophy. Monitoring progress at this level remains important to see the effects of changes in practices and culture. Counting is passive, however, and does little to bring about change that can be measured. On the other hand, change is disruptive and likely to create some resistance. In the future, strategies for improving women's participation in philosophy should be directed toward understanding and challenging the cultural factors leading to the loss of women students at undergraduate and postgraduate levels. We need to look beyond the numbers and look to the culture and practices of philosophy for ways of explaining and rectifying women's participation in philosophy. The practical steps suggested above are first steps to redress the chilly climate of philosophy departments and the philosophy curriculum. We acknowledge that some philosophers will be more and others less enthusiastic about taking these steps, as they require reconsideration and review of familiar practices and philosophical "moves". Those philosophers who assume philosophy to be gender-neutral and to view their own pedagogic practices as non-discriminatory are likely to point to the large numbers of women at undergraduate level and the shining examples of women who excel at advanced and postgraduate level to demonstrate that all is well with the state of philosophy as they practice it. The fact that that argument has been trotted out for three decades gives it no purchase in the face of the persistent evidence that there is a real problem in philosophy and how it is taught. We view our suggested recommendations as ways to normalise the presence of women in philosophy—as philosophers, within the advanced student and academic body, and in the syllabus—as well as ways to challenge the narrowness of what is understood as "philosophy", how good philosophy is evaluated, and who can be a good philosopher, in order to enrich the discipline of philosophy and ensure that it does not lose good philosophy students.

References

Allen, Margaret, and Castleman, Tanya (2001) "Fighting the Pipeline Fallacy", in Alison McKinnon and Ann Brooks (eds.) *Gender and the restructured University: changing management and culture in higher education*, Buckingham, UK: Society for Research into Higher Education and Open University Press, 151–165.

AVCC (Australian Vice Chancellors' Committee). (2006) "Second AVCC Action Plan for Women Employed in Australian Universities 2006–2010", available at http://www.universitiesaustralia.edu.au/resources/427/407.

Bell, Sharon, and Bentley, Ronda (2005) "Women in Research", discussion paper prepared for the AVCC National Colloquium of Senior Women Executives, November.

Bellon, Christina, ed. (2009) *APA Newsletter on Feminism and Philosophy*, Vol. 8, No. 2, 1–26.

Berryman, Sue E. (1983) "Who Will Do Science? Trends, and Their Causes in Minority and Female Representation among Holders of Advanced Degrees in Science and Mathematics, A Special Report". New York: Rockefeller Foundation.

Burns, Linda, and Agar, Nick (1991) "Survey of Australian Philosophy Postgraduates". Report to Australasian Association of Philosophy (AAP).

Calhoun, Cheshire (2009) "The Undergraduate Pipeline Problem", *Hypatia*, Vol. 24, No. 2, 216–223.

Chilly Climate Collective (eds.) (1995) *Breaking Anonymity: The Chilly Climate for Women Faculty.* Waterloo, Ontario, CA: Wilfred Laurier University Press.

Gannaway, Deanne, and Trent, Faith (2008) "Nature and roles of arts degrees in contemporary society: Project final report". Sydney, AU: Australian Learning and Teaching Council, available at www.dassh.edu.au/ba_scoping_project/project_resources.

Gatens, Moira (1986) "Feminism and Philosophy, Riddles without answers" in Carole Pateman and Elizabeth Gross (eds.) *Feminist Challenges, Social and Political Theory.* Sydney, AU: Allen & Unwin, 13–29.

———. (1991) *Feminism and Philosophy.* Cambridge, UK: Polity.

Goddard, Eliza (2008) "Improving the Participation of Women in the Philosophy Profession", on behalf of Dodds, Sue, Burns, Lynda, Colyvan, Mark, Jackson, Frank, Jones, Karen, and Mackenzie, Catriona. Report to Australasian Association of Philosophy (AAP), available at http://www.aap.org.au/Womeninphilosophy.

Goddard, Eliza (2010) "Forward Thinking: Learning and Teaching Philosophy in Australian Universities", with Ravenscroft, Ian (director), Dodds, Susan, Diprose, Ros, Duke-Yonge, Jennifer, Lumsden, Simon, Mackenzie, Catriona, Menzies, Peter, and Parsell, Mitch. Report submitted to the Australian Learning & Teaching Council (ALTC), available at www.aap.org.au/forwardthinking.

Goddard, Eliza, Dodds, Susan, and Ravenscroft, Ian (2010) "Forward Thinking: Learning and Teaching Philosophy in Australian Universities—Final Report", Strawberry Hills: NSW, Australian Learning & Teaching Council (ALTC), available at http://www.olt.gov.au/project-forward-thinking-teaching-flinders-2007.

Grant, Barbara (2002) "'I thought philosophy was a girl thing', The Curious Case of Women Students in a Department of Philosophy", *Teaching Philosophy*, Vol. 25, No. 3, 1–14.

Hanson, Sandra L., Schaub, Maryellen, and Barker, David P. (1996) "Gender Stratification in the Science Pipeline: A Comparative Analysis of Seven Countries", *Gender and Society*, Vol. 10, No. 3, 271–290.

Haslanger, Sally (2008) "Changing the Ideology and Culture of Philosophy, Not by Reason (Alone)", *Hypatia*, Vol. 23, No. 2, 210–223.

Hugo, Graham (2005) "Academia's Own Demographic Time-bomb, The Australian Universities", *Review*, Vol. 48, No. 1, 16–23, available at http://search.informit.com.au/documentSummary;dn=129573089342688;res=IELHSS.

Lloyd, Genevieve (1984) *The Man of Reason*. New York: Routledge.

MacColl, San, Tapper, Marion, Lloyd, Genevieve, and Roxon, Barbara (1982) "To investigate the special problems concerning women in the philosophy profession", Report to Australasian Association of Philosophy (AAP).

MacColl, San, and Russell, Denise (1991) "To update the recommendations of the 1982 report concerning women in the philosophy profession", Report to Australasian Association of Philosophy (AAP).

Schiebinger, Londa (1999) *Has Feminism Changed Science?* Cambridge, MA: Harvard University Press.

Tapper, Marion, and Thompson, Janna (1990) *Employment of Women 1983-9*, Report to Australasian Association of Philosophy (AAP).

Valian, Virginia (1998) *Why So Slow? The Advancement of Women*. Cambridge, MA: MIT Press.

8

Women In and Out of Philosophy
Catriona Mackenzie and Cynthia Townley

1. The Challenge of Diversification

In Australia and throughout the Anglophone world, there has been a resurgence of interest in the gender (im)balance within philosophy.[1] Recent work on women in philosophy has drawn attention to the continuing underrepresentation of women in Ph.D. programmes and in the profession, and the so-called undergraduate pipeline problem—the drop-off of female students between first year and the major and honours years. At the same time in Australia, a major government-commissioned review of higher education in 2009 highlighted the need to diversify higher education and recommended sector-wide incentives aimed at increasing diversity (Bradley et al. 2008; DEEWR 2009). These initiatives focus on increasing the participation in higher education of students from rural and remote areas, indigenous students, and students from underrepresented ethnic communities and less advantaged socioeconomic backgrounds. This social-inclusion agenda poses a challenge for disciplines that have markedly inequitable gender patterns, such as philosophy, to think seriously about how to ensure that women from diverse backgrounds do not face a "double exclusion" problem: on the grounds of social background and on the grounds of gender.

Our argument in this chapter is that in order to meet this challenge, we need to extend the debate about women's participation in philosophy beyond current concerns about gender representation within the profession. Our discussion is certainly not intended to undermine, bypass, or dismiss these concerns; we think that addressing them is critical for the future of the profession. But in doing so, we should take care that our focus is not overly inward-looking. Our concerns about the profession should certainly prompt us to look critically at it and the mechanisms by which it reproduces itself, many of which are exclusionary, not

---

[1] See, for example, Calhoun (2009); Goddard (2008); Haslanger (2008). See also the Women in Philosophy Taskforce on Facebook: http://feministphilosophers.wordpress.com

only of women but also of ethnic minorities and individuals who are not from the middle class. However, these concerns should also prompt us to look beyond the profession and engage in more broad-ranging reflection on the value of a philosophy education: for our students—and not just for those students who will major or pursue postgraduate studies in the discipline but for the much larger group of students we teach—and for the communities to which they belong. As we discuss later, we think that taking inclusion and diversity seriously in the classroom leads to a more pluralist conception of philosophical research, but our primary focus in this chapter is philosophical pedagogy.

If there are clear drop-off points in women's participation in philosophy—from first year to third year, from third year to honours, and from honours to postgraduate study—then we need to be able to explain why this is a problem, not just for the profession but for the students themselves. In other words, we need to be able to answer the following questions: Why does philosophy matter? Why is a philosophical education valuable? Why is it important for philosophy to be more inclusive, not just for the sake of students, but for the discipline and the profession?

If we can't answer these questions convincingly, this may indicate that there is a conflict between the interests of our profession in reproducing and maintaining itself, and the interests of our (potential and increasingly numerous, increasingly diverse) students. As professionals with a duty of care for our undergraduate and graduate students, we are obliged to confront this possibility because continuing education (an honours year or postgraduate study) carries opportunity costs. Even the best-off students (those with scholarships or research and teaching opportunities) are earning significantly less than many of their peers, and for those who complete a Ph.D., this low-income period frequently extends to insecure casual and/or contract employment for at least a year, and frequently longer post-Ph.D. Women typically have lower lifetime earning expectations than men, so these low-income years place them at a disproportionate disadvantage.

The challenge of diversification is hence to consider both what a diversified philosophy discipline can be like—that is, to think beyond replacing the familiar (white, male, and middle-class) faces with some currently less familiar ones (female, non-white, low socioeconomic status), which could be mere cosmetic change absent significant cultural change within the profession—and what the discipline of philosophy can offer to those who study it, to the communities from which they come, and to society more generally. In the following sections of the chapter, we argue that taking up this challenge requires a critical examination of the prevalent narrow criteria of success for philosophy programmes and an expansion of our conceptions of what a successful, rich, and flourishing philosophical culture might be like. In the next section, we critically appraise the dominant conception of successful outcomes for philosophy graduate students, and in particular the implicit messages we convey to students in our

Ph.D. programmes. In the third section, we suggest that addressing problems of underrepresentation in the discipline requires expanding our conception of the relevance and value of a philosophy education at the undergraduate level: to address the undergraduate pipeline problem, we need to think beyond the pipeline. Here we agree with Dodds and Goddard (this volume), but whereas they focus on the culture of philosophy as encountered by those within the discipline, we focus on the perceived relevance of the discipline to those outside of it. In the fourth section, we consider the implications and challenges of an expanded conception of success for the career mentoring of women and other underrepresented groups.

2. Expanding Conceptions of Success for Graduate Students

Saul (this volume) analyses in detail how implicit bias and stereotype threat are likely to be at work in women's career trajectories, and she makes some important cautionary remarks about strategies that are unlikely to succeed in remedying bias, as well as suggesting strategies that might work. One suggestion Saul makes toward the end of her essay, namely "Stop talking about who's smart", resonates with our concerns about the way that philosophers and philosophy departments measure the success of our students, particularly graduate students.

As Saul remarks, philosophers are very prone to making hasty judgments about who is smart and who is not, on the basis of very limited information and evidence. For reasons that Eric Schwitzgebel (2010) has highlighted, these judgments are likely to provoke stereotype threat in women and minority group members, and are likely to be based on implicit bias, given that those identified as "smart" are usually confident young white males who have gone to graduate school at a select group of elite universities. We think these judgments point to a wider problem within the discipline: that we operate with a very narrow and inward-looking conception of success. This narrow conception is evident in a range of troubling ways in which the discipline reproduces itself. Connected to the "who's smart" judgments is the phenomenon, more pronounced perhaps in the U.S. than in Australia, whereby certain recent graduates from Ph.D. programmes (again usually white males working in a narrow range of philosophical fields) are identified as "stars", with fierce competition among elite universities to offer them jobs. Then there is the phenomenon of the U.S.-based Leiter Report, which evaluates departments according to their "placement success"—the extent to which graduate students are employed in philosophy jobs.[2] Although this view of success has

---

[2] For example, the U.S.-based Philosophical Gourmet Report, http://www.philosophicalgourmet.com/jobplace.asp, emphasises employment in academic philosophy jobs, but says very little about where students might otherwise end up. At the same time, issues about options for philosophy graduates are discussed; see, for example, http://leiterreports.typepad.com/blog/2008/04/will-demographi.html.

become entrenched in the profession, we think it conveys a troubling message to graduate students—that if they don't succeed in obtaining a job in philosophy once they have obtained their Ph.D., then they are failures.

An important and rewarding part of our professional role is to bring a new generation into the profession, and thus there are good reasons for departments to be concerned about the placement of our Ph.D. graduates and to take seriously our professional responsibilities to enculturate students into the standards and practices of the discipline. Caring for our students means that we have an obligation to encourage, reassure, and motivate them to stay with the programme. And, if they are to have a chance of being competitive in a very tight job market, it is important that we provide them with information and advice about publishing and presenting their work at conferences, how to put together a curriculum vita, how to write a job application, postdoctoral opportunities, and so on. It is also important that we are candid with them about the competitiveness of the job market. This responsibility is not just incumbent on individual academic supervisors, but on departments and the profession as a whole. In recent years, the Australasian Association of Philosophy (AAP) has responded to this responsibility via a series of workshops at its annual conference and with online information.[3]

These kinds of activities are very important. However, as they are currently conducted, they also tend to convey the message that the natural and most desirable pathway from the Ph.D. is into academic philosophy, preferably at an elite institution. This message is highly problematic, however, especially in the current context where there is a massive gap between the number of Ph.D. completions and the number of job openings in philosophy.[4] Given this gap, if we persist in seeing our responsibilities just in terms of assisting our students to be as competitive as possible, so that they might be one of the lucky few, then we are setting them up for failure. Unfortunately, anecdotal evidence suggests that this sense that in all likelihood they will fail to be one of the lucky few is a common experience for many students who attend the AAP workshop. We think this is a serious problem. It demoralises our graduate students and can undermine their motivation to complete the degree.

As a profession, we therefore have a responsibility to expand our conception of what counts as success, both for individual students and for a graduate programme. In addition to making pathways into the philosophy profession less opaque to graduate students, we need to ensure that students are given a wider view of the opportunities for professional success that are available

---

[3] For example, Mark Colyvan's advice at http://homepage.mac.com/mcolyvan/careeradvice. html.

[4] In Australia in 2008, 46 Ph.D.s were awarded in philosophy. By our reckoning, this is equivalent to about ten years' worth of continuing positions in philosophy in Australia. Source: DEEWR Report.

to them in non-academic contexts, such as in public policy work, business, or the not-for-profit sector. Presumably, most people pursue philosophy because they love it. But other jobs can incorporate the appeal of philosophical practice. Even though these other areas of work may be outside the experience and comfort zone of many academic philosophers (and we tend to speak mainly from what we know), we have an obligation to educate ourselves about other professional career paths for our students and to convey the message that these other career paths may be just as rewarding, perhaps more so, as the academic pathway. Many of us will have students who have pursued these other career paths and used their education in philosophy to make important contributions outside the discipline. These should be celebrated as successes for philosophy, not failures. When organising workshops about career options, it is therefore crucial that we identify for philosophy graduates "happy choices" outside the academy and present such alternative career choices as both individually rewarding and as making positive social contributions.

A further problem with the message that the natural and most desirable pathway from the Ph.D. is into academic philosophy is that, in a context of increasing casualisation in the sector, our practice tacitly endorses insecure, casualised jobs as the "best available option"—the next best thing to the elusive "proper academic job". Such positions can provide important opportunities for recent graduates to gain teaching experience, which may assist them in obtaining longer-term jobs. However, they are often not good options in themselves, but rather place graduates in a "holding pattern" while awaiting the promise of a "real job", which may never eventuate.[5] Because many philosophy programmes rely on having a pool of highly qualified Ph.D. graduates available to fill casual teaching positions, in presenting such positions as "the best available option", our departmental and professional self-interests combine with unexamined assumptions about good and acceptable outcomes to implicate us in exploitative labour relations with our students and former students. Departments are hostage to financial imperatives from the larger institution that promote increased casualisation of teaching, rather than additional continuing positions. Early career research positions tend to be contract-based, and though attractive, they still amount to precarious employment. Neither casual teaching nor contract-based research is a good long-term option for recent graduates. When the main value of the work done by sessional staff accrues to the institution, not to the worker, the situation is exploitative: the secure jobs of continuing staff are supported by the work of a group whose interests are not well served. This is particularly

---

[5] There are perhaps some cases in which a person only wants casual employment. Perhaps the flexibility is appealing because they have other pursuits and interests that are not compatible with a full-time job. However, insecure income is rarely good for a person who wants to set up a family, and long-term commitments are hard to manage with a patchy and unreliable income.

pernicious when these jobs are in no sense "stepping stones" on the way to a "real job".

Given the pressures on philosophy departments in the current global higher education context, departments may not be able to completely eliminate exploitative teaching conditions. However, by openly acknowledging the potential conflicts between our own self-interests and the interests of our graduate students, we may be able to find ways to reduce exploitation. These include ensuring that our students are fairly renumerated for all aspects of their teaching-related duties (this would seem a minimal requirement, but one that is often breached); trying to provide a range of different teaching and research-related forms of employment to strengthen students' CVs; and being vigilant about not overloading students with casual teaching, which may compromise their ability to complete their Ph.D. on time. Once students have graduated, departments also have a responsibility to provide employment opportunities in the immediate post-Ph.D. period and to provide support and assistance in finding employment elsewhere. However, it is important that we also challenge the assumption that any kind of academic role, no matter how insecure or badly paid, is the best outcome for graduates. Hence, it is imperative that we do not encourage students to remain in the "holding pattern" position of insecure casual and contract teaching for long periods of time, and that we make sure students recognise a need to plan for alternative options. One way that departments might make this need visible and salient would be to consider sunset clauses for post-Ph.D. employment.

What are the implications for women and members of other underrepresented groups of these reflections on the need for an expanded conception of success for a Ph.D. programme? Haslanger's and Saul's discussions of implicit bias suggest that in a tight market, it is members of these groups who may be most likely not to succeed in highly competitive contests for the few available jobs unless strategies are put in place to counter implicit bias, as well as outright discrimination. Their discussions of stereotype threat also suggest that members of these groups are more likely to internalise the message that they won't succeed, and that if they don't succeed, they are failures. It is therefore crucial that the expanded conception of success we are advocating does not inadvertently reinforce current inequities in the profession, setting up the expectation (conscious or unconscious) within the profession, and among group members themselves, that women and members of other underrepresented groups are the ones who are more likely to end up in professional fields outside philosophy. For this reason, the focus by Haslanger, Saul, and others on highlighting current inequities within the discipline and devising strategies to improve women's opportunities and positions in philosophy is essential. Below, we discuss mentoring in detail, but here it is worth noting that mentoring needs to include support for non-traditional pathways and finding ways for students to flourish intellectually and professionally beyond academic environments. In acting as mentors, however, we must take care not to steer members of some groups more than others toward non-academic positions and away from philosophical careers.

We have argued that in addition to combating gender and other inequities within the profession, we also have an obligation to our students to expand our horizons as a profession and not to represent alternative career pathways as "second best". Taking these suggestions seriously has implications not only for the way we advise and guide students, but also for our conception of the nature and function of a philosophy department and our professional roles. In research-intensive institutions, it is of course important that research excellence is taken seriously. But this is often taken to mean that the most important thing a philosophy department does is to publish research; that when it comes to academic appointments, only research matters; and that when it comes to measuring the success of our students (majors and graduates), what counts is how many "star" researchers a department has produced. Our argument suggests that these assumptions are problematic. Research and "placement" success cannot be the only markers for the success of a department. Success must also be measured by the extent to which a department provides a supportive and encouraging environment for its academic staff, postdoctoral researchers, and graduate students; enables its graduate students to complete high-quality Ph.D.s and achieve a broad range of good employment outcomes; and attends to the importance and value of teaching, focusing on not only what is taught, but how it is taught and the consequences for students beyond their learning in particular classes. Taking these broader measures of success into account in appointments, promotions, and assignment of responsibilities, we suggest, will make a difference to the kinds of departments and departmental cultures we create.

In the next section, we suggest that in order to address issues of underrepresentation in the discipline, we also need to expand our horizons at the level of undergraduate education.

3. Diversification in Undergraduate Philosophy Curricula

Calhoun (2009) has recently expanded the focus of discussions concerning gender and the profession to the so-called undergraduate pipeline problem: fewer female undergraduates leads to fewer female postgraduates; fewer female postgraduates leads to fewer female academics, and so on. Because women are the most visibly underrepresented group, systematic data collection in philosophy has concentrated on gender, but it does not take much observation to see that philosophy faces similar problems with respect to the inclusion of other underrepresented, stigmatised, or negatively stereotyped groups.[6] Visible minorities

---

[6] Empirical work is still needed. Getting precise data about participation gaps is necessary for tracking changes to representation and evaluating strategies.

are largely absent from professional philosophy, and in Australian universities, class also seems to be significant.

The pipeline analysis of gender inequity in professions has been criticised, however, for failing to address systemic gender inequities in institutional and social structures. Dodds and Goddard (this volume) apply this critique to the philosophy profession, arguing that its masculinist culture is a major reason for the continuing patterns of gender inequality within the discipline. We focus on a different problem with the pipeline model, namely the presumption that well-qualified students 'should' filter through into the profession. Although attempts to improve diversity and representation within the undergraduate philosophy community are welcome, seeing the issue of undergraduate diversity exclusively in terms of the number who continue in the profession leaves many if not most students out of consideration. Most students who enrol in an undergraduate class will not complete a major, let alone a graduate qualification in philosophy. Exclusive focus on retention would see the main task as increasing the number and diversity of majors, and would particularly emphasise encouraging impressive and exceptional students who might go on to graduate study. (Problematically, it will be easier to identify promising students who fit the schema for philosopher, so this approach is inherently fraught.) However, focusing on these students and on the need to attract and retain potential professional philosophers leaves us with an awkward silence about the interests of the majority of undergraduate students—those who will not pursue advanced study in philosophy. Even if the so-called pipeline problem were to disappear, leaving perfectly representative cohorts at every level, a question remains concerning the benefits of a philosophy education for students who will not go on to graduate level study or even undertake a major. Thinking about the interests of these students, and about patterns of underrepresentation, can therefore constructively challenge standard views of philosophy and its benefits and motivate a revision of traditional approaches to teaching philosophy.

Traditional views of the intrinsic and instrumental benefits of philosophy present these benefits as relevant and available to all. Studying philosophy is said to be good for its own sake, for the intrinsic value of the skills of clear thinking and reasoning, and for the pleasure of doing one's best thinking in conversation with peers and with reference to the best efforts of past thinkers. Philosophy values openness to diverse ideas and challenges, the capacity to work with abstract ideas, and the ability to engage critically, rigorously, and constructively with others and their reasons. Thinking for oneself is the heart of philosophical practice and, so the story goes, can be cultivated by any student in any moderately well-conducted philosophy class. In practice, however, it seems that we do less well at engaging students from underrepresented groups in this kind of practice than we do at engaging a more traditional student base.

Other often-cited instrumental benefits of philosophy include those identified with a liberal arts education. Defences of liberal arts education in the
European and U.S. traditions explicitly claim that citizens need such an education in order to develop skills and acquire the information they need to participate in democratic processes and debates.[7] "The idea that Higher Education's
contribution to democracy lies first and foremost in the education of enlightened, informed and critical citizens, also plays a prominent role in more recent
discussions about the role of Higher Education in democratic societies" (Biesta
2007, 469). Philosophical studies are well suited to encourage or enable citizens
to be informed participants in political and civil life.[8]

Most likely, philosophical training (a bachelor or higher degree) is not the
only way to achieve skills for public and civic participation, and perhaps it
must be supplemented by training or experience in other areas. However, the
"concept mongering" that is at the heart of (much) philosophy—that is, the
effort to develop clear understanding of ideas that, while abstract, are vitally
important—is a necessary part of clear thinking about the shape of our world
and possibilities for change. "For UNESCO, philosophy provides the conceptual bases of principles and values on which world peace depends: democracy,
human rights, justice, and equality" (Shino 2004). Like philosophy's intrinsic
benefits, however, access to these instrumental benefits is delivered less well to
members of underrepresented groups.

Ensuring that philosophy delivers its benefits broadly and fairly requires us
to address questions of access and inclusion, and there are numerous ways to
do this. By challenging and contesting implicit bias, schemas, and stereotypes,
we can make philosophy fairer for its students and practitioners. By expanding
the canon, philosophy teaching can become more relevant to a more diverse
body of undergraduate students. Increasing the visibility of philosophers from
socially diverse groups can help members of underrepresented groups to engage
with the discipline. Widening the range of contributors to philosophy and the
kinds of thinking we recognise as philosophical could make the discipline more
relevant and less alienating for its non-traditional students, such as those from
indigenous or culturally and linguistically diverse backgrounds. It will also be
instructive to ask what students from underrepresented communities can bring
to philosophy and what they take away from it. Do their experiences match our
intentions that by taking our classes, they come to think better, or become better local and/or global citizens? The perspectives and standpoints of students

---

[7] For a recent discussion, see Nussbaum (2010).

[8] There is some cause for caution about these claims. Eric Schwitzgebel (2008) has found
little evidence that philosophers in general and ethicists in particular are better behaved than are
comparison groups of non-philosopher academics or non-ethicists. (Good behaviour is identified
with such things as voting when it is not compulsory, vegetarianism, and responding to student
e-mails.)

themselves can usefully inform better philosophical practice. We expand on these strategies below.

Expanding the curriculum can help to ensure that currently underrepresented groups can access the benefits of philosophy, and philosophy already has resources for such expansion. Philosophical research in the 21st century is less exclusively "Western focused" than its history has been—various voices from indigenous groups, non-Western traditions, and religions are coming into the conversation.[9] Metaphysical concerns (such as the nature of time and personhood) and of epistemology (such as different kinds of justification) have been considered in indigenous cultures and other non-European traditions. Philosophy already engages with concerns such as entrenched inequalities, and these can be of direct importance to the lives of various social groups. In Australia, at least, these possibilities are rarely made explicit to students. Our curriculum content has tended to lag behind philosophy's evolution, and although non-Western philosophical perspectives are now making their way into the curriculum, there is little undergraduate teaching on philosophy of race or indigenous thought. Perhaps this is because teachers look to an established body of work, and often for good reason. But it is possible and it can be pedagogically sound to adopt a more progressive approach. Bringing students to new kinds of content informed by recent research could help them to see themselves as philosophers, and in doing so, challenge philosophy itself to become truly global and genuinely open to all.

It is not only students, however, who benefit from such expansions to the curriculum. We would argue that the inclusion of diverse philosophical perspectives is necessary to reinvigorate the discipline itself. Feminist philosophy, for example, has transformed many areas of the discipline, such as ethics, social and political philosophy, and epistemology. Rather than thinking of feminist philosophy as an add-on to an essentially unchanged discipline, we would argue that feminist and non-Western perspectives ought to be *integrated* into our teaching across the curriculum. This means that we don't just teach a dedicated 'Feminist Philosophy' course, but we include work by feminist philosophers in courses on ethics, metaphysics, epistemology, continental philosophy, and so on. Further, the responsibility to integrate diverse perspectives into the curriculum should not just be left up to individual teachers with a specific interest in doing so. Taking diversity seriously means taking seriously a commitment to philosophical pluralism, and this can only be achieved at the level of departments as a whole. This may seem utopian, given the fractured nature of philosophy and the dysfunctional nature of some departmental cultures. But in a higher education context in which we cannot assume that institutional administrators understand the relevance and value of philosophy, the future of

---

[9] See, for example, Garfield and Edelglass 2011.

departments that eschew pluralism or cannot function as effective self-governing collectives may be imperilled.

Visibility, in terms of both curriculum content and diversity of teaching staff, is another way to make philosophy more relevant to diverse student groups. Visibility in curriculum content is relatively easy to address for women. Because author name is often a direct indicator of gender, expanding the proportion of women philosophers on course reading lists can be a good start. For example, the Australasian Association of Philosophy hosts *Women's Works*, a database of writings by women in philosophy, designed to facilitate greater gender balance in undergraduate reading lists.[10] Presentation of counter-stereotypical examples by including more work by women philosophers in undergraduate curricula will help women students to see themselves as philosophers. Highlighting contributions of philosophers from underrepresented groups other than gender is also important, albeit harder to do by author name alone. Showing non-white and non-European faces of authors is one option, and exposing students to narratives about class or socioeconomic status and about "first in family" university students can also help to illuminate explicit pathways from feeling out of place to familiarity, establishing a less daunting and exclusionary environment for students.

Visibility in terms of better gender-balanced departments and better representation on faculty of ethnic and racial minorities is harder and takes much longer to achieve because it requires transforming departmental cultures. We agree with Samantha Brennan (this volume) that such transformation must be incremental and involves addressing numerous micro-inequities. But as Brennan points out, small changes that begin to address these micro-inequities can make a difference. Some ways to make issues of gender more visible at the level of our teaching practice that are easy to implement include instituting a prize for the best-performing female undergraduate student and reporting at departmental examination meetings on the gender profile of the top-performing students in our classes. This strategy can help to prompt reflection on the nature and quality of our teaching practice. Are we ensuring that implicit bias or entrenched aspects of philosophical practice (such as the adversarial method)[11] don't disproportionately discourage members of underrepresented groups? Do we devote too much attention in tutorial classes to aggressive or insistent male students? Standpoint theory would suggest that some students may be well placed to identify some of our unconscious biases, as they might be highly sensitised in relevant domains. Perhaps there are discrepancies between what we think we are doing and the environment students perceive and encounter that could be uncovered by focus group or similar research. Alongside

---

[10] The database can be found at http://women.aap.org.au/papers/index.html.

[11] For the classic critique of the adversarial method, see Moulton (1983). For a more recent exploration of this issue, see Rooney (2010).

"de-gendering" the philosophy profession, we need to think about subverting the schema for philosopher that is not just male, but also white, middle class, and otherwise socially privileged. Information from the diverse standpoints of students can help us to do this. Cross-disciplinary comparisons with other disciplines that have made greater and faster progress in redressing gender and other forms of inequality might also provide useful models of how to achieve disciplinary transformation.

We have suggested that making philosophy more relevant to a diverse range of students can help to challenge the schema for philosophy. One way to change the perception of philosophy is to change philosophy itself. People with some experience of philosophy but who remain outside the profession are both best placed to broaden public perceptions of philosophy and are much more numerous than philosophy professionals. If students who take just one or two subjects from a philosophy programme encounter an enriched, diverse, and relevant discipline, the schema for philosophy might evolve accordingly. Although, as Calhoun has noted, the schema for philosopher does not begin with an undergraduate class, changes to the schema can be initiated there.

4. Mentoring within and beyond Professional Philosophy

Alongside issues such as the importance of critical mass, visibility, counter-stereotypical exemplars, and so on, mentoring is often identified as crucial for supporting and encouraging the members of underrepresented groups to persevere in professional contexts where they are in the minority. Many philosophers from underrepresented groups cite the influence of supportive mentors as one of the main reasons for their professional success. Although mentoring is often crucially important for professional success in philosophy, there are nevertheless reasons to be cautious about it, both for provider and recipient, and we should be wary of thinking that gender inequities in the profession can be addressed by simple identity-based assignments of mentors to mentees.

Taking on mentoring roles cannot be presumed to be without cost, when in fact mentoring is time-intensive, highly demanding, and not always equally distributed, especially among underrepresented groups. If it is assumed that only women and others from underrepresented groups bear the responsibility for encouraging and supporting colleagues from similar groups, then the demands of mentoring would overwhelm and overburden the small pool of women (or members of other underrepresented groups) available to be mentors. For women in particular, assumptions about suitability and availability for caring, supportive, and nurturing roles align with pernicious stereotypes. It is therefore both impractical and unfair to impose further burdens on such individuals.

More insidiously, as Jacqui Poltera (2011) points out, uncritical assumptions about the benign influence of mentors are problematic. Not all members of underrepresented groups are always supportive of others. Some are not even pleasant or polite. Perhaps even the nicest among us are not always as collegial, as inclusive, as unbiased, or as generous as we might be. Successful academics, in philosophy as elsewhere, have succeeded in a competitive field; necessarily, we have made efforts and sacrifices for this achievement, and typically we need to continue to build on these individual achievements. In real (and likely differently perceived) ways, the competitive character of the profession and the often egoistic and obsessive nature of philosophical activity can manifest itself in relations between colleagues and peers, and across levels of experience. Gender bias enacted by women can complicate this kind of pattern:

> When women are required to fit into tightly defined feminine roles in order to be accepted, those who are willing to act as expected often end up in opposition to those who aren't. Women who behave in traditionally feminine ways may find women who behave in traditionally masculine ways off-putting, and vice versa.... Likewise, professional women who have succeeded by playing by men's rules may have a lot invested in proving that "that's what it takes to be a serious professional." Women who seek to change the old rules may feel shocked and betrayed if more established professional women don't support them.[12]

Furthermore, seniority and success in a profession need be no protection against internalisation of gender or other schemas that inhibit or conflict with recognising the professional qualities of members of underrepresented groups. This remains so even when the established colleague is herself a member of such a group. Unconscious associations between professional excellence and maleness, for example, can in spite of our express and sincere commitments to inclusion, equality, and fairness, affect—even contaminate—our conduct and judgment, skewing these to reflect and reinforce the very patterns that we are seeking to undermine (Saul, this volume). Thus, while taking gender into account means that all mentors need to be mindful of gender issues and the effects of subtle forms of exclusion, implicit bias, stereotype threat, and the like, taking gender into account does *not* mean that all women should be mentors, nor that women are always best mentored by other women, who can be presumed to be sympathetic and supportive.

In addition to these reasons for being cautious about identity-based mentoring, there are positive reasons for encouraging cross-group mentoring. Although mentoring across social groups can be difficult, as differences of culture, style, demeanour, and the like can lead to misunderstanding, often the

---

[12] The Center for WorkLife Law (2010).

most suitable mentor will be someone who does not share the mentee's social group identity but is best suited because of their relevant expertise or professional contacts, or because the mentee trusts and feels comfortable with that person. Other benefits of cross-group mentoring include transferring knowledge about the experiences of women and other underrepresented groups to mentors who lack direct access to such experience. As mentors learn from their mentees, as well as providing support and advice to them, wider awareness of bias, chilly climate, and the like can be distributed into the philosophical community and can foster a broad-based critical mass of good practice.

Those in mentoring roles or who occupy positions of leadership are not thereby immune to implicit bias, and goodwill is neither an inoculation nor an antidote. Thus, mentors whose mentees are members of underrepresented groups in philosophy must be particularly alert to issues of power, structural inequity, and patterns and practices of professional and social exclusion within the profession. But making these explicit in the context of a mentoring relationship might in some ways be at odds with the professional enculturation that a mentor is tasked to provide. There is therefore a tension between the different demands placed on those in mentoring roles: to assist a colleague to meet professional expectations and norms while at the same time contesting the aspects of those expectations and norms that reproduce patterns of privilege. Can one responsibly mentor a colleague into becoming highly sensitised and resistant to the tacit norms of the discipline and institution? Would this help or hinder a career? Clearly, feminist or otherwise politically informed and just mentoring does not mean ignoring structural and local inequities, nor does it require so much attention to injustice that professional development is obstructed. Yet the solution is not just an Aristotelian middle path, though a balance between conformity and subversion might be important. Rather, this tension reveals that the mentoring context is wider than the relationship between two individuals. Within a department, faculty, or institution, issues of marginalisation and professional exclusion, implicit (and explicit) bias, and resources to contest and combat them are of collective concern. A concern for equity within the discipline needs to be manifest in the wider practice of mentoring and in the broad context in which enculturation takes place. A critical and critically engaged culture is required, and hopefully an expanded conception of success will help to foster this.

This critical mass and reflective culture depend on goodwill, but good intentions are not enough. Current work on implicit bias, schemas, and unconscious influences, cited earlier, is beginning to illuminate the challenges and possible solutions to problems that can be hard to recognise. Poltera makes the useful point that philosophy's acknowledgment of underrepresentation as a problem of numbers needs to be supplemented by qualitative inquiry. What discrepancies are there between the experiences of those for whom seeing oneself as a philosopher is easy and those for whom it is difficult? Do more experienced philosophers from underrepresented groups eventually forget that discomfort, and then dismiss, ignore, or fail to see it in others? Does experience in philosophy entrench or challenge our attitudes? Investigations of limitations to our current practice need to be carefully researched, and inquiries and solutions need to be taken up at collective (including departmental, institutional, and discipline) levels.

Mentoring can best contribute to resolving patterns of underrepresentation and ameliorate (though not eliminate) its problematic aspects if it is part of a reflective community of practice. Three areas for research and action are the distribution of mentoring labour; how best to cultivate shared attention to mentoring and its outcomes, particularly to identify and offset any tendency for mentoring to replicate or entrench group-based disadvantage in philosophy; and developing a learning culture with respect to identifying and overcoming implicit bias.

The need to broaden our horizons and those of our students beyond the profession and to develop an expanded conception of what counts as success raises additional challenges for mentoring beyond those discussed above. For example, if we are to provide our Ph.D. graduates with realistic alternative career options, then philosophers need to establish networks with a broad range of other professions in which our graduates might pursue a career, as our expertise is typically limited to the academic field. We think these challenges can only be met by concerted action by departments and the broader profession.

Conclusion

The dominant view of what counts as success for a philosophy programme focuses on disciplinary reproduction. We want to attract good students to our undergraduate programme, to encourage a significant number of these students into the major and to continue onto an honours year. We then want our best honours students to pursue philosophy at graduate level, to undertake a Ph.D., and, with luck, enter the profession. Clearly, success of this kind is crucial for a thriving philosophy programme and should be one of our goals. What we have suggested, however, is that in addition to this conception of success, it could also be a mark of success for a programme that it succeeds in disseminating philosophical skills and values into the wider community; not only that our profession attracts a representative range of people from various social groups, but also that the skills and values we claim to be valuable are disseminated broadly across a range of social groups and employment contexts. Alongside addressing the pipeline problem, meeting the challenge of diversification involves the cultivation of a flourishing public culture in which philosophy is important and making visible the wide range of areas in which philosophical contributions can be useful.

References

Bradley, D., P. Noonan, H. Nugent, and B. Scales (2008), *Review of Higher Education in Australia: Final Report*. Canberra, AU: Australian Government.

Biesta, G. (2007), "Towards the knowledge democracy? Knowledge production and the civic role of the university", *Studies in Philosophical Education*, 26: 467–479.

Calhoun, C. (2009), "The Undergraduate Pipeline Problem", *Hypatia* 24(2): 216–223.

Center for WorkLife Law (2010), "Gender Bias Learning Project", UC Hastings College of the Law, http://www.genderbiaslearning.com/stereotype_genderwars.html.

Department of Education, Employment and Workplace Relations (DEEWR) (2009), *Transforming Australia's Higher Education System*. Canberra, AU: Australian Government.

Garfield, J., and W. Edelglass (eds.) (2011), *Oxford Handbook of World Philosophy*. Oxford, UK: Oxford University Press.

Goddard, E. (2008), "Improving the Participation of Women in the Philosophy Profession", on behalf of Susan Dodds, Lynda Burns, Mark Colyvan, Frank Jackson, Karen Jones, and Catriona Mackenzie, professional report submitted to the AAP, http://aap.org.au/women/reports/index.html, accessed 08/08/08.

Haslanger, S. (2008), "Changing the Ideology and Culture of Philosophy: Not By Reason (Alone)", *Hypatia* 23(2): 210–212.

Moulton, J. (1983), "A Paradigm of Philosophy: The Adversary Method", in S. Harding and M. Hintikka (eds.), *Discovering Reality*. Dordrecht, NL: Reidel, 149–164.

Nussbaum, M. (2010), *Not for Profit: Why Democracy Needs the Humanities*. Princeton, NJ: Princeton University Press.

Poltera, J. (2011), "Women and the Ethos of Philosophy: Shedding Light on Mentoring and Competition", *Hypatia* 26(2): 419–428.

Rooney, P. (2010), "Philosophy, Adversarial Argumentation, and Embattled Reason", *Informal Logic* 30(3): 203–234.

Schwitzgebel, E. (2010), "On Being Good at Seeming Smart", http://schwitzsplinters.blogspot.com/2010/03/on-being-good-at-seeming-smart.html.

Schwitzgebel, E. (2008), "The Moral Behavior of Ethics Professors", http://schwitzsplintersethicsprofs.blogspot.com/.

Shino, M. (2004), "Why a Philosophy Day?" *SHS Newsletter 04—Foresight: the future in the present*, January–March 2004,http://www.unesco.org/new/en/social-and-human-sciences/themes/human-rights/philosophy/philosophy-day-at-unesco/why-a-philosophy-day/.

9

Rethinking the Moral Significance of Micro-Inequities

THE CASE OF WOMEN IN PHILOSOPHY

Samantha Brennan

Micro-inequities are small, unjust inequalities often pointed to as part of the larger story about the unequal place of women in the workforce. This chapter sets out to examine micro-inequities in the context of women's careers in the academic discipline of philosophy. It also offers a philosophical analysis of micro-inequities, looks at some explanations about why moral philosophy has struggled with the problem of small harms, and argues that we need to rethink their moral significance. I argue that we should not treat acts and their results only on an individual basis. The existence of micro-inequities highlights a significant problem with doing so as cumulative effects are easily ignored when we do this. A final section offers some suggestions about solutions appropriate to the kind of wrongs that micro-inequities are.

1. The Context: Women in Philosophy in Canada

Looking at the situation of women in philosophy, it is helpful to begin with some numbers.[1] The situation of women in philosophy is much closer to that of women in the sciences than that found in any other arts and humanities discipline. In Canada, outside of the STEM fields (science, technology, engineering, and mathematics), only theology fares worse than philosophy in terms of numbers of women. At the top 54 U.S. research/doctoral schools, the percentage of women on faculty according to the Philosophical Gourmet Report is a mere 18.49 percent. Things are better at less elite schools and better as well in

---

[1] For a more complete picture in terms of numbers, please see Bishop et al., this volume, appendix 1.

Canada. The Canadian Philosophical Association's most recent equity survey puts the numbers at about 30 percent, but not all schools report data. While we do not know this, we might reasonably worry that the schools reporting data are better than average in terms of equity. Those are the departments that think it is important to fill in and return the form. I have not included data about women moving through the ranks here, but the pattern is much as one might expect. Women typically take longer to tenure and move more slowly from associate to full professor, if they do so at all. A further worry is that women retire earlier than their male colleagues and so spend much less time at the academy's highest ranks. These numbers affect further honours such as the numbers of women who are fellows of the Royal Society of Canada or who become Tier I Canada Research Chairs.[2]

However, one important difference between the American and Canadian contexts is the degree to which equity goals have found widespread support among Canadian philosophy departments and among Canadian universities more generally. Although there are of course individual faculty members who disagree[3] at the university and government level, there is significant support for the goal of equity in hiring. The Canadian Government's Federal Contractors' Program (FCP) requires provincially regulated employers with 100 or more employees bidding on federal contracts of $200,000 or more to certify that they will implement employment equity measures. Created in 1986, the FCP applies to universities, so Canadian universities are required to take steps to increase the representation of four specified groups in the workforce: women, visible minorities, aboriginal peoples, and people with disabilities. A 1991 Report of the Canadian Philosophical Association (CPA) Equity Committee (philosophers Kathleen Okruhlik, Lorraine Code, Wayne Sumner, and Brenda Baker were among its members) made the following recommendations that were passed by the CPA membership at its annual general meeting:

(1) By the year 2000 at least twenty-seven percent of permanent or probationary faculty in any unit should be female, and by the year 2010 at least forty percent should be female.

(2) In any decade in any department, at least fifty percent of new permanent or probationary positions should be filled by women.

(3) The first goal takes precedence over the second. (So, for example, if achieving twenty-seven percent female faculty by 2000 requires a hiring rate for women that is higher than fifty percent, the higher rate should be implemented.)

---

[2] For a discussion of equity and the Canada Research Chairs Programme, see Wendy Robbins, Rosemary Morgan, John Hollingsworth, Judy Stanley, and Michèle Ollivier (2001), *Ivory towers: feminist and equity audits.*

[3] See, for example, philosopher Andrew Irvine's May 27, 2010, editorial in the Ottawa Citizen, which claims that discrimination against men is the real problem in philosophy.

Now, nearly 20 years later, it is obvious that Canadian philosophy departments have fallen far short of these goals. So, why in the face of goodwill and political commitment have philosophers failed to meet goals to which we have collectively committed?

There are a number of different pieces to this puzzle. Many people think we need to find factors that make philosophy as an academic career special. But many of these roads lead to dead ends if one thinks that these explanations will tell the complete story on their own. Some people focus on general worries about academic career paths and the extent to which typical male lifestyles and patterns are taken as normative. For example, the typical academic career path with very heavy pre-tenure workload expectations does not fit very well with the pattern of women's lives in which those same years are also often the only years available for childbearing and raising. But although this is true and no doubt an issue, it's not unique to academic careers. Doctors and lawyers face similar challenges in terms of life stages that coincide with exceptional work demands, and the number of women in these fields continues to climb. At many medical and law schools, women outnumber men, and it is women's life patterns that drive recent trends in career paths for doctors and lawyers. Likewise, whatever is going wrong in philosophy, the explanation cannot come from the academy in general, because the numbers of women in certain academic fields is on the rise. Within the sciences, biology is the obvious example of a field with growing numbers of women. Some feminist philosophers focus on the content of our discipline—the study of the writings of dead white men—and wonder whether that affects the numbers of women. But here too we are not alone. Classical studies, English, and history struggle with masculine canonical texts as well, and those disciplines are rather more balanced in terms of gender.

Other explanations of the gender gap in philosophy focus on the hostility of our working environment, looking at some clear examples of outright discrimination and sexual harassment. Although I do not doubt these situations exist—indeed I know firsthand that they do—such infringements of women's basic rights to a safe and non-discriminatory workplace will not be the focus of my chapter. It is not because they are not serious; they are very serious. But the wrongness itself and its source are not puzzling from the viewpoint of ethical theory. Usually, such acts involve bad intentions, are against justified moral rules, and have bad results. On most moral theories, they will come out to be wrong and their wrongness is over-determined. I am much more interested in the question of why people who are committed to doing the right thing end up failing.[4]

---

[4] It is the same reason why, out of all the books on just distribution of work in home, my favorite is Rhona Mahony's *Kidding Ourselves: Breadwinning, Babies, and Bargaining Power*. Mahoney attempts to answer the question of why men and women who set out with egalitarian commitments end up with an unequal distribution of housework and childcare responsibilities (Mahony 1995).

The most compelling explanations of the situation of women that do not focus on intentional wrongdoing, such as harassment and deliberate discrimination, look to the twin causes of implicit bias and micro-inequities.[5]

The Barnard Report on Women, Work, and the Academy, citing a 1999 MIT report, describes these twin causes of women's inequality in the academy in these terms:

> The first is that biases operating below the threshold of deliberate consciousness, biases in interaction that are unrecognized and unintended, can systematically put women and minorities at a disadvantage. Second, although individual instances of these "micro-inequities" may seem trivial, their cumulative effects can account for large-scale differences in outcome; those who benefit from greater opportunity and a reinforcing environment find their advantages compounded, while deficits of support and recognition ramify for those who are comparatively disadvantaged (Wylie et al. 2007, 2).

My focus in this chapter is on understanding micro-inequities and their moral importance. To be clear though, it is not because I think micro-inequities tell us the whole story of why there are so few women faculty members in philosophy. There are many different factors at play, and some of them might not be significant if they were the only such factor. What happens, I think, is that these factors are compounded. So, yes, there are real worries about the numbers of women who start off in philosophy in the first place; there are legitimate concerns about the masculine shape of the academy's career path; there are some serious issues with sexual harassment and gender-based discrimination; and it probably does make a difference that our canon is almost entirely composed of white male authors. I also think it's quite likely that philosophy and other disciplines don't differ all that much with respect to their micro-inequities (deep-seated biases are similar across the professions), but micro-inequities do play a significant compounding causal role, and altering them could go some way toward rectifying the imbalance. As such, we should be aware of micro-inequities and act to minimize their effects, rather than argue about what makes philosophy different. I also think that understanding the moral importance of micro-inequities will have other payoffs in moral theory as well.

---

[5] Sally Haslanger's well-known paper "Changing the Ideology and Culture of Philosophy: Not by Reason (Alone)" examines both of these explanations but focuses mainly on implicit bias (Haslanger 2008). Alison Wylie's equally excellent "What Knowers Know Well: Women, Work and the Academy" looks at micro-inequities from the perspective of feminist standpoint theory and is a wonderful contribution to work in feminist epistemology of social change (Wylie 2011).

2. Understanding Micro-inequities

Why do those who try to do the right thing nevertheless fail? For example, why do Canadian philosophy departments that have endorsed equity goals fail to achieve equity in hiring? I think that micro-inequities are part of the answer. Because of their size, micro-inequities are very easily overlooked by both the perpetrator and victim. One reason they are overlooked is because when we do moral philosophy, we engage in a kind of individualism about acts and their results that prevents us from seeing cumulative harms. In what follows, I look at some examples of micro-inequities, including everyday workplace interactions, and look to their cumulative effects in support of the claim that we should reconsider the moral importance of small inequities.

Micro-inequities are small, unjust inequalities often pointed to as part of the larger story about larger-scale inequalities such as women's unequal place in the workforce. However, one doesn't find anything close to a precise definition of a micro-inequity in the literature on workplace ethics and equity. What exactly is a micro-inequity? People often contrast inequities with mere inequalities, where the former are taken to be unjust inequalities. The latter, inequality, is a neutral term, whereas inequity assumes that there is some injustice involved. An inequity is a harm that derives its wrongness from being an undeserved inequality. Micro-inequities are very small inequities. As far as I know, there are inequities and micro-inequities. No one talks about mini-inequities, which would be halfway between a full-sized inequity and a micro-inequity. So we'll use "micro-inequity" for any inequity that falls shy of counting as a full-blown inequity on the basis of its size. The following are some definitions of micro-inequity from the literature on workplace climate:

(1) According to Bernice Sandler, "micro-inequity" refers to the ways in which individuals are "either *singled out*, or *overlooked*, *ignored*, or *otherwise discounted* based on an unchangeable characteristic such as sex, race or age" (Sandler 1986, 3; emphasis in original). A micro-inequity generally takes the form of a gesture, different kind of language, treatment, or even tone of voice. It is suggested that the perceptions that cause the manifestation of micro-inequities are deeply rooted and unconscious. The cumulative effect of micro-inequities can impair a person's performance in the workplace or classroom, damage self-esteem, and may eventually lead to that person's withdrawal from the situation.

(2) Mary Rowe defines micro-inequities as "apparently small events which are often ephemeral and hard-to-prove, events which are covert, often unintentional, frequently unrecognized by the perpetrator, which occur wherever people are perceived to be 'different'" (Rowe 2008, 45). Rowe is the person who first coined the term "micro-inequities." Rowe named one of her articles "Saturn's Rings" because the planet Saturn is

surrounded by rings, which obscure the planet, but are made just of tiny bits of ice and sand (Rowe 1974). Rowe writes that her interest in these phenomena began with an incredible opportunity:

"In 1973 I took a job at MIT, working for the then new President and Chancellor. I was charged, among other things, with learning how the workplace could improve with respect to people who were under-represented at MIT—as examples, men and women of color, white women, and people with disabilities. As an economist I had expected to learn about big issues standing in the way of progress" (Rowe 2008, 45).

She writes that she did find a few big issues, but not as many as she expected and not enough to account for the scope of the problems. What struck her instead were all of the "little issues." She writes that little acts of disrespect and failures in performance feedback seemed to corrode some professional relationships like bits of sand and ice.

Why do micro-inequities have such wide-ranging effects? One part of the story concerns expectations and the feedback pattern between expectation and success. There is a passage from philosopher/poet Michael Frayn's work on this subject that I think resonates with these themes. Frayn writes: "It's not excellence which leads to celebrity, but celebrity which leads to excellence. One makes one's reputation, and one's reputation enables one to achieve the conditions in which one can do good work" (Chotiner 2010). In academic contexts, this quotation made me think about the issue of the philosophy job market and who becomes an academic star. Many people think that because those people so identified as intellectually "hot" do go on to achieve great things that our ability to spot brilliance is dead on. Some philosophers do act as if they possessed personal "genius detectors" that allow them to judge on the basis of one good question, one brow furrowed just the right way at just the right time, or one speedy reply to a tough question that so-and-so is *really smart*. But I often have a thought like the Frayn quotation above: At least in some cases, the hot shots become real hot shots because we expect more of them. We follow their careers, read their papers, and attend their talks with heightened expectations. Of course, they also tend to get the jobs at pressure-cooker universities with high research demands, little teaching to get in the way, and a "publish or perish" environment. A colleague once commented that he suspected you could take any of the candidates in the top half of the academic job market, plunk them down into that environment, with that amount of attention and expectation, and they would go on to achieve great things. Years after, we could pat ourselves on the back, say what a good job we have done, and note how well our genius detectors work. Of course, this is speculative, and it would be difficult to test, but we ought to consider whether and what role expectation plays in success.

There are a variety of micro-inequities at play in the hiring scenario I sketched. Those of us concerned about equity wonder about the epistemic basis of these quick and certain judgments. A member of an appointments committee I sat on once asked us to consider whether the philosophers' preference for the quick reply could be any more than an aesthetic preference. Doesn't it matter more how good the reply is, not how fast it comes? Others worry whether those of us who are socialized to smile, to always make others comfortable, can ever really look smart in that deep-in-thought, furrowed-brow kind of way. (Maybe there's a kind of anti-botox that could give you brow wrinkles temporarily, kind of like an appearance-enhancing drug for academic job interviews.) Philosopher Sandra Bartky writes about how she battled the tendency, when she started teaching, to think of the graduate seminars she taught as "tea parties" she was hosting in which it was her job to smile, to welcome everyone, and make sure that all of her students got along (Bartky 2002, 14). The University of Western Ontario equity guide for people on hiring committees asks if we can "hear" soft voices, southern accents, and lilting speech as "smart." Never mind the tendency to discomfort if the candidate is disabled, outside prevailing norms for gender, or clearly of a non-standard sexual orientation. It may be that the ideal of a serious academic is masculine, and individuals who don't share the traits associated with the masculine professor are unjustly disadvantaged in campus visits.

These effects of differential expectations are also cumulative. Over a period of time, the differences become real. Some people call this the Matthew effect from the following biblical passage in the gospel of Matthew, chapter 13, verse 12: "For to all those who have, more will be given, and they will have an abundance; but from those who have nothing, even what they have will be taken away." In the sociology of science, "Matthew effect" was a term coined by Robert K. Merton to describe how, among other things, eminent scientists will often get more credit than a comparatively unknown researcher, even if their work is similar; it also means that credit will usually be given to researchers who are already famous (Merton 1968). One sees this especially in the granting of honours and awards. I have a fair bit of experience in this area because I served as chair of my department for eight years, and one of the things you do a lot of as department chair is to nominate your colleagues for awards, honours, and grants. Some of the awards are very clearly meant to go in a sort of order. At my university, you're a "faculty scholar" before you're a holder of the "Hellmuth prize" and before you're a "Distinguished University Professor." The teaching awards work similarly. It would be hard to jump in late in the game and get the career-capping award without having also received any of the lesser awards that go before. Committee members may lament the lack of qualified female candidates for various awards. I often hear people say, "We'd nominate a woman but she'd never get it. There are no qualified women." There may be a very real sense in which that is true, but it is true as a result of decisions made much earlier. Here the parallel with the equal distribution of work in the home is striking. Yes, at the time an opposite-sex couple sits down to make the decision as to who stays home to look after very young children and interrupt their career, it may be that the obvious and efficient choice from an economic perspective is that the woman do so. Yet this is only obvious and efficient in light of a whole series of educational and career choices in which taking time off with children figured into her plan but not his.

The person who thinks women are not suited for a career with a heavy research or administrative load may find his opinions confirmed by the truth of these perceptions in the case of senior women, and thus find his views about women in general reinforced. If these views then inform his views about junior colleagues, the cycle repeats. I find the same thing to be true in a variety of academic contexts—from teaching awards, to research honours, to appointments to meaningful and important administrative tasks. We might start out not seeing the junior women as qualified, and then later we look and there are no senior women who are qualified. There was a point at which I thought it was best to "protect" younger female colleagues from some of the more demanding aspects of academic careers such as academic administrative committees and large class teaching, but I now think such protection is mistaken. Later success depends on early success in ways that were not clear to me when I first started to think about women's careers and choices. It is often the case that the later judgment—"There are no qualified senior women"—is correct even though our earlier judgment made it so.

To see how this sort of vicious cycle can manifest in practice, consider the example of the Canada Research Chairs (CRC) program. These research awards show that micro-inequities can compound as part of a self-confirming process. In the first years of the Canada Research Chairs program, only 22 percent of Tier II Chairs and 10 percent of the senior, more prestigious Tier I Chairs went to women. Wendy Robbins, in a February 16, 2010, posting on the FedCan blog "Equity Matters" notes that all of the top program officials were men, as were 83 percent of its international panel of peer reviewers. In 2003, a team of eight women from across Canada registered a formal complaint, alleging discrimination before the Canadian Human Rights Commission. *Cohen et al. v. Industry Canada* was settled in 2006 by a negotiated agreement. The agreement required adherence to basic fair-employment practices, such as advertising vacancies so that the pool of qualified applicants is as large as possible. Yet data still show that women, who are a third of full-time faculty in Canada, continue to be underrepresented in CRC appointments.[6]

---

[6] Although the percentage has slowly risen, reaching 25 percent in 2009, this represents only 17 percent of Tier I and 31 percent of Tier II Chairs. No data are reported for other equity groups—aboriginal peoples, racialized minorities, and persons with disabilities—despite their inclusion in the settlement agreement.

In 2008, the government invested $200 million in the Canada Excellence Research Chairs program, which seeks "to attract and retain the world's most accomplished and promising minds." Not only were there no women in the final 19 researchers selected, there were none in the shortlist of 36 proposals either. Now, some better news: The government asked three leading female academics to probe what happened. Likely the government is acting both from a concern for justice and the cause of fairness for women researchers, and the wish to avoid another human-rights challenge of the Canada Research Chair program. The report's authors—University of Alberta president Indira Samarasekera, Elizabeth Dowdeswell, head of the Council of Canadian Academies, and granting council head Suzanne Fortier—made recommendations to improve female participation. These include introducing a "rising stars" category, as well as one for "established leaders," a move that would change the aim of a program billed as a magnet for top talent. They also recommend broadening the areas of the search and introducing an "open" category. Limited time was also a factor, they say. With very short deadlines, the old boys' network was more likely to play a role in who was considered. They also recommend a shorter list of nominees, as women may be reluctant to take part in a nomination process in which the odds of success are around 50 percent. Obviously, several factors resulted in the very low numbers of women, but the point I am trying to make is that these factors don't work independently. If at each step along the way—from beginning an academic career to arriving at the career stage of senior researcher—one encounters micro-inequities, there may be very few women in the research chair applicant pool. Further, when we compound these micro-inequities with the micro-inequities in the CRC process itself, one can see how the result isn't shocking or surprising. Rather, given micro-inequities and the ways in which they compound, one should expect these results.

Over time, these processes affect the candidates themselves. Judgments about performance can erode the self-confidence and self-esteem of women academics. What was initially perceived as a slight may just become business as usual, the norm. Women may come to see themselves as not deserving of the top awards or honours. People suffering the effects of micro-inequities may also experience themselves as shut out from others in their workplace. Writes Rowe: "Micro-inequities exert influence both by walling out the 'different' person, and by making the person of difference less effective" (Rowe 1990, 156). In other words, micro-inequities can lead to poor performance—when we have low expectations of those we work with, those people have a tendency to deliver what is expected of them. "It's a downward spiral; the more I behave in ways that devalue you, the less confident you feel. The less confident you feel, the less you'll risk confronting issues or contributing innovative ideas. And the less you contribute, the less I'll value you" (Moynahan 2009, 2).

A common response to micro-inequities is to give alternative interpretations or explanations of the event. We might also wonder why the person is so sensitive. Or we might deny that the event in question is so significant. The blogger known as "Female Science Professor" writes that "[e]very time [she posts] an anecdote about a possible situation in which [she] may or may not have been treated in a way that could perhaps be described at least in part as sexist," she receives these responses and is then accused of man-hating. She describes her examples of mistreatment as mostly falling under the category of micro-inequities:

> There is a complete spectrum between the mini-incidents and the big unambiguous ones that most people would agree are sexist or racist. Clearly we need to eradicate the big unambiguous examples of discrimination, but are some (most?) people willing to accept micro-inequities because the incidents are, in many cases, so ambiguous? Where do you draw the line between deciding that someone is oversensitive vs. the target of habitual disrespect?[7]

One thing we might wonder is how micro-inequities are related to the problem of implicit bias. Recall that the Barnard Report cited at the start of this chapter referred to micro-inequities and implicit bias as the twin causes of women's inequality. These categories will often overlap though they need not. Not every micro-inequity will be the result of implicit bias and not all cases of implicit bias will result in micro-inequities. The inequalities that result from bias might be large and substantial. Likewise, a micro-inequity could stem from intentional discrimination or implicit bias. For example, a lecturer who repeatedly passes over female students' contributions could be aware of doing so and intend to because of a conviction that the contributions will not be valuable, or could be entirely unaware of doing so. In either case, each time a female student is not called on is a micro-inequity.

If it turns out that some rather large differences in terms of women's participation in the discipline of philosophy can be explained as the accumulated effects of many, many actions with small results, most of which were unintentional harms stemming from implicit bias, then we ought to pay more attention to micro-inequities both in terms of understanding them as a moral phenomenon and in terms of practical solutions.

3. Paying Attention to Small Harms as a Problem in Moral Philosophy

The problem of small harms is not new. Indeed, moral and political philosophers have worried about small harms and the tendency of moral theories to overlook them. Our moral frameworks—whether consequentialist or

---

[7] See the September 7, 2009, entry on her blog "Musings of a Science Professor at a Large Research University" at http://science-professor.blogspot.com.au/.

deontologist in nature—tend not to see small harms. When we see the moral world through these frameworks, small harms do not appear, though for very different reasons.

Let's consider deontological ethics first. Many rights theorists have difficulties with rights against small harms because of a commitment to absolute rights. Charles Fried is a champion of absolute deontology (Fried 1978). He articulates and defends the view that all rights are absolute. And on Fried's view, there can be no right not to be pinched. Being pinched is never an injustice. That's because such a right would protect a very small harm and as all rights are absolute, there would be an absolute right not to be pinched. Clearly, that's absurd, writes Fried. Things like being pinched fly under the radar of the language of moral rights. Now we might reject Fried's particular view about where the right not to be harmed kicks in, but for each rights theorist, there will be some point at which harms become large enough to be appropriately protected by a moral right. (There are also issues regarding rights against risk of harm that are relevant, but I set these aside for now.) In an academic context, it may well be that we all have an equal right to respect from our colleagues. Swearing at someone or physically touching them in an aggressive way will count as a violation of the right to equal respect. But what about something the effects of which are smaller and harder to measure? How long I hold eye contact with someone when speaking is a form of acknowledgment, and it may be that I treat men and women differently in this regard. Indeed, it's quite likely that I do. If I cut off someone's gaze prematurely, have I harmed that person? It may be a form of disrespect, but it will difficult to say that I have a right to equal eye contact.

While rights theorists are deontologists who focus on act type in determining wrongness (whether B's rights have been violated, for example), other versions of deontological ethics focus on intention instead. But here too there are some rather obvious problems. In most cases involving implicit bias, the moral agent whose actions bring about the harm won't have intended it. At best there is a duty to try to fix such mistakes in our thinking, but it's still up for debate which methods are most successful. Again, to consider an example from my own experience in academia, it's quite likely that I call on male students to speak more often than I call on female students. Apparently, it's something we all do. These sorts of mistakes, like the bias demonstrated in various CV evaluation studies, are not limited to men. And yet it seems unlikely that I intend to harm my female students in any way. Again, if intention is our focus, then it seems we may miss out on micro-inequities.

One might think that small harms would fare better in a consequentialist analysis. After all, consequentialist moral philosophers are concerned with outcomes and the overall good. Small harms and small benefits are part of the overall results. But consequentialists too have tended to ignore very small harms. I can have my interests set back, or have some very small negative experience, but if it is too small to register for me, then some consequentialists want to say that I haven't been harmed. To insist otherwise is to move to an objective standard of well-being. On this way of thinking, harms have natural boundaries, and very small harms may be too small to register and hence cannot count in determining the overall good.

Derek Parfit draws our attention to this mistake in his book *Reasons and Persons* (see chapter 3, "Five Mistakes in Moral Mathematics," in Parfit 1984). Parfit considers a series of mistakes in moral mathematics, including at least one that is relevant to our purposes. The fourth mistake is ignoring small or imperceptible effects. Even if imperceptible, bad effects with sufficient extent or repetition can be very terrible indeed. Parfit's examples concern environmental issues such as overfishing and pollution, but his lesson can be just as important for small injuries and insults that are part and parcel of academic life for some people. If we view each act individually, we might miss out on the aggregate effects and the patterns that are relevant to understanding bias and discrimination.

Another useful resource in this regard is Andrew Kernohan's analysis of cumulative harms in his book *Liberty, Equality, and Cultural Oppression* (Kernohan 1998). Kernohan's main interest is in Mill's harm principle as a justification for liberty-restricting legislation, and his main target, like Parfit, is environmental harm. He's interested in what happens when individuals commit acts that would not be harmful were each act the only one of its kind, but when considered together produce harmful effects. Each act itself would not pass the harm test, but if we consider the set of acts together, we see that they produce cumulative harms. This doesn't quite match our problem, but the concept of cumulative harm is useful. In our case, we can think of the harm as being to an individual. The first few micro-inequities may not have a huge effect, but over time, like drops of water on stone, a person's interests can be set back significantly.

We can thank Parfit and Kernohan for drawing our attention to this error common in contemporary ethics, but there is another mistake at play here as well. Some feminist critics of moral philosophy typically fault contemporary moral theory for its individualism, focusing on persons as separate, autonomous, and not connected to one another in meaningful ways. But I have argued there is a more pernicious kind of individualism that can be found in contemporary ethics, and it plays a role in contributing to our inattention to small harms such as micro-inequities. This kind of individualism applies to acts and their results. Consider the case of a very small slight or benefit, something so trivial that on its own it merits no particular moral attention. Frances Kamm, for example, argues that if we are choosing between turning a trolley down a track that has one person who will be killed on one side and one person and some flowers on the other, that the flowers can make no moral difference (Kamm 1996, 158). Morally speaking, we are faced with a tie; likewise for small harms. I have a medicine that can cure one person of cancer and fix his hang-nail or cure one other person who doesn't also have a hangnail; here again I'm faced with a tie. Flowers and hangnails are too small to make a moral differ-ence. But surely it makes a difference if the benefits and burdens, no matter how small, are distributed such that some people get a great many small benefits and others get a great many small burdens. We may allow benefits and burdens to add up within a person's life even if they are too small to make a moral differ-ence when considered across persons (Brennan 2006, 259–261).

My position is that the question of whether some benefits and burdens are so small that they don't count morally cannot be answered outside of the con-text in which they occur, and that we lose sight of morally important factors if we push all of the time to see wrongness in its smallest possible units. It is an important theoretical question how micro-inequities relate to the larger wrongs of which they are part. We might ask the following question: Is it the case that the micro-inequities are not morally objectionable taken in isolation, but they cumulatively cause the morally objectionable inequality? Alternately, one might think that each micro-inequity that forms a large-scale unjust inequality is also wrong, and the wrongness of the larger inequality is composed entirely of the sum of the wrongness of its parts. In the middle, one might think that the micro-inequities are each a little bit wrong, but the wrongness of the whole is greater than the sum of the parts.

But although this question is important, I worry that focusing too much on it may cause us to lose sight of the forest for the trees. My own answer is that some-times the individual micro-inequities will be wrong, even though we may not be in a position to blame anyone. Other micro-inequities may be neither wrong nor blameworthy. Some might worry that not addressing the wrongness of individ-ual micro-inequities may seem to be letting people off the hook too easily, but it does allow us to shift our focus to collective solutions to the problem. As a group we have responsibilities for the outcome, and group-based solutions are likely to be much more effective than individual ones. Finally, some may worry that the focus on micro-inequities lets us all off the hook for the large-scale culpable wrongs that do occur in the academy. There are also important questions about why we have the implicit biases that we do. Aren't we as a society responsible for our sexist, racist, homophobic, and ableist beliefs even if they are implicit in our thinking? My answer here is that there are questions both larger (societal beliefs that inform implicit bias) and smaller (individual responsibility), but that the most practical place to address the issues is at the level of the group in which we find ourselves, at the department and university level.[8]

---

[8] Another advantage of the mechanical responses that I propose in this section seems to be that while it could be very difficult to hold anyone responsible for, for example, the length of time they hold eye contact with someone, it is much easier to hold someone responsible for failing to adhere to a mechanical policy.

4. What Should We Do to Help?

An obvious first step in addressing such bias is to take micro-inequities more seriously, both in our capacities as moral theorists and as advocates for equity in the academy. This doesn't mean, as some have assumed, that we need to take steps to outlaw or legislate against micro-inequities. Even self-regulation doesn't look like it will be particularly effective. Because the whole point is that many such actions occur below the threshold of conscious decision-making, it would be unfair to target individual actions. That said, it's appropriate within the workplace to raise awareness of the problem of micro-inequities, but we need to do it in a way that doesn't involve tracing each and every act back to specific individuals.

There are hard and interesting questions here about collective responsibility and workplace climate that I don't have the expertise to address and that fall outside the scope of this chapter. Cleary, however, there are things that groups can do.

First, as a group we can decide to change some environmental factors that might be affecting our decision-making. If unconscious bias is more of an issue when we face tight time constraints, then we should do what we can to loosen those constraints. In some cases, but not all, we can remove the information that's causing bias to occur. We should all read students' papers anonymously and grade them without access to names. Some things that help may seem at first to be beneath us as serious scholars. It turns out that environmental factors do make a difference. So, for example, being surrounded by pictures of dead white male scholars does influence our decisions.[9] And that's something we can easily fix.

Second, some rather mechanical solutions will turn out to be the right approach, given how it is that the problems occur. For example, my university has a salary anomaly fund to which faculty members can apply (or deans and chairs can apply on their behalf) when they think their salary is anomalously low when compared to faculty members with similar qualifications and achievements. Very often, not surprisingly, women are the beneficiaries of this fund. Some faculty members, with good intentions, lament the existence of this fund, arguing that we ought to be able to get things right the first time. Indeed, we might wonder how such inequities come about and try to fix the process that yields unequal salaries. Yet given that the mistake is likely an aggregate of a number of very small mistakes, sometimes the errors will be hard to find. The committee that decides on anomaly fund salary adjustments is not in any better position regarding implicit bias, but by the time matters make their way to this committee, the mistakes are larger and easier to spot. Let me give one more

---

[9] See Saul, this volume.

example of a rather mechanical solution. It's my solution to the problem of calling on men and women equally. Again, rather than carefully examining my own motives and intentions about who I'm calling on or worrying about effects of my actions, I simply alternate genders on a speakers' list. Sometimes I have done this as well when chairing department meetings or when chairing talks as a way of trying to ensure that women's voices are heard.

Third, we can think about small, positive differences we can make. Mary Rowe and others have also studied successful workplaces that see increased participation and involvement by women, and one notable difference is the presence of micro-affirmations. These are the opposite of micro-inequities and are defined similarly. Writes Rowe:

> Micro-affirmations—apparently small acts which are often ephemeral and hard-to-see, events that are public and private, often unconscious but very effective, which occur wherever people wish to help others to succeed. Micro-affirmations are tiny acts of opening doors to opportunity, gestures of inclusion and caring, and graceful acts of listening. Micro-affirmations lie in the practice of generosity, in consistently giving credit to others—in providing comfort and support when others are in distress, when there has been a failure at the bench, or an idea that did not work out, or a public attack. Micro-affirmations include the myriad details of fair, specific, timely, consistent and clear feedback that help a person build on strength and correct weakness (Rowe 2008, 46).

Fourth, we can extend the range of characters on whose shoulders moral responsibility falls. Maureen Scully and Mary Rowe suggest that we need to train bystanders in the workplace. She writes that "a bystander could be any-one who sees or otherwise becomes aware of behaviour that appears worthy of comment or action" (Scully and Rowe 2009, 1). In the past, much workplace training has focused mainly on three cohorts: people who do or say something (whether positive or negative) that might merit a response; people who are impacted by what is said or done; and supervisors. There is a fourth cohort that is also important: There may be one or more *bystanders* present who can influ-ence the workplace climate. Bystanders can highlight positive acts that might otherwise be invisible or overlooked. They can redirect or de-escalate negative acts that might be problematic. Bystanders might be peers or teammates. They might be subordinate or senior to the person whose comment or behaviour war-rants reaction. Training that encourages "active bystanders" takes into account the different power dynamics and contexts that may be involved. Bystander training is designed to help people in all cohorts to note—and to commend—the achievements of their fellow workers. Such commendations often matter a lot to the person concerned and are thought to be useful in encouraging future socially desirable behaviour.

In conclusion, micro-inequities are not the complete explanation of women's situation in philosophy, but they are part of the problem that we can understand and do something about. At the same time, it is my hope that a better understanding of micro-inequities and their moral significance will be useful for other areas of moral philosophy.

Acknowledgment

Thanks to David Wiens, Tracy Isaacs, Rachel Brown, Fiona Jenkins, Katrina Hutchinson, Holly Lawford-Smith, and the participants at the Under-Represented Groups in Philosophy (SWIP-UK/BPA Conference in Cardiff, November 2010) for comments on various versions of this chapter. Thanks also to the departments of philosophy at the Research School of Social Sciences, Australian National University, and at the University of Otago where I was a visiting faculty member while working on this paper. Thanks as well to very many colleagues in feminist philosophy for comments on early drafts.

References

Bartky, Sandra. 2002. *"Sympathy and solidarity" and other essays.* Lanham, MD: Rowman & Littlefield.

Bishop, Glenys, Helen Beebee, Eliza Goddard, and Adriane Rini. 2013. Appendix 1, this volume.

Brennan, Samantha. 2006. Moral lumps. *Ethical Theory and Moral Practice* 9: 249–263.

Chotiner, Isaac. 2010. Fleet Street blues. Review of *Towards the end of morning*, by Michael Frayn. *The New Republic*, March 3.

Fried, Charles. 1978. *Right and wrong.* Cambridge, MA: Harvard University Press.

Haslanger, Sally. 2008. Changing the ideology and culture of philosophy: not by reason (alone). *Hypatia* 23: 210–223.

Kamm, Frances. 1996. *Morality, mortality: rights, duties, and status.* Toronto: Oxford University Press.

Kernohan, Andrew. 1998. *Liberalism, equality, and cultural oppression.* New York: Cambridge University Press.

Mahony, Rhona. 1995. *Kidding ourselves: breadwinning, babies, and bargaining power.* New York: Basic Books.

Merton, Robert K. 1968. The Matthew effect in science. *Science* 159: 56–63.

Moynahan, Brigid. 2009. Engaging employees: pay attention to messages you're overlooking. *Workforce Diversity Network*, http://www.workforcediversitynetwork.com/docs/Articles/Article_EngagingEmployees_Moynahan_3.09-3.pdf.

Parfit, Derek. 1984. *Reasons and persons.* Toronto: Oxford University Press.

Robbins, Wendy, Rosemary Morgan, John Hollingsworth, Judy Stanley, and Michèle Ollivier. 2001. *Ivory towers: feminist and equity audits.* Ottawa: Canadian Federation for the Humanities and Social Sciences (CFHSS).

Rowe, Mary. 1974. Saturn's rings. In *Graduate and Professional Education of Women.* Washington, DC: American Association of University Women.

Rowe, Mary. 1990. Barriers to equality: the power of subtle discrimination to maintain unequal opportunity. *Employee Responsibilities and Rights Journal* 3: 153–163.

Rowe, Mary. 2008. Micro-affirmations and micro-inequities. *Journal of the International Ombudsman Association* 1: 45–48.

Sandler, Bernice. 1986. *The campus climate revisited: chilly for women faculty, administrators, and graduate students.* Washington, DC: Association of American Colleges.

Scully, Maureen, and Mary Rowe. 2009. Bystander training within organizations. *Journal of the International Ombudsman Association* 2: 1.

Side, Katherine, and Wendy Robbins. 2007. Institutionalizing Inequalities in Canadian Universities: The Canada Research Chairs Program. *NWSA Journal.* Special issue: Women, Tenure, and Promotion. 19(3): 163–81.

Wylie, Alison, Janet R. Jakobsen, and Gisela Fosado. 2007. *Women, work and the academy.* New York: Barnard Center for Research on Women.

Wylie, Alison. 2011. What knowers know well: Women, work and the academy. In *Feminist epistemology and philosophy of science*, ed. Heidi E. Grasswick. New York: Springer.

10

The Silencing of Women
Justine McGill

When those who have the power to name and to socially construct
reality choose not to see you or hear you...when someone with the
authority of a teacher, say, describes the world and you are not in it,
there is a moment of psychic disequilibrium, as if you looked in the
mirror and saw nothing. It takes some strength of soul—and not
just individual strength, but collective understanding—to resist
this void, this non-being, into which you are thrust, and to stand
up, demanding to be seen and heard.

Adrienne Rich

Statistics reveal that women who show aptitude for philosophy nevertheless
abandon study or work in this field at markedly higher rates than men.[1] They
fall silent, as it were, when they might have been expected to go on speaking.
Why? The hypothesis of this chapter is that in some cases, at least, the decision to stop speaking altogether comes after repeated experiences of having
speech acts fail. As J. L. Austin points out, there are many ways in which
a speech act can go wrong or turn out unhappily (Austin 1962). The kinds
of failure and unhappiness that interest me here are those associated with
the sense that the speaker has been 'silenced' and that this silencing is not
an isolated case or accident, but the effect of a culture that is to varying
degrees hostile to or dismissive of women. My contention is that within the
culture of academic philosophy, presuppositions are regularly invoked that
are prejudicial to women's participation. This approach to understanding
silencing is modelled on that found in the work of Rae Langton and Caroline
West (Langton & West 1999). In what follows, I discuss their account of how

---

[1] I refer to the findings of the Australasian Association of Philosophy 2008 Reports on
"Improving the Participation of Women in the Philosophy Profession": http://aap.org.au/
women/reports/index.html [accessed 28/08/2010].

pornography works to silence women and then make use of their illuminating analysis of the mechanisms of silencing to explore the question of how women are silenced in philosophical contexts, as well as what might be done to remedy this.

Some might suppose that this level of analysis is superfluous; the best approach to overcoming gender-based silencing tactics would simply be for women to ignore them and carry on speaking, proving their philosophical skill by cumulative, irrefutable demonstration. At first glance, this appears to be the message of the Soma Sutta, an ancient text that depicts a woman of knowledge confidently overcoming an attempt to silence her. I take these verses as a starting point for my discussion, but argue that on closer analysis, Sister Soma's story indicates that if contemporary women aspire to follow her example, we need more than a liberal feminist approach to overcoming barriers to women's success in philosophy. We also need to recognise and combat the prejudices that linger like shadowy but powerful ghosts in the 'blind men's groves' of contemporary academia, threatening women's ability to survive and flourish in these places.

1. In Blind Men's Groves: Does Gender (Still) Matter?

The Soma Sutta is one of a collection that records the experience and teaching of early Buddhist nuns. This brief text paints the portrait of a woman who seems to have little trouble neutralising the power of negative views about women's capacity for wisdom:

> Then, in the morning, the bhikkhuni Soma dressed and, taking bowl and robe, entered Savatthi for alms. When she had walked for alms in Savatthi and had returned from her alms round, after her meal she went to the Blind Men's Grove for the day's abiding. Having plunged into the Blind Men's Grove, she sat down at the foot of a tree for the day's abiding. Then Mara the Evil One, desiring to arouse fear, trepidation, and terror in the bhikkhuni Soma, desiring to make her fall away from concentration, approached her and addressed her in verse:
> "That state so hard to achieve
> Which is to be attained by the seers,
> Can't be attained by a woman
> With her two-fingered wisdom."
> Then it occurred to the bhikkhuni Soma: "Now who is this that recited the verse—a human being or a non-human being?" Then it occurred to her: "This is Mara the Evil One, who has recited the verse desiring to arouse fear, trepidation, and terror in me, desiring to make me fall away from concentration."

Then the bhikkhuni Soma, having understood, "This is Mara the Evil
One," replied to him in verses:
"What does womanhood matter at all
When the mind is concentrated well,
When knowledge flows on steadily
As one sees correctly into Dhamma.
One to whom it might occur,
'I'm a woman' or 'I'm a man'
Or 'I'm anything at all'—
Is fit for Mara to address."
Then Mara the Evil One, realizing, "The bhikkhuni Soma knows me,"
sad and disappointed, disappeared right there. (Bodhi 1997)

The verse of the Buddhist nun Soma suggests that a woman who is concentrated on the pursuit of wisdom will not be bothered by those who attempt
to disturb her with disparagements or discouragements based on her status
as a woman or any other aspect of identity. She will not be silenced by such
tactics. Instead, her own understanding will allow her to rise confidently above
such claims and calmly demonstrate their falsity, leaving those who attempt to
undermine or distract her, including voices in her own mind, to become sad and
disappointed, and disappear.

Applied to the question of how women working in philosophy might respond
to gender-based disparagement or exclusion, this suggests that women should
not get upset or angry, or allow themselves to be distracted from doing philosophy by any tactics or experiences that tend to make them fearful or doubt their
own abilities. In particular, Soma's story implies that we should not allow ourselves to be seduced into accepting a perspective that insists on gender as significant to the ability to do philosophy. Soma completely sidesteps the question
of the relationship between being female and being able to attain to knowledge
and wisdom. She doesn't attempt to defend herself as a woman or give a more
positive account of the capacities of women. Instead, she directly demonstrates
her own abilities and implies that she is not "fit for Mara to address"—that is,
she will not allow him to define her as a woman or anything else, regardless
of what content or associations, positive or negative, might be attached to his
categories. Among other advantages, this means she doesn't have to concern
herself with the problematic question Simone de Beauvoir poses at the beginning of *The Second Sex*: "What is a woman?"

Soma's supremely calm and confident response to Mara may seem attractive but hard to emulate if you're not a nun warding off Mara, the Lord of
Sensuality, but a woman studying or working in a philosophy department,
dealing with men who do not usually disappear right there and then when you
refute their arguments. It may seem that Soma's strategy is a bit too pure and

otherworldly to be practical and effective in the contemporary secular setting of a university. On more principled grounds, many feminists would insist on the fact that in spite of their aspirations to attain to universal reason, all philosophers are undeniably embodied, and the gendered aspect of embodied experience is something that must be recognized and addressed, not dismissed as irrelevant to philosophical achievement.[2]

On this argument, Soma might even be reproached for buying in to the privileged male philosopher's fantasy that his body doesn't matter, a fantasy traditionally supported by the fact that women or servants do most of the work to keep his body healthy and comfortable, so that his mind is free for more abstract adventures.[3] Mara has won if he has convinced Soma to abandon or devalue what he calls "women's two-fingered wisdom," that is, a wisdom based on practical recognition of the embodied nature of human existence (the two fingers of the expression are said to refer to the two fingers needed to press a grain of rice to see if the rice has been well cooked[4]). On this reading, we might suspect that Mara actually disappears quite pleased with himself, only feigning dejection, because maintaining the fiction that gender makes no difference to one's ability to succeed as a philosopher is one way to cover up the practical problems that make it difficult for women to survive and flourish in this field. It is a view that will tend to stymie from the outset any practical measures to identify and overcome gender-based discrimination or philosophical cultures that are inhospitable to women. It also maintains the elitist view that the philosopher has nothing to learn from the cook, and that practical wisdom is subordinate to more abstract forms of knowledge.

However, if we look at Soma's response more carefully, and also consider that her verse was composed in a context in which the concept of a mind-body split was still many centuries away, we can see that she doesn't claim that womanhood or gendered bodies don't matter at all. Rather she implies that womanhood has no significance under a specific set of conditions, that is

When the mind is concentrated well,
When knowledge flows on steadily
As one sees correctly into Dhamma.[5]

This suggests that we can stop worrying about things like gender once we've established conditions that allow concentration of the mind, an uninterrupted

---

[2] See, e.g., Lloyd 1984; Irigaray 1993.

[3] These days, this is a fantasy that privileged women in the developed world may share, thanks to the fact that much of the menial labour required to produce consumer goods takes place in the developing world.

[4] Venerable Tejadhammo, of the Association of Engaged Buddhists in Sydney, is my source for this interpretation (personal communication, August 2010).

[5] Dhamma is a Pali term used in Buddhism to refer to teachings leading to enlightenment, and also to the laws of nature.

flow of knowledge, and clarity of intellectual and ethical vision (i.e., once we've achieved a peaceful, energized state conducive to philosophical inquiry). However, before these conditions have been attained, we may very well need to take into account the needs of an embodied self. Notice that the sutta begins by mentioning how the bhikkhuni dresses (in a monastic robe) and how she obtains food for the day (by going on an alms round). It also specifies the place where she goes to find enough calm and seclusion to enter into her practice of meditation.

These details indicate that the material needs of this woman have been met before she enters into her philosophical debate with Mara. The way in which her needs are supplied also indicates a positive level of social connectedness: The bhikkhuni's food is provided on a daily basis by a community that is supportive of her way of life. It is worth noting that there is no discernible difference in the way the bhikkhuni Soma has her material needs met and the way a bhikkhu, or male monastic, would have his needs met. This suggests that she finds herself in a social and cultural environment in which men's and women's aspirations to monastic achievements are valued and supported without any distinction based on gender.

To this point, the lesson of Soma's story for women pursuing study or careers in philosophy appears to be that it is essential to ensure equal access to relevant resources, whether material or social. Once this is achieved, then gender ought to—and can finally—be regarded as irrelevant to the pursuit of philosophy, just as Soma suggests that a well-concentrated mind will be immune to identification with either gender. There are some indications that this form of justice has been achieved for women working or hoping to work in philosophy in Australia—for example, statistics indicate that women are appointed to ongoing positions in proportion to the numbers applying, which suggests that any previous bias in selection committees in favour of men has been effectively overcome. We might wonder, nevertheless, whether this is enough to show that women and men have equal access to all relevant resources for succeeding in philosophy. Such doubts are worth pursuing and addressing. But they do not take us beyond the liberal feminist goal of ensuring equal access to resources and structures that in themselves are not interrogated or expected to change in any significant way. Is this as far as Soma's story can take us?

Let us consider the place into which Soma 'plunges' for her day's 'abiding.' It has a significance that is not immediately apparent, but depends on knowledge of its history. The Blind Men's Grove was given this name after a nun was raped here by a group of men. On leaving the grove, the men discovered an unexpected effect of their violence: All of them had become blind. So the bhikkhuni Soma is courageously entering a place in which the threat of sexual violence and male 'blindness' in relation to women have played themselves out in an explicitly embodied way, and not merely in the form of clever arguments put by Mara. This is the space in which she sits down to meditate—a space that,

202 Women in Philosophy

though quiet and secluded, is not remote from the problems of male-female relations in the wider world.

The magical blinding of the rapists of Blind Men's Grove is reminiscent of the self-inflicted blindness of the ancient Greek figure of Oedipus, who puts his eyes out after discovering that he has unwittingly fulfilled the prophecy that he would kill his father and have sex with his mother. This literal blinding is a self-punishment for his previous failure to 'see' in the sense of recognising or understanding the proper form of his relationships with others. In the case of Oedipus, the punishment may seem harsh to us. How could he have avoided his errors when the identity of the other people involved was hidden from him? In light of the modern concept of personal responsibility that is tightly tied to consciousness, Oedipus is innocent, but this does not shield him or others from the distressing consequences of his actions.

Similarly, we might see the actions of the ancient Indian rapists as driven or at least powerfully endorsed by common cultural assumptions about women who spend time alone in forest groves. In this respect, their blindness reflects not exceptional individual failures or faults, but a collective inability to see beyond prejudicial images of women to the reality of a woman's actual capacities and vulnerabilities. The problem is cultural, but this does not shield these individuals from the consequences of their violation of the nun. In acting on the figurative blindness concerning women in their culture, they gave this blindness physical form, harming themselves, as well as their victim.

Is there a similar blindness at work in the world of academic philosophy? Can we identify a culture of prejudicial assumptions about women and their philosophical capacities that causes individuals to treat women poorly, doing harm to women, and in the process compromising their own ability to see or hear clearly (capacities of particular interest to philosophers)? The remainder of this chapter explores this possibility, arguing that such 'blindness' or 'deafness' constitutes a crucial dimension of the problems currently facing women in philosophy departments and elsewhere.

2. The Silencing of Women

Over many centuries, the Western tradition of philosophy has been a conversation between men, in which women's voices have rarely been heard. These days, things are different. Women are able to speak as philosophers, in principle on an equal footing with their male counterparts. But this does not mean that the heritage of centuries during which women were denied the right to philosophical speech has been obliterated, or that prejudicial views of women as intrinsically incapable, or less capable, of doing philosophy have lost all their power. Not so long ago, one could find these opinions overtly expressed by living philosophers, and they remain embedded in the texts of many dead ones.[6]

Even if today, few would explicitly defend such ideas, I argue that they remain in play as implicit assumptions, with the effect that women who attempt to speak philosophically are systematically liable to have their speech acts go wrong in mystifying ways—mystifying because the reason for the failure is not immediately apparent. A woman may find that she is permitted, even encouraged or required to speak, only to have her speech dismissed or ridiculed as incompetent. She may speak and have her speech misinterpreted or ignored in spite (or even because) of the competency she displays. Such responses (or failures to respond) frustrate the aims that motivate speech and can render her effectively, and eventually literally, silent.

Ambiguous modes of silencing in which speech is systematically dismissed or misinterpreted can be more painful to endure than simply being denied the right to speak, because they tend to throw responsibility for the failure of communication back onto the one who has been silenced. Perhaps it is her fault that her speech was not well received; perhaps it really was hopelessly incompetent or uninteresting; perhaps she is personally unsuited to work in philosophy. Or perhaps she is just unloved by the people she is addressing; for reasons of their own, they want her to stop making her philosophical speeches, however competent, to them. In any given case, any or all of these hypotheses may be plausible enough; indeed, some variation on them may seem like the most reasonable explanation to everyone involved.

The tendency to locate personal responsibility for communicative failure with the woman who finds herself silenced, or with other individuals (male or female) who are suspected of personal hostility toward her, turns attention away from the question of collective or cultural responsibility for the silencing or exclusion of women in philosophy. Energies are wasted in debilitating personal doubts and conflicts, and meanwhile, the collective Mara of the philosophical world goes unrecognised. Rather than being banished, he is able to continue his destructive work. Instead, it is the women who one by one disappear, saddened and disappointed by their experiences in academia.

One way to bring the collective dimension of the situation to light is to think of Western philosophy as a 'language game' (the concept is borrowed from Lewis 1979) that commonly involves implicit assumptions that are prejudicial to women. Rae Langton and Caroline West have used a parallel approach in their work on how women can be 'silenced' by the effects of pornography (Langton & West 1999). They show that pornography is a clear and pervasive example of how certain constructed images of women and what women are capable of, or what role they can be expected to play, have effects on real

---

[6] See Lloyd (1984) for a seminal study of the philosophical construction of the thinker as 'man of reason.'

women. Even if individual women do not recognize themselves in these images, they may nevertheless have to struggle with them within the domain of their own identity, as well as in their relations with others. As Langton and West remark, the implications of this interpretative framework "go beyond the debate about pornography" (Langton & West 1999: 305). I adopt it in order to think about how damaging stereotypes or fixed views of women operate in the world of academic philosophy, and what can be done about them.

2.1. LANGTON AND WEST ON HOW WOMEN ARE SILENCED BY PORNOGRAPHY

The starting point for Langton and West's analysis is an American legal debate over whether pornography ought to be protected as free speech. This question arose as the result of a feminist proposal to introduce anti-pornography legislation in the United States, an initiative led by Catherine MacKinnon, a high-profile lawyer and philosopher whose work has been pivotal in bringing about tougher regulation of pornography in Canada. In response to her uncompromising arguments about how pornography subordinates women, the American court responded with an equally uncompromising appeal to the right to free speech, rejecting the proposed legislation on the grounds that it was in breach of the First Amendment. (We can imagine that similarly defensive appeals to freedom of expression might greet any attempts to censor or otherwise control imagery or ideas prejudicial to women in philosophy.) West and Langton seek to occupy the middle ground in the conceptual space staked out by this stark opposition, by showing that the Court's interpretation of pornography *as speech* (a definition rejected by MacKinnon) can be held together with MacKinnon's view that pornography works to silence women.

At the nub of their argument is a view of speech that is influenced by J. L. Austin's theory of speech acts. Austin points out that a lot of speech is not constative—it doesn't make statements that can be assessed as true or false. Rather, many utterances are performative: They are ways of doings things, like getting married, to take one of his favourite examples. If you say "I do," in the course of a marriage ceremony, this utterance isn't true or false, it doesn't report anything about the world, but it does something to change your status and the social organization of your world (Austin 1962).

Langton and West apply this insight to the debate over pornography to make the point that if we follow the Court and consider pornography to be a form of speech, it is necessary to take into account the fact that we "do things with words" and consider not just what pornography might say, but what it is that pornographic speech does, and how it does it. If one of the things it does is to silence women, as Langton and West maintain, then there is a conflict between pornographers' right to speak and women's right to speak that cannot be resolved simply by invoking the right to free

speech: This rhetorical move to defeat proposals for the regulation of pornography ought to fail.

Political philosophers such as Ronald Dworkin who defend pornography as
an exercise of free speech compare it to speech "advocating that women should
occupy inferior roles" or expressing an opinion that "women are submissive, or
enjoy being dominated, or should be treated as if they did" (Dworkin 1991: 104,
105). These messages may be unpalatable, but they think we shouldn't attempt
to censor them; if we want to combat them, we ought to do so by speaking up
against them. As good liberals, we should counter these views with our own
persuasive arguments. We should let the Lord of Sensuality have his say, and
then do our best to demolish his perspective with superior logic. One problem
with this approach is that in our society, logic seems to have little power against
Mara's 'speech acts'. The video porn industry in the U.S. is worth substantially more than Hollywood,[7] and with the Internet, pornography is more readily available than ever before. Nevertheless, on this view, pornography doesn't
silence anyone; it just presents a set of views that seem to be extremely popular.

If this approach doesn't seem entirely satisfying, you might think that this is
because a mistake has been made at the outset in supposing that pornography
is properly considered as speech. Do pornographers really want to persuade us
of anything that can be compared to a political position? Aren't they just trying to stimulate certain libidinous responses? Doesn't pornography operate on
a less than fully conscious, fully rational level? From this perspective, we might
still be skeptical that pornography silences women, but instead concerned that
it could lead to problems of addiction that might inhibit the free and rational aspects of the speech or choice of which a regular user of pornography is
capable. The real problem might be that users of pornography who indulge in
pleasure gained from seeing women sexually degraded and humiliated begin
to lose their sight, like the men of Blind Men's Grove—the repetitive power of
pornographic imagery inhibits their ability to see beyond this to appreciate the
ways in which living women and men differ from the images. On this interpretation, pornography doesn't silence women; rather, it incrementally blinds the
people who use it (whether they are men or women).

This could be said to amount to the same thing, however, because the sense
of silencing that interests West and Langton is not literal. It's obvious that
our society is flooded with pornography. It's also obvious that women are still
speaking. We haven't literally fallen silent. But it may be the case that along
with pornographically induced blindness comes an etiologically related deafness. The people affected can no longer hear women's speech clearly, because
the sight of a woman's body triggers pornographic images that interfere with

---

[7] See David Foster Wallace, 2005: 4–5. In 2005, he estimated the value of the U.S. adult-film
industry at $3.5–4 billion, compared with $2–2.5 billion for legitimate mainstream American
cinema.

the ability to pay attention to what she is saying. So a woman may speak and not be heard, or be misheard, or be heard but ignored. When such responses become systematic, they amount to a comprehensive silencing of women, as women's speech itself becomes equivalent to silence. Under certain circumstances, it may become impossible for a woman to say 'no' to an unwanted sexual advance, for instance. Of course, she can still utter the word 'no,' but it will not be heard as signifying refusal, or as signifying anything at all. It is not only pornography that can give rise to this kind of problem; any strongly held prejudice will tend to operate in this way. No matter what an individual who is targeted by prejudice says, this person's speech will be filtered or distorted or completely silenced by the operation of the powerful image with which he or she is identified by others, and perhaps even by him or herself.

This is the kind of result that concerns Langton and West, but they take a different route to arrive at the problem of the silencing of women. Rather than supposing that the power of pornography operates at an unconscious level, they grant the legal contention that pornography can be considered to be a form of speech and remain open to the idea that it produces its "effects on belief, desires and behaviour in a manner that is not utterly different from other forms of speech." (305) They then draw on David Lewis's model of speech situations as language games to analyse how pornography works as a language game that has the effect of silencing women.

Like other games, language games are rule-governed. But one of the most intriguing things about language games is that they include a 'rule of accommodation,' which, simply put, operates to make any unchallenged move acceptable. If I say something and no one challenges it, it becomes a valid move, and will shift the conversational 'score' of the game. An important way in which new moves are accommodated is by importing implicit presuppositions that support them as valid. In order to make sense of the language game of pornography, the viewer is typically led to supply presuppositions such as the idea that women are inferior to men, that they are sexual products on a market in which men are the buyers, and that sexual violence is normal and legitimate (gang rape is the example that most concerns Langton and West). It is worth noting that such presuppositions will be all the more readily supplied if they are "in the air," as it were, already familiar, although possibly unconscious elements of a shared culture.

Langton and West point out that in all language games, presuppositions are typically harder to challenge than explicit statements. Because they are implied, the suggestion is not only that they are true, but that their truth is something that can be taken for granted: "it is widely known, a matter of shared belief among the participants in the conversation, which does not need to be asserted outright" (309). This analysis suggests two reasons why the presuppositions implied in language games are powerful—they are elicited from the listener, rather than imposed upon him or her explicitly, so they become part of a move in the game in which the listener actively, if inarticulately, participates. And when the listener makes this move, he or she has a sense that it is initiated and supported by others. It's not an individual decision for which a person might feel personally responsible, but a comfortable (or perhaps anxious) joining in, a going with the flow.

If pornography is viewed as a language game that operates largely at the level of implicit presupposition, this goes some way to explaining both how it is that pornography says things about women and why the presuppositions it introduces are powerful enough to persist in other speech situations in ways that prevent women from making certain intended moves in these different but connected language games. Women may speak, but in a social language game that is to any significant extent continuous with pornography, there will be certain speech acts they can no longer successfully or easily perform. Langton and West give some examples: A woman may say 'no' in a sexual context, or she may describe a sexual ordeal with the intention of seeking justice or making a protest, but in each of these cases, her intended move may fail to count as 'correct play.'

Interestingly, the rule of accommodation seems to fail at this point. It is not the case that the woman's move in the language game is accepted unless and until challenged. Certain implicit presuppositions governing the situation have become more powerful than the explicit utterances of the speaker, and she is unable to import the different presuppositions that are required to support her own intended move. Langton and West explain this by concluding that women, "as participants in conversations where rape myths are presupposed as a component of conversational score, are silenced and subordinated" (318).

I would question whether women are even granted the status of 'participant' in these kinds of conversations. Insofar as the consumption of pornography of the type described by Langton and West can be understood as involving a conversation, this is a conversation between men, and one of its most fundamental presuppositions is that women are not the kind of creatures that are fit to take an active part in it. Women, or rather women's bodies, are the major topic of the conversation; women are not participants in it. Whatever men's pornography may 'say' about women, the content of its presuppositions is structurally related to the fact that it systematically excludes women from the conversation.[8]

This provides another way to understand why the liberal argument put forward by Dworkin and others fails. Pornographic speech, whatever its content, whether derogatory or appreciative of women, is not equivalent to statements of opinion expressed on the open market of liberal democratic political debate.

---

[8] Of course, this is not true of all pornography, some of which is directed toward women or both genders. However, these (rarer) kinds of pornography do not raise the issues that concern Langton and West.

It does not make statements or import presuppositions that women are invited to debate and counter with their own views. A story in a men's magazine describing a gang rape is not attempting to communicate anything to women (this is one of the examples examined by Langton and West). It is not designed to elicit women's agreement or disagreement with presuppositions such as 'Rape is acceptable and enjoyable sexual behaviour.' Rather, it represents a private mode of conversation between men in which women do not have standing to participate.

Women can speak, in other contexts, *about* pornography, although even this language move is likely to be considered ridiculous and annoying by many male users of pornography. But women, as women, cannot take part in the pornographic language game as it goes on between men. If, as Langton and West suggest, this language game extends into the courtroom, the bedroom, the world of publishing, and so on, it is logical that when this takes place, women will find that they are not able to engage effectively in the conversation as it is carried on in these contexts either. A woman's speech will either be ignored, treated as incompetent, or it will be heard as if it had been scripted by a man. In the last case, a host of assumptions common to the pornographic language game will be used to reinterpret the sense of her speech, against her own intentions. Thus a woman's indignant or clinical description of a sexual ordeal she has undergone can be remarketed as more pornography (see Langton and West 1999: 314).

If Langton and West are correct in contending that a significant and disturbing effect of pornography is to silence women, then in a society in which pornography has become a major and growing cultural influence, we are exposed to a real threat of having women's power to speak eroded. The silencing of women in pornographic 'language games' is likely to reinforce or ignite the potential for women to be silenced in other communicative situations. The world of academic philosophy, however refined it may be in some respects, is not immune to this problem, but such spill-over effects of pornographic speech in academia are not my central concern here.

Rather, I wish to draw upon this analysis of how pornography works to exclude and silence women to shed light on how women are silenced by images and presuppositions that are commonly accepted features of philosophical discourse. As shown by the debate over pornography, such silencing is invisible from the perspective of a purely liberal analysis. If we do not go beyond this, the persistent, systematic failure of women's speech acts remains mysterious, and will consequently tend to be explained by reference to crude prejudices that reinforce rather than illuminate the problem. To understand the silencing of women in philosophy requires a focus not just on the content of what is said in philosophical speech, but on what such speech acts do: whom they include or exclude, whose points of view they valorise, and whose perspectives are rendered incomprehensible or simply inaudible.

2.2. THE SILENCING OF WOMEN IN THE LANGUAGE
GAME OF PHILOSOPHY

Like pornography, philosophy is a language game that tends to invoke assumptions that are prejudicial to women's participation. This is not to suggest that the assumptions invoked in the two language games are the same or even comparable; the extreme and often violent objectification of women that takes place in much heterosexual pornography has no legitimate equivalent in philosophical discourse. The presuppositions that function to silence women in philosophical contexts are much more limited in scope; they point only to the idea that women are incapable or less capable than men of philosophically valuable speech. Compared to the treatment of women in pornographic 'speech,' this may seem a relatively benign prejudice, but it is capable of handicapping and even driving women out of the highly culturally valued domain of philosophy.

When and how are presuppositions prejudicial to women's participation invoked in philosophy? A crucial factor is that like pornography, philosophy has traditionally been a language game reserved largely for men. In philosophical texts and symposiums that are dominated by male voices, the reader or listener may well be led to supply implicit presuppositions that involve the idea that women are unlikely or incompetent participants in philosophical conversations.

How does one make sense of the fact that almost all seminal texts in the 'language game' of Western philosophy are written by men? When this question is not raised and addressed thoughtfully, it is likely to be met by the unexamined assumption that women simply aren't as good as men at philosophy. As we have seen in the case of pornography, such a view need never be explicitly articulated; indeed, its influence in leading to the silencing of women will typically be greater and more difficult to combat (and to recognize) when it is not. When such ideas come into play, the results will parallel those we have seen in the discussion of the effects of pornography: a woman's expression of philosophical ideas is likely to be ignored, treated as incompetent (by others or herself), or to be heard as if her speech had been scripted by a man.

Helen Beebee provides a thought-provoking example of how this happens in contemporary analytic philosophy. In conceptual analysis, certain intuitions (about what counts as knowledge, for instance) that are standardly valorized as typical or shared turn out upon investigation to be more widely shared by men than by women (see Beebee's chapter in this volume). The authority of the philosophical text or teacher operates to trigger the implicit assumption that those who do not share the intuition—predominantly women—are philosophically deficient. This example is useful, because it shows that it can take considerable effort even to see that assumptions that are prejudicial to women in philosophy are being evoked in an apparently gender-neutral text or teaching environment. Students or readers who feel excluded by the assertion that 'we share' a certain intuition will not usually articulate this, or if they do, they will commonly be heard as expressing confusion that calls for clarification of the philosophical point being made, rather than an alternative perspective that poses a philosophical challenge to that teaching. Silenced by the effect of the assumption, they will not discover how many others also feel excluded—or that the exclusion is systematically related to gender, and not dependent on personal failings or differences.

The imagery and examples chosen by philosophers to illustrate their theoretical ideas are another point at which signals are emitted regarding who is granted standing to participate in the philosophical conversation.[9] Consider John Searle's oft-quoted example of metaphor: 'Sally is a block of ice.' As Robyn Ferrell testifies, such an example can engender 'wordless anxiety' in a woman attempting to engage with philosophical thought, an anxiety that will do nothing to enhance her ability to produce successful speech acts. While Searle, disavowing the sexual innuendo of his example, explains that the meaning of the metaphor is that Sally is 'unusually unemotional and unresponsive,' Ferrell suggests that the woman in philosophy evoked and provoked by Sally might alternatively ignite 'as hysterical and alive to paranoia in every philosophical utterance.'[10]

Ferrell's description of Sally invites the suspicion that the real problem here might not be the suggestiveness of the metaphor so much as the sensitivity of the woman who (over)reacts to it. To extend the point, might talk of implied presuppositions that operate to silence women, while possibly useful in the case of pornography, amount to a form of paranoia when applied to the more refined and rational discourse of philosophy? The skeptic might wonder whether it is the philosophical text or the hysterical feminist gloss on it that is liable to provoke the kind of anxiety that might make an impressionable woman feel that she has no place in a philosophy department. Have we lost sight of the example set by women like Soma who calmly demonstrate the ability to rise above the effects of potentially disconcerting modes of speech?

If women in philosophy are disconcerted to the point of hysteria by examples like that of the metaphorical Sally, I would suggest that this reflects not merely personal sensitivity, but a predictable, even inevitable response to the stresses inherent in a context that proclaims to be open to and supportive of women's participation, but regularly undermines women's abilities to 'do things with words.' Hysteria and paranoia are precisely the symptoms to be expected in a situation in which women, particularly articulate women who reasonably expect to succeed, repeatedly find that their speech acts fail for no easily identifiable reason. Apparently innocuous images like that of Sally then come to

---

[9] The work of Michèle Le Dœuff is especially instructive in this regard (see Le Dœuff 1990).

[10] These remarks by Robyn Ferrell come from an unpublished conference paper "Sally is a block of ice: Revis(it)ing the figure of woman in philosophy."

seem like coded signs of secret rules in a language game that women cannot win because in spite of appearances, they haven't been given a fair chance to play.

It is important not to succumb to a hysterical or paranoid perspective, but it is equally important not to dismiss such reactions as indications of merely personal weakness. Evidence of bias against women in philosophy is provided not only in anecdotes of women's experiences, but also in statistics that indicate that the introduction of blind peer review of articles submitted to philosophy journals results in an immediate increase in the number of papers authored by women that are accepted for publication.[11] This shows that blind review is useful in excluding gender bias and allowing philosophers to appreciate the worth of women's work, but it also confirms the hypothesis that when philosophers can see that it is a woman who is writing or speaking, prejudicial presuppositions frequently intervene to distort their vision or dull their hearing. Artificially blinding ourselves in order to mitigate this problem is a crude and partial, if ancient, solution. Thorough-going change will only be achieved when the prejudicial presuppositions that create the problem have been removed.

3. Overcoming Silencing: A Middle Way

What can be done to dispel the damaging presuppositions that tend to silence women in philosophy? The proposal to ban or regulate the 'language game' in question, which may appear viable to some as an answer in the case of pornography, seems clearly undesirable in the case of philosophy. Nor is it enough to suggest that women should simply try harder to make their perspectives heard. It is vital to acknowledge that, just as no amount of personal integrity could shield a nun from the danger of being raped while meditating in Blind Man's Grove, no amount of personal brilliance, emotional fortitude, or sheer hard work can protect a woman from being silenced in a context in which implicit shared assumptions about the relevance of her gender operate to leach her words of their power. The suppression or distortion of women's speech is a collective, cultural problem that needs to be addressed as such.

In order to think through how this might be achieved without compromising the freedom of thought and speech that are a crucial condition for philosophical inquiry, let us turn back to conceptual resources developed in the debate over how to address the silencing of women by pornography. In this context, Judith Butler argues that the problem of silencing will not be solved by legislating "lines of necessary continuity among intention, utterance, and deed" (Butler 1997: 93). This is how she characterizes Langton's approach to

---

[11] See the findings of the Australasian Association of Philosophy 2008 Reports on "Improving the Participation of Women in the Philosophy Profession": http://aap.org.au/women/reports/index.html [accessed 28/08/2010].

the question of how to overcome practices of silencing and guarantee effective political agency and citizenship (in Langton 1993). More generally, Butler opposes the Habermasian solution of introducing "idealizing suppositions" that would constrain in advance the kinds of interpretations to which utterances are subject (Habermas 1987: 198).

Instead, she insists on the "equivocity of the utterance," which "means that it might not always mean in the same way, that its meaning might be turned or derailed in some significant way" (Butler 1997: 87). The modes of silencing encountered by women in philosophy depend in part on this kind of equivocity. They are one way in which the meaning of utterances can be significantly "derailed." However, for Butler this is not a reason to attempt to eliminate equivocity. She maintains that some of the most promising forms of contemporary political agency arise from strategies that exploit the equivocal nature of speech, turning the language of power against itself, interrupting and redirecting it, just as it interrupts and redirects the speech of the less powerful. This leads her to a conclusion that is not far from that of the liberal theorists who see pornography as speech that is entitled to protection and should be combated not by censorship but by alternative views traded on the free market of democratic discourse: "Insurrectionary speech becomes the necessary response to injurious language, a risk taken in response to being put at risk, a repetition in language that forces change" (163).

Butler's analysis is helpful in that it points to the fact that the equivocity of speech is basic to its power. To attempt to eliminate it would be like trying to freeze the ocean. She is also eloquent in evoking the inevitable risks associated with the act of speech: "[I]f one always risks meaning something other than what one thinks one utters, then one is, as it were, vulnerable in a specifically linguistic sense to a social life of language that exceeds the purview of the subject who speaks" (87). This kind of vulnerability is necessary and productive.

But some speakers are vulnerable in more than "a specifically linguistic sense," and the social life that conditions such vulnerability is not merely a matter of language. It is also a matter of social and material resources, physical space, and the reverberations of acts of kindness or violence. The structure of this extra-linguistic social life affects the question of who is given the chance to cultivate the capacity for skilled and effective speech. Along with the "social life of language," it also generates implicit presuppositions that determine how speech acts are received. Butler may well be right that the best counter to injurious language is insurrectionary speech, but this does not address the question of what to do about injurious presuppositions that remain unspoken, but which nevertheless leach explicit utterances of the power to achieve their intended effects. Insurrectionary speech can work only if it manages to cross the threshold created by the kinds of silencing we have been considering. To achieve this, a battle also needs to be fought at the level of the implicit presuppositions that govern whose speech can be heard as they intend.

I think Butler is right when she suggests that it is vain and dangerous to attempt to "legislate" how people speak and listen to one another. The silencing of women in philosophy is a problem that necessarily exceeds the purview of the legal reforms that have been successfully used to overcome other hurdles to women's participation in this field. On the other hand, it is not clear that risky, inflammatory speech is the key to a solution here. Insurrections tend to be bloody and exhausting; there is typically a high price to be paid for the temporary triumph of inflicting injury on the powerful. Guerrilla warfare, if superficially more glamorous and exciting, is no more attractive in the long term as a model for bringing about change than the imposition of dictatorial control.

Rather than attempt to combat silencing practices through mechanisms of control or provocation, I would suggest that lasting change is more likely to be brought about simply by patiently and persistently exposing the unexamined presuppositions that structure these practices, as well as the harm they do in inhibiting both the success of women in philosophy and the free development of ideas. If an unexamined life is not worth living, an unexamined supposition is not worth relying upon; any philosopher will agree to that. This is an attitude not notably shared by the consumers of pornography or respected on the battlegrounds of politics; in the field of philosophy, on the other hand, it represents a valuable resource for bringing about cultural change. Here, the unarticulated notions that compromise women's ability to speak effectively can be held up to the transformative light of philosophical scrutiny.

For example, the effects of gender-specific language and imagery in philosophical texts and discussions can be consciously noted and examined.[12] The possibility of bias in favour of men's voices in philosophy can similarly be noted, tested, and challenged, for example, by observing the effect of blind reviews of articles for publication and similar practices when marking students' work (or when students assess one another's work). Attention can also be given to the question of whether women's works are represented on course reading lists (and if not, why not?). More generally, it is valuable simply to raise the issue of silencing and encourage individuals to speak up about it when they feel it is happening, in order to find solutions adapted to the particular circumstances. As in Soma's dialogue with Mara, the crucial first step is to recognise and name the problem. Once this occurs, the presuppositions that work to silence women in philosophy are likely to appear sad and disappointing, to philosophers of any gender, and consequently to disappear.

---

[12] The most memorable and transformative philosophy course I took as an undergraduate was a course on philosophical and feminist biblical hermeneutics. The teacher, Dr. Erin White, asked us to practice a reading strategy that involved consciously noting the presence and effect of any gender-specific language in the texts we were reading for this course and any others we were following. It was a simple instruction, but one that had a dramatic effect in raising my awareness of this aspect of philosophical writing and its ambivalent effects.

Conversely, as long as prejudicial views of women go unchallenged, they rein-force the silencing of women across our culture as a whole. Efforts to challenge and defuse the power of negative attitudes toward women in privileged contexts, such as philosophy departments, are important not only because of the interests that a small group of women have in being able to pursue careers in philosophy, although this might be considered reason enough to make such efforts. They are important also to the message that is carried out beyond the academy to the wider society, in which the needs of women to have their speech respected and understood by men are connected to fundamental issues of safety and physical integrity. Until women's voices receive the same respect as men's in the elite domains of philosophy and religion, in which the most abstract forms of knowledge and deepest values of our culture are defined and debated, the chance that women's speech will be fully and reliably effective in other areas of life is slight.

References

Austin, J. L. (1962) *How to do things with words*, the William James Lectures delivered at Harvard University in 1955, ed. J. O. Urmson, Oxford, UK: Clarendon.

Bodhi, Bhikkhu (1997) *Discourses of the Ancient Nuns (BL 143)*, translated from the Pali by Bhikkhu Bodhi, Kandy, LK: Buddhist Publication Society.

Butler, Judith (1997) *Excitable Speech: A Politics of the Performative*, New York and London: Routledge.

Dworkin, Ronald (1991) "Two Concepts of Liberty," in Isaiah Berlin: A Celebration, eds. Edna and Avishai Margalit, London: Hogarth.

Habermas, Jürgen (1987) *The Philosophical Discourse of Modernity*, trans. Federick Law-rence, Cambridge, MA: MIT Press.

Irigaray, Luce (1993) *An Ethics of Sexual Difference*, Ithaca, NY: Cornell University Press.

Langton, Rae (1993) "Speech Acts and Unspeakable Acts," *Philosophy and Public Affairs*, 22(4): 293–330.

Langton, Rae, and West, Caroline (1999) "Scorekeeping in a pornographic language game," *Australasian Journal of Philosophy*, 77(3): 303–319.

Le Dœuff, Michèle (1990) *Hipparchia's Choice: An Essay Concerning Women, Philosophy etc.*, trans. Trista Selous, Oxford, UK: Blackwell.

Lewis, David (1979) "Scorekeeping in a Language Game," *Journal of Philosophical Logic*, 8: 339–359.

Lloyd, Genevieve (1984) *The Man of Reason: 'Male' and 'Female' in Western Philosophy*, London: Methuen.

Rich, Adrienne (1986) *Blood, Bread and Poetry: Selected Prose, 1979-1985*, New York: W. W. Norton.

Wallace, David Foster (2005) "Big Red Son," in *Consider the Lobster and Other Essays*, London: Abacus.

11

Finding Time for Philosophy
Michelle Bastian

In his collection of essays, *Infancy and History*, Giorgio Agamben makes the intriguing claim that "every culture is first and foremost a particular experience of time and no new culture is possible without an alteration in this experience" (1993, 91). This suggests that in responding to the question 'what needs to change?' one answer would be 'the particular experience of time that informs the culture of philosophy'. In many ways, this claim chimes strangely with much of contemporary philosophy, where time is often treated either as an objective phenomenon (as within much of metaphysics) or in its subjective and/or experiential aspects (as within phenomenologically inspired philosophy). Within sociology and anthropology, however, there is a well-developed recognition that our experiences and understandings of time are influenced and shaped by social life. The study of 'social time', in particular, seeks to understand "the ways in which social experience defines the forms, meanings and relevance of time" (Greenhouse 1996, 25). Importantly, while within philosophy, 'public time' has often been treated as synonymous with an objective, apolitical clock time, work in the social sciences suggests that time plays a much more varied and significant role in public life, including in social methods of inclusion and exclusion (e.g., Nespor et al. 2009; Urciuoli 1992) and political legitimation (e.g., Boyarin 1994; Greenhouse 1989; Hutchings 2008; Lloyd 2000). Thus in my work (e.g., 2009, 2011), I am interested in developing a dialogue between philosophical accounts of time on the one hand, and accounts of social time developed in anthropology and sociology on the other, in the belief that this work provides a rich and underutilised body of research that has important implications for political and ethical philosophy, as well as potentially significant challenges for metaphysics.

In this chapter, then, I want to bring insights from the social sciences about the role of time in exclusionary practices into debates around the underrepresentation of women in philosophy. I suggest that part of what supports the exclusionary culture of philosophy is a particular approach to time, and thus that changing this culture requires that we also change its time. Importantly, although the naturalness of categories such as sexuality, race, and gender have been widely challenged, the time of social life is only rarely treated as a normative and politicised discourse within philosophy. As a result, there continues to be an assumption that social life plays out against a backdrop of 'real' or 'objective' time that is itself linear, one-dimensional, and all-encompassing. However, this is far from being the case, as is demonstrated in a wide variety of work, in areas such as political theory (Pierson 2004; Connolly 2005), feminist theory (Diprose 2009; Hesford and Diedrich 2008), post-colonial theory (Chakrabarty 1992; Ganguly 2004), and queer theory (Dinshaw et al. 2007; Freeman 2010). What this work suggests is that understanding time as an all-encompassing, linear, immutable succession of moments is deeply problematic, particularly when utilised in the explanation of social life. Thus, in this chapter, I argue that assuming that time is the same for everyone works to hide a number of exclusions produced within professional philosophy. In particular, such an assumption denies the diverse and contradictory temporal processes that characterise the profession. I suggest that linear temporality is only available to certain types of idealised persons and as a result should be read not as an objective account of how things are, but as a normative and political discourse that is supportive of some while excluding many others.

Ways of thinking about and enacting time underpin a myriad of other elements of social life including identity, causal explanations, history, social coordination, and projections into the future. Thus, in order to show how understandings of time are bound up in mechanisms of exclusion, I analyse a number of key issues that have already been highlighted as reasons for women's exclusion from philosophy, in order to draw out the way particular assumptions about time compound these issues further. I begin with Christine Battersby's challenge to the notion that embodied experiences make little difference to the philosophy one produces. Inspired by her critique of the Kantian conception of space for its male bias, I develop a similar challenge to his conception of time that helps to illustrate the point that the experience of time as linear is far from being universal. I then move to the question of gender schemas, particularly the seeming disconnect between the schemas for 'woman' and 'philosopher'. In this case, I am particularly interested in the importance of the iterative, rather than linear, character of identity. Finally, I look at issues to do with the history and future of philosophy in order to question the way women are continually refused a place in the flow of philosophy's time. I conclude by arguing that a more representative philosophy would be guided by a more complex approach to time, one that would recognise and actively support the multiple and contradictory temporalities that must be negotiated by the discipline and those who practice it.

1. Embodying Philosophy

Despite the extensive work feminist philosophers have produced on the subject, the notion that the underrepresentation of women is not a problem because philosophy is supposedly not affected by contingent factors such as gender continues to arise in discussions on the issue. Yet, as Helen Beebee argues in this volume, one of the most central tools of analytical philosophy—the notion of intuition—cannot be treated as non-situated or free from gender bias. Even the ideal of reason itself has been shown to be intertwined with idealised notions of masculinity and the repudiation of feminised traits (Lloyd 1993). For Christine Battersby (1998), taking sexed embodiment seriously troubles many of the assumptions that permeate metaphysics. In her *Phenomenal Woman*, Battersby argues that identity, space, and time have been theorised from the vantage point of a particular idealised body. She questions the pervasive treatment of the male body as the norm, and instead explores how metaphysics would be transformed if philosophy's starting point was the body that could give birth. Importantly, she is careful not to assume that all women can or want to give birth, but contends that once the embodied experiences of women are taken into account, traditional metaphysical accounts can no longer be viewed as objective or universal. She suggests that these seemingly logical or intuitive accounts are not derived from a shared experience of the world, available to all, but are accounts specific to an idealised sense of male embodiment (1998, 39).

In a particularly striking example, Battersby describes the way different mobilisations of the Kantian account of embodiment (where space is external to the self) create a "shock of strangeness", leaving her to wonder "what it would be like to inhabit a body *like that*" (1998, 41). Referring to Mark Johnson's and George Lakoff's work in cognitive semantics in particular, she questions their assumption that a fundamental characteristic of embodiment is the experience of boundedness or containment (1998, 40). Instead, she discusses her own experiences of her body as multiple and fragmented, where different 'zones' become differentiated and may war with each other (1998, 44). Further, extrapolating from interviews with female anorexics who experience their bodies as alienated and threatening, she points out that even the normalised female body is experienced as permeable and only ambiguously protected against the 'outside' (1998, 44–46). These and other examples in Battersby's work suggest that the notion that there is a clear boundary between the internal and the external, between inner time and external space, does not rest upon an intuition that is immediately obvious to all, but rather only to specific kinds of humans. As a result, her work challenges the failure of much of philosophy to recognise the way it has been developed in reference to a very particular experience of embodiment and so needs to interrogate its claims to universality.

Although Battersby's focus in the arguments I've cited is space in particular, I want to suggest that the Kantian account of time also arguably draws on an idealised account of embodiment. I, too, feel a 'shock of strangeness' when I read Kant's account of time. His assumption that linear time is an intuition common to us all, regardless of language, culture, or embodied experience both ignores the cultural particularity of his account of time and fails to encompass the experiences of many of those within Western culture itself. To summarise briefly, Kant suggests in the *Critique of Pure Reason* that our experience of time accords with a number of axioms, specifically that (1) all parts of time belong to the same time; (2) no specific moment of time is simultaneous with any other, but is always successive; and (3) that time is one-dimensional (1998 [1787] A31/B47). Like Battersby, I can't help but wonder what it would be like to inhabit a body that experienced time *like that*. In relation to my own experiences, Kant's characterisation of time is profoundly counterintuitive. The problem of negotiating the clash between social expectations around motherhood and professional expectations in philosophy—an issue that is recognised as an important element in the underrepresentation of women in philosophy— provides an illustrative example. As an embodied woman philosopher caught between (at least) two sets of social expectations, each with their own version of which events are significant in my past and future, and their own accounts of which actions I must enact in the present, I am arguably caught between two different times. Because, as I draw out below, the recommended ways of living one's time for mothers and for philosophers often appear to be in direct opposition. Attempting to fit both into one's life often produces a sense of time as multiple, disjunctive, and inadequate, rather than one-dimensional and all-encompassing.

The connection between particular modes of embodiment and assumptions about the flow of time was brought home to me quite vividly by a story presented on the "BBC Breakfast Show" in 2009 on the increase of Down's Syndrome births. In a story in disagreement with itself, the presenters reiterated the common narrative of the failure of women to have children 'at the right time' and recounted, once again, the dramatic increase in the likelihood of a Down's pregnancy between the ages of 30 and 40. However, the presenters also touched on an earlier debate over whether the U.K. had become a more welcoming place for people with Down's Syndrome. On the one hand, the apparent 'punishments' of mistiming pregnancy were reiterated, and women were admonished not to leave pregnancies until too late. And yet, on the other hand, the presenters appeared to be suggesting that this threat was simultaneously a thing of the past, given the supposedly more positive and supportive environment in the U.K.

For me, these kinds of stories, which form part of the incessant recounting of the dramatic drop-off in fertility rates after 30, create a context in which I, as a female human "tied to a body that could birth", do not meaningfully experience time in accordance with any of the three axioms Kant attributes to it. First, my experiences suggest to me that all parts of time *do not* belong to the same time. My time is marked by ruptures. Upon turning 30, I was forever divided from the possibility of being a woman who enacted a timely procreation and instead became the 30-plus woman who can only procreate in an untimely fashion, having spent too much time on selfish occupations such as postgraduate study.

Second, I *do* experience different moments of time *as* simultaneous with each other. Specifically, the supposed timely moment in the mid-to-late 20s is also the same untimely moment when pregnant employees and students are given up on by their employers or supervisors as wasted talent. In my experience, there is no right time. Due to the competing messages received from the different institutions that shape one's life and the diverging understandings of social time implicit within these institutions, a decision I might now make about having a child would be both too early and too late *at the same time*.

Finally, I would argue that within this context, it is in fact *not* commonplace to experience time as one-dimensional. Instead, as sociologist Georges Gurvitch argued, "[S]ocial life always takes place in divergent and often contradictory manifestations of social time" (1964, 13). As already suggested above, this is because within the variety of social relationships and social institutions that we participate in, 'time' comes to be expressive of different values and expectations. Time is instead experienced as multiple and contradictory.

What I would like to suggest then, is that Kant's account of the intuition of time and its rules is not so intuitive when one examines the competing times that need to be negotiated within embodied social life. Although I do not have the space here to explore the full implications of this analysis, it raises questions about the neutrality and universality of Kant's account, suggesting that embodied experience is not external to philosophy, but shapes some of its most central concepts. Further, it suggests that insofar as accounts of time such as Kant's guide a commonsense notion of public time, and particularly, guide the implicit temporal assumptions that structure institutional life, then they actually work to hide the competing values and contradictions that must be negotiated by those who do not embody the 'typical' philosopher. Importantly, as I explore in the rest of this chapter, assuming that time is the same for everyone means that disadvantages faced by philosophers negotiating the multiple and often conflicting times they experience can be read as nonsensical or misguided, or simply go unrecognised.

2. Timing Professionalism

Looking at work already available on the issue of women in philosophy provides further examples of how seemingly commonsense notions of time mask inequalities within philosophy in multiple ways. The first follows directly from the above discussion and helps to further illustrate the way the clash between the health profession's recommended timeline for mothers and the academic timeline for philosophers is often unrecognised, or is addressed inadequately. In her contribution to Linda Martín Alcoff's collection on women in philosophy, *Singing in the Fire*, Martha Nussbaum recounts the difficulties of being a junior academic and a mother. She writes that although the birth of her daughter created a great number of changes for her, "meanwhile, in the philosophy department...life went on as if no children existed. Colloquia were routinely scheduled at five, after the childcare centres closed" (2003: 104). This example is particularly interesting, because it highlights a form of exclusion that is not necessarily explicit or deliberate. Rather, it rests on an inadequate understanding of the way something as simple as scheduling provides a medium for supporting some ways of life over others. The philosopher whose only key responsibility is to co-ordinate themselves with other philosophers may thus find it very easy to experience time as a one-dimensional medium that encompasses all their important activities. However, for those who need to coordinate themselves with other philosophers *and* dependants *and* care providers *and* other institutions such as schools, sports associations, healthcare providers, etc., time is multiple and conflicting.[1]

Further, although it might seem that an adequate solution to this problem would be to reschedule meetings at a better time, this is not actually a sufficient response to the types of inequalities being produced in the clash of responsibilities. To assume so would be to overlook the broader social meanings that are attributed to time use. Timing is not simply about logistical coordination, but also signals whether one conforms to a variety of social norms. The importance of timing in regard to hospitality, gift-giving, or forgiveness provides good examples of this. In this particular case, one's use of time feeds into broader understandings of what it is to be a professional, where the ability to fulfil this role is bound up with conforming to modes of time use. Specifically, even while the professional may nominally work according to a schedule, they are nonetheless expected to be ready to act in their professional capacity at any time.[2] In a context where one must signal one's constant availability, to be unavailable thus comes to be construed as being unprofessional.

Importantly, this does not affect everyone equally, but disadvantages those more tenuously recognised as professionals because of their deviance from what is considered to be the norm. As Nussbaum notes, while men in her department proudly left early to pick up children from hockey practice, she was unable to do so as her actions were more likely to be interpreted unfavourably

---

[1] For a further example, see Genevieve Lloyd's analysis of the differing temporal dilemmas experienced by Descartes and Elisabeth (2006, particularly 309).

[2] In relation to the medical profession, for example, see Zerubavel 1979, 53.

(2003: 105).[3] Thus, the conflict Nussbaum points to is not only a conflict of schedules, but also a conflict of values and expectations that are bound up in implicit and explicit social temporal norms. This means that institutional temporal practices may fail to recognise the way that philosophers with caring responsibilities may be disadvantaged by being unable to attend certain scheduled events; they may also support the misrecognition of this problem as one of timing, rather than one of being unable to meet implicit temporal assumptions that guide understandings of professionalism and department fit. This background assumption that time is the same for everyone provides a good example of why there needs to be a greater awareness of time as multiple and conflicting if the culture of philosophy is to change.

3. Iterations of Identity and Causation

A second example of how linear accounts of time may contribute to the misrecognition of exclusionary mechanisms within philosophy is bound up with the problem of identity, specifically the question of who is recognised by others as a philosopher and who can most easily identify themselves with this role. The blog "What is it like to be a woman in philosophy?" for example, provides a variety of accounts of women philosophers being misrecognised as a school administrator, as another philosopher's girlfriend/wife, or the babysitter. But the failure to recognise women *as* philosophers is not restricted to personal encounters such as these and feeds into the more widespread problem of women's philosophical work being ignored or downplayed. As others have already convincingly argued, these kinds of exclusions arise, in part, because the historical schema for 'philosopher' does not map onto the schema for 'woman' (Valian 2005; Haslanger 2008; Calhoun 2009). However, a further point to be contributed to the analysis of this problem has to do with the production of identity itself. As Samantha Brennan's discussion of micro-inequities reveals, one's identity within social life is not stable, but is supported or undermined by the many small affirmations or inequities that one experiences in daily life (see chapter 10 in this volume). This iterative character of identity is not well reflected within a framework that emphasises the linearity of time rather than its repetitive character. Indeed, what I suggest in this section is that an understanding of time as one-dimensional and sequential may be at work in both the failure to notice the micro-affirmations that support some philosophers' identities over others, as well as the commonsense denial of the causative power of micro-inequities.

The question of when one becomes a philosopher, a question to do with status and recognition, but also a question of timing, might seem to have a

---

[3] See also Jennifer Saul's discussion of this point in chapter 2, §2.6, this volume.

fairly straightforward answer: 'When one has met the generally recognised criteria'. In the case of professional philosophy, this might be once one has completed the Ph.D., when one is first published, or when one has a permanent position. So, from the perspective of a nominally linear social time, where one moment unproblematically follows the other, the shift from student to philosopher should theoretically occur in the moment successive to that when the criteria are fulfilled. However, in the case of 'when does a woman become a philosopher?' time is suddenly not so docile. I have met the first two of these criteria and yet I still feel uncomfortable describing myself as such. This is in no way unique to me. Instead, it appears that for many, the moment when one becomes a philosopher never actually arrives, but either continually recedes into the future or is simply unachievable. As Cheshire Calhoun has written, "[W]hile I might enjoy philosophy and be good at it, I couldn't authentically, convincingly, unproblematically be a philosopher. I could study, do, and teach philosophy, but not be a philosopher. (To this day, I almost never say I am a philosopher; I say I teach philosophy)" (2009:219–220).

So, rather than simply happening automatically, the temporal logic involved in 'becoming a philosopher' does not follow the traditional logic of linear time. The linear representation of time suggests that time moves from the past toward the future in a single sequence of non-repeatable moments. However, when it comes to one's sense of self, to one's personal identity, this logic does not really seem to apply. Within linear time, it is logical, for example, to claim that once an event has happened, it will always have happened. However, although I might always be able to say that I had an article or book published, the social meaning of this event is not stable. For this event to be able to be reliably selected as the causal event that enabled me to identify myself as a philosopher, it needs to be supported by a host of subsequent events in which I am recognised as a philosopher by others and treated as such. Without these subsequent events, the original event does not retain the same meaning. What this means is that the temporal logic of identity is not a sequence of non-repeatable events, but its opposite, a sequence of repeated recognitions, affirmations, and identifications. Lack of awareness of these non-linear mechanisms can help to hide the support particular philosophers are able to regularly draw on, as well as the subtle discriminations that undermine the confidence of those who do not fit.

In order to further explain what I mean by this, I want to pick up on Brennan's argument that, in looking for the causes of exclusion, attention needs to be paid to the systematic micro-inequities that operate within professional philosophy. However, as she points out, the small repeated incidents of disrespect, dismissal, and misrecognition are one of the less obvious modes of discrimination within philosophy. Instead, our first instinct when attempting to discern the cause of the problem seems to be to look for causes in relatively self-contained events that can be tied to deliberate agents. We appear less likely to recognise the cumulative causative power of small, repeated acts. Arguably, this tendency is itself based on a certain social understanding of how change happens over time and how to assign responsibility for these changes. Our inability to respond adequately to the massive threats of climate change and resource depletion is a key example of our tendency to ignore the effects of cumulative events. But in regard to the problem of the exclusions within professional philosophy, this tendency appears to hide the way the identity of 'philosopher' has to be actively produced and continuously reinforced. That is, certain iterative mechanisms of identity are ignored because our implicit theories of causation are guided by a model in which change occurs as a result of significant events enacted by conscious agents, rather than insignificant repetitive events enacted relatively unconsciously. Specifically, the micro-affirmations received by certain philosophers are as likely to go unrecognised as are the micro-inequities experienced by others. Further, philosophers attempting to highlight and acknowledge particular micro-inequities can be dismissed as being too sensitive because such acts are not deemed to be significant enough to have really caused any kind of harm. In order to fully recognise this problem, therefore, we need to recognise that discussions focused on micro-inequities are not just about specific events, but also about examining and challenging implicit temporal models of identity and causation.

4. Histories

The importance of recognising the multiple and conflicting times that must be negotiated in professional life, as well as the importance of repetition in affirming identity, come together in the issue of philosophical legacies. Closely bound up with more structural aspects of the discipline, the question of who takes part in the legacy, both in the past and the present, raises issues to do with philosophy's own particular 'social time'. As with the issue of identity above, the institutional structures of philosophy do not follow a trajectory where one moment follows unproblematically from another, but instead work to restrict access to this trajectory such that only some philosophers are able to see themselves as participating in the next 'moment' of philosophy. Donna-Dale Marcano's comments in an interview with George Yancy make this particularly clear. For instance, she claims:

> I could never imagine myself as a Plato. And I wanted to. That's a real obstacle.... To want to be Socrates or Plato, or whoever your white male embodiment of philosophy is, may seem ambitious at best or foolish at worst. But it is not trivial, especially for a black woman.... My white male students may never articulate their aspirations to be a Socrates or Plato, and yet it is not unusual for many of them to envision themselves as purveyors of the tradition (Yancy 2008, 165).

Raising issues to do with identity and identification, Marcano is here also pointing toward the way 'philosophical time' flows from the past into the present. Again, far from being all-encompassing, as Kant's account might indicate, her comments suggest that within philosophy, the ability to enter into successive moments of philosophy (to be successors) does not occur merely due to the flow of time, but is restricted by the repetitive affirmation of iconic white male philosophers as the true representatives of the discipline.

The limits produced in the present are, of course, bound up with the stories told about 'our' arrival in it. Rather than tell the complex story of a practise that has inspired a broad range of philosophers and philosophical approaches, thus supporting a broader range of 'successive moments', the canon has largely remained a sequential list of well-known white male philosophers. One problem with challenging the exclusions of the canon, however, is that from a certain temporal perspective, it seems perfectly logical. Indeed, a great many mainstream history of philosophy courses fit well within the progressive logic of linear time. This is not to say that philosophical history is itself without disagreements or rifts, but that there is considerable consensus around what the canonical sequence is and who should be included in it, particularly through to the 19th century (see Warren 2009, 5–6). Within this logic, the inclusion of non-white philosophers and white women philosophers can be dismissed as a supplementary move aimed at pacifying critics, rather than being a step guided by what counts as 'good' philosophy. Understanding this kind of practice as an attachment to a particular kind of logic, rather than an objective account of the best philosophers, might go some way toward explaining why, as Margaret Walker has argued, the work of women philosophers "cannot be counted upon to find its way into the permanent record" (2005, 155).

In fact, the seemingly self-evident practise of developing a hierarchical list of 'important' philosophers could also be read as a tool for simplifying the history of the discipline, in line with a particular value set, while simultaneously passing as objective. It thus becomes essential to ask why stories of successive progression seem to make sense so easily, despite the fact that they fail to accurately represent the true diversity of philosophical thought. Importantly, I would argue that such methods of producing history only seem credible when told in a context where time is conceived of as linear progression. When time is instead thought of in its fullness of varying, contradictory processes, a linear story of philosophy does not seem so straightforward. Instead, such a story would be more readily interpreted as simplistic and dangerously misleading. Indeed, to present the history of philosophy in a more comprehensive and accurate manner, we need to recognise the way it consists of multiple traditions with varying trajectories, which cannot be confined to a single canonical sequence. Challenging the way the legacy is portrayed may thus require challenging the implicit temporal assumptions that enable linear accounts to appear as a perfectly reasonable, requiring also that we more fully recognise the way 'commonsense' accounts of time are utilised within methods of exclusion.

5. Philosophers of the Future?

By way of bringing this chapter to a close, I'd like to move from the question of legacies to briefly consider a final theme that arises in literature on women in philosophy—their place in its future. Cheshire Calhoun, for example, has suggested that women are less likely to develop an easy identification with and attachment to philosophy and, as a result, women's understandings of their future possibilities within philosophy are largely not the same as those of male students. One reason for this is suggested by Marcano, who writes that

> [d]espite the disorientation inherent to one's initial engagement with philosophical discourse, white male students nonetheless have models in their professors and through the authors of various texts to help them find their mastery in the discipline. I had no models and still struggle to find models who can represent my ability to overcome that disorientation (2008, 165–166).

As suggested above, her comments suggest that the narrowness of the philosophical legacy problematically restricts the possibilities open to philosophy in the present, as well as the future. Although it is undoubtedly the case that ensuring there are more role models and mentoring programmes is important for remedying the inability of many women to anticipate a future within philosophy, the issue I'm particularly interested in here is the way the future itself is conceived within institutional philosophy.

What I want to suggest is that in many ways the discipline of philosophy continues to be guided by a narrow vision of the future that only admits of a particular kind of philosopher. Rather than relating to the future as a force that may profoundly transform it in ways that cannot be anticipated in the present, the discipline stubbornly resists calls to change. The persistent failure of the discipline to recognise its structural exclusions, even while other disciplines have made active commitments to increase diversity, suggests that there is still no anticipation that the discipline may need to reconsider its current trajectories. Instead, the onus continues to be placed overwhelmingly on women to prove that they are fit to be recognised as contemporaries, even while colleagues continue to doubt their capacity for reason, their interest in philosophy, their professionalism, and the status of the issues they research.[4] Interestingly, in his *Politics of Friendship*,

---

[4] One of the reviewers of this volume, for example, felt it important that contributors address the question of women's rational capacity and their interest in philosophy, as they had colleagues who had recently argued that these were valid reasons for women's underrepresentation.

Jacques Derrida has traced the way this notion that women are somehow 'not yet' ready for philosophy has resonated throughout the discipline. He argues that there has been a repeated insistence that women have somehow fallen behind, remain delayed, or simply cannot be thought of as contemporary with men. Analysing the way concepts of male friendship guard the entry to both politics and philosophy, Derrida notes that a wide range of writers, including Michelet, Montaigne, Nietzsche, and Aristotle, presume that women are 'not yet' ready for proper, virtuous friendships, and thus cannot be considered to be suitable politicians or philosophers in the present. He thus argues that "the form or the pretext of 'not yet'" is a key method in the exclusion of women from the public realm (1997, 291, see also 281).

Unlike a number of his other temporal tropes, Derrida does not develop a full analysis of the characteristics and consequences of the 'not yet', but I would argue that it is bound up with an assumption that those 'leading the way' have already forged the most appropriate path into the future. If others are excluded from this future, it is for them to rectify. In this sense, the legacy of the 'not yet' continues into present-day philosophy in multiple ways. If women have a harder time identifying with philosophy and anticipating their future within it, it may thus also be because this future has already been colonised by and for a particular kind of philosopher. Part of rectifying the problem of anticipation that Calhoun points toward then is moving toward a conception of the future as unpredictable and surprising, what Derrida calls the 'to come'. This kind of future contrasts strongly with the 'not yet', which assumes a future continuous with the present and so forecloses the possibility that the future might be completely unexpected and transformational. An institutional philosophy that faced up to its continuing discriminations would thus need to begin to welcome the possibility that the future may well be very different from the present.

6. Finding Time

By considering a range of issues including embodiment, professionalism, identity, causation, historical legacies, and future anticipations, I hope to have illustrated why it is important that philosophers come to recognise that the discipline is not situated within a single, all-encompassing temporal process, but rather is characterised by multiple disjointed and contradictory processes. I have suggested that while for some, the work of managing this multiplicity is hidden, by virtue of their ability to fit into certain disciplinary expectations, many more others are disadvantaged by the lack of these implicit support structures. For those who don't fit, the work of being a philosopher includes negotiating seemingly mutually exclusive demands simultaneously, demands that multiply with each further element of exclusion. As Jacqueline Scott vividly attests in an interview with George Yancy, these contradictions can be so great that simply being fully present seems impossible:

> I find myself expending a lot of energy on insisting on actually existing. By this I mean that I am often seen as a contradiction in terms and given that traditionally in philosophy we don't like contradictions, I am either overlooked or they take away the parts that are illogical (having a Ph.D. for example). In order to have my full self acknowledged then I need to insist on the existence of all parts of me. We have talked about the difficulty of embodying the *simultaneity* of being a woman and being a philosopher, and being black. We see this as a seamless category— maybe there are some seams but it kind of goes together for us in our saner, happier moments. But I think that a lot of people continue to want to put some slash marks in there and say, "We'll allow the woman part but we won't allow the black part." Or "We'll allow the philosopher part but not some of the other parts." And so we need to insist on bringing that together. (My emphasis, Yancy, 2008, 178)

The traditional philosophical aversion to contradiction, well illustrated by a preference for an all- encompassing linear time, risks leaving philosophy unable to respond adequately to the complexities of the world in which it is practiced. Gloria Anzaldúa, for example, has written extensively on the way the Western logics of identity and history are fundamentally unable to deal with the embodied realities of social life. Her work challenges the way social categories (that others use to politically situate her) cut and fragment her own sense of wholeness; because, as Scott points out, to be whole within a traditional Western metaphysical framework is to be without contradiction. As I have argued elsewhere (2011), Anzaldúa's work thus seeks to claim a conceptual space for contradictory identities, in part by challenging linear temporal models that do not allow one to be more than one thing within any one moment. Her work instead suggests the importance of recognising a notion of 'contradictory simultaneity', which resists the urge to separate out differences across time and instead insists that we recognise seemingly contradictory differences within the 'same' moment. Although Scott's comments could, of course, be read in terms of schema clashes, I want to suggest that she is also pointing to a need for a broader conception of temporality. When time is understood to be a sequence of 'nows', within which one can only do or be one thing at a time, then the multiplicity and diversity of lived, embodied philosophy is obscured. This again suggests that if professional philosophy is to act on the exclusion of women and minority men, then it will need to rethink the implicit temporal assumptions that guide it.

The key transformation I have argued for is a greater awareness of the problems involved in adopting a 'commonsense' notion of linear time when seeking to understand the complexities of social life. Instead, professional philosophy needs to be guided by an understanding of time as normative and political, as supportive of certain ways of living over others. In particular, there needs to be a greater awareness of how linear accounts of time, in their pretence of being all-encompassing, actively hide the multiple processes, expectations, responsibilities, and histories that must be negotiated in order for women and minority men to be 'philosophers'. As Derrida argues in the interview 'Negotiations', "there is not an 'at the same time,' there is not, period...there are simply differences, multiplicities of rhythm. In the phenomenon, or in what has the appearance of 'at the same time,' there are already differences of rhythm, differences of speed" (2002, 28). As a result of this, he suggests that

> in political or institutional action one must not only make several speeds cohabit with each other, one must also enable the multiplicity of speeds (there are not only two, there are more than two speeds) to be rendered, not only possible, but necessary and enable diversities to cohabit in an institution (ibid.).

Understanding the time of philosophy in this way would more easily support the kinds of calls for change that have been made by women in philosophy. A reworked history of philosophy could be seen as more accurate, rather than an additive attempt at appeasement. Micro-inequalities could be read as significant events, rather than as small meaningless incidents. It would also become clearer why the linear pipeline model of increased participation is as woefully inadequate as Eliza Goddard and Susan Dodds point out (this volume, chapter 7). The emphasis on quick repartee in seminar discussions that Beebee and Brennan both critique can also be clearly understood as problematic when we understand that temporalised concepts are not value-free. But above all, a philosophy guided by multiple speeds may be better able to recognise those philosophers who are 'not yet' as the philosophers of the future that the discipline so desperately lacks.

References

Agamben, Giorgio. 1993. "Time and History: Critique of the Instant and the Continuum." In *Infancy and History: The Destruction of Experience*, ed. Giorgio Agamben. London: Verso, 91–105.

Bastian, Michelle. 2009. "Inventing Nature: Re-writing Time and Agency in a More-than-Human World." *Australian Humanities Review* 47: 99–116.

———. 2011. "The contradictory simultaneity of being with others: Exploring concepts of time and community in the work of Gloria Anzaldúa." *Feminist Review* 97(1):151–167.

Battersby, Christine. 1998. *The phenomenal woman: feminist metaphysics and the patterns of identity*. New York: Routledge.

Boyarin, Jonathan, ed. 1994. *Remapping memory: The politics of timespace.* Minneapolis: University of Minnesota Press.

Calhoun, Cheshire. 2009. "The Undergraduate Pipeline Problem." *Hypatia* 24 (2):216–223.

Chakrabarty, Dipesh. 1992. "Postcoloniality and the Artifice of History: Who Speaks for 'Indian' Pasts?" *Representations* (37):1–26.

Connolly, William E. 2005. *Pluralism.* Durham, NC: Duke University Press.

Derrida, Jacques. 1997. *Politics of Friendship.* London: Verso.

———. 2002. "Negotiations." In *Negotiations: Interventions and Interviews, 1971-2001,* ed. E. Rottenburg. Stanford, CA: Stanford University Press, 11–40.

Dinshaw, Carolyn, Lee Edelman, Roderick A. Ferguson, Carla Freccero, Elizabeth Freeman, Judith Halberstam, Annamarie Jagose, Christopher Nealon, and Nguyen Tan Hoang. 2007. "Theorizing Queer Temporalities: A Roundtable Discussion." *GLQ: A Journal of Lesbian and Gay Studies* 13 (2–3):177–195.

Diprose, Rosalyn. 2009. "Women's Bodies Giving Time for Hospitality." *Hypatia* 24 (2):378–399.

Freeman, Elizabeth. 2010. *Time binds: queer temporalities, queer histories.* Durham, NC: Duke University Press.

Ganguly, Keya. 2004. "Temporality and postcolonial critique." In *The Cambridge Companion to Postcolonial Literary Studies,* ed. N. Lazarus. Cambridge, UK: Cambridge University Press, 162–179.

Greenhouse, Carol J. 1989. "Just in Time: Temporality and the Cultural Legitimation of Law." *Yale Law Journal* 98 (8):1631–1651.

———. 1996. *A Moment's Notice: Time Politics across Cultures.* Ithaca, NY, and London: Cornell University Press.

Gurvitch, Georges. 1964. *The Spectrum of Social Time.* Dordrecht, NL: D. Reidel.

Haslanger, Sally. 2008. "Changing the ideology and culture of philosophy: Not by reason (alone)." *Hypatia* 23 (2):210–223.

Hesford, Victoria, and Lisa Diedrich, eds. 2008. *Feminist time against nation time: gender, politics, and the nation-state in an age of permanent war.* Lanham, MD: Lexington.

Hutchings, Kimberly. 2008. *Time and World Politics: Thinking the Present.* Manchester, UK: Manchester University Press.

Kant, Immanuel. 1998 [1787]. *Critique of Pure Reason.* Cambridge, UK: Cambridge University Press.

Lloyd, Genevieve. 1993 [1984]. *The Man of Reason: 'Male' and 'Female' in Western Philosophy.* 2nd ed. Minneapolis: University of Minnesota Press.

———. 2000. "No One's Land: Australia and the Philosophical Imagination." *Hypatia* 15 (2):26–39.

———. 2006. "Busy Lives: Descartes and Elisabeth on Time Management and the Philosophical Life." *Australian Feminist Studies* 21(51): 303–311.

Nespor, J., D. Hicks, and A. M. Fall. 2009. Time and exclusion. *Disability and Society* 24 (3):373–385.

Nussbaum, Martha. 2003. "'Don't Smile Too Much'—Philosophy and Women in the 1970s." In *Singing in the Fire: Stories of Women in Philosophy,* ed. Linda Martin Alcoff. New York: Rowman & Littlefield, 93–108.

Pierson, Paul. 2004. *Politics in time: history, institutions, and social analysis.* Princeton, NJ: Princeton University Press.

Urciuoli, Bonnie. 1992. "Time, Talk and Class: New York Puerto Ricans as Temporal and Linguistic Others." In *The Politics of Time*, ed. H. J. Rutz. Washington DC: American Anthropological Association, 108–126.

Valian, Virginia. 2005. "Beyond Gender Schemas: Improving the Advancement of Women in Academia." *Hypatia* 20 (3):198–213.

Walker, Margaret Urban. 2005. "Diotima's Ghost: The Uncertain Place of Feminist Philosophy in Professional Philosophy." *Hypatia* 20(3):153–164.

Warren, Karen J. 2009. "2,600 Years of the History of Western Philosophy without Women: This Book as a Unique, Gender-Inclusive Alternative." In *An Unconventional History of Western Philosophy: Conversations between Men and Women Philosophers*, ed. Karen J. Warren. Lanham, MD: Rowman and Littlefield, 1–26.

Yancy, George. 2008. "Situated Voices: Black Women in/on the Profession of Philosophy." *Hypatia* 23(2):160–189.

Zerubavel, Eviatar. 1979. *Patterns of Time in Hospital Life*. Chicago and London: University of Chicago Press.

Seeing the Trends in the Data
Glenys Bishop, with Helen Beebee, Eliza Goddard, and Adriane Rini

1. Introduction

To underpin the arguments and discussions in the preceding chapters, we have compiled data from Australia, New Zealand, United Kingdom, United States of America, and Canada. Each country has provided data from different sources. These datasets all have their own shortcomings, and the data are not directly comparable.

However, it is possible to use all these datasets to provide a picture of various aspects of women engaged in philosophy. The emphasis of this appendix is to use the available data to draw out some of the issues.

The situation in Australia is examined in some detail in section 2. Data from New Zealand, the United Kingdom, Canada, and U.S.A. are presented in sections 3 to 6, and finally the issues that have arisen in the discussion of each country are compared and summarised in section 7.

2. Australia

STAFF

As part of its Benchmarking Collection, the Australasian Association of Philosophy (AAP) collects data on an annual basis from university philosophy programmes in Australia and New Zealand. For the purposes of the collection, a programme in philosophy offers philosophy taught at undergraduate and research doctoral levels with discipline-specific staff. Information collected includes numbers of staff engaged in both teaching and research, student loads,

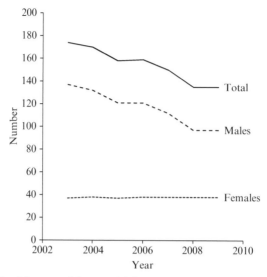

FIGURE 1 *FTE for full-time and fractional full-time philosophy teaching and research staff in philosophy programmes in Australian universities, 2003–2009, by gender.*
Data Source: AAP Benchmarking Collection (philosophy)

research higher degree completions, and research inputs and outputs. The data are collected from heads of departments and so should be regarded as self-reporting, albeit comprehensive.[1]

Figure 1 shows total counts of teaching and research staff employed in full-time and fractional full-time (FFT) contracts as full-time equivalents (FTE), and these totals are also broken down by gender. The number of females is flat (37 or 38) from 2003 to 2009, whereas the number of males decreases by an average of 7.1 ($\pm$1.2)[2] per year in that time period. The total number also decreases at this rate. Details of statistical analysis are shown in appendix 2.

Because of this reduction in male staff, the percentage of female staff has increased despite the fact that the numbers have not changed. Nonetheless, females still only comprised 28% of staff in 2009.

---

[1] Universities included in this collection are Australian National University (Faculties and Research School), University of Adelaide, Australian Catholic University, University of Ballarat, Deakin University, Flinders University of South Australia, Griffith University, La Trobe University, Macquarie University, Monash University (Philosophy and Bioethics), Murdoch University, University of Melbourne, University of Newcastle, University of New England, University of New South Wales, University of Notre Dame, University of Queensland, Swinburne University of Technology, University of Sydney (Philosophy and HPS), University of Tasmania, University of Western Australia, and University of Wollongong. These are the Australian universities with 'philosophy programmes' as defined by the AAP.

[2] Figure in () is 2 standard errors. Subtract this number from the estimated average decrease and add it to the estimated average decrease to create an interval. We can be 95% confident (as opposed to 100% sure) that the actual average decrease is somewhere in this interval.

It is informative to consider the numbers at each level in figure 2 (below). The largest group of females is at level B (lecturer), whereas the largest group of males is at levels D (associate professor or reader) and E (professor). The number of males exceeds the number of females at all levels in most years.

There is a dip in the number of females and males employed at level A (associate lecturer) and level B in 2005 and a sudden decline in the number employed at level C (senior lecturer) in 2006, more pronounced for males. At the same time, the highest numbers of staff, mainly male, employed at levels D and E occurred in these two years. There is an increase in females at level C from 2006 to 2008 at the same time as a decrease in numbers of females at level B.

Although these changes may be due to random fluctuations, some knowledge of events in philosophy departments would be needed to tease out the issues in these two years. For instance, was there a wave of promotions to levels

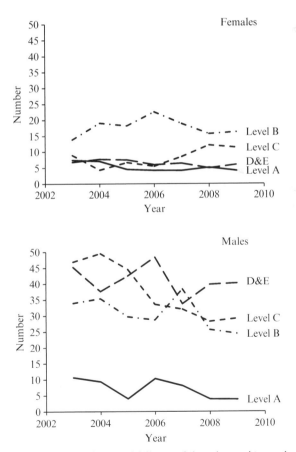

FIGURE 2 *FTE for full-time and fractional full-time philosophy teaching and research staff in philosophy programmes in Australian universities by level and gender.*

Data Source: AAP Benchmarking Collection (philosophy)

TABLE 1 FTE appointments to teaching and research contracts by level and gender for 2005 and 2006 combined

Level	Females	Males	Total	%Female
A	4.4	10.1	14.5	30%
B	5.3	3.8	9.1	58%
C, D, E *			1.0	

Data Source: Goddard, Eliza (2008).

* *Numbers too small for publication.*

D and E in 2005 and 2006, or were staff recruited to this level? Were most pro-motions or recruitments males? Was there a wave of retirements from level C in 2006? What proportion of the staff leaving level C in 2006 gained promotions to level D? Were women promoted from level B to level C at this time?

Unfortunately data showing numbers of retirements and promotions by gender are not available. Appointments data for contract positions (full-time and fractional full-time) were obtained for 2005 and 2006 and are shown in table 1. However, these do not include appointments to continuing positions, and so it is difficult to draw conclusions that would illuminate the patterns seen in figure 2. For the two years, at level A, 14.5 FTE contract appointments, of which 30% were females, were made. Of the 9.1 FTE staff appointed to level B in the two years, 58% were female.

One could argue that women's homemaking and child-caring roles inhibit their ability and willingness to seek promotions. However, this is not borne out by the academic female participation rates in all disciplines. We do not have access to directly comparable data, but figures for 2009 were obtained from the staff dataset published by the Department of Education, Employment and Workplace Relations (DEEWR). Their data are collected from each univer-sity's official statistical collection and include academics employed in teach-ing or research or both. As already mentioned, the philosophy data from the AAP used in this chapter are for academics engaged in both teaching and research (i.e., not those engaged in only one of these) and have been reported by department heads.

Data for all disciplines combined, at the abovementioned universities that teach philosophy, are compared with the data for philosophy only in figure 3. It shows that women's representation in philosophy is considerably lower than their representation in the sum of all academic disciplines at all levels.

STUDENTS

A possible reason for relatively low numbers of women being employed as aca-demics in philosophy could be that fewer women are studying philosophy. The AAP obtained data on student load and completions of degrees in philosophy

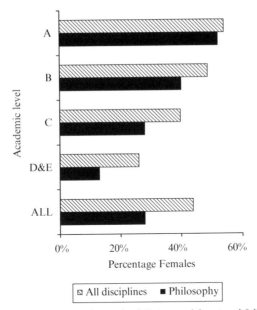

FIGURE 3 *Females as a percentage of FTE for full-time and fractional full-time staff by level in 2009 at the Australian universities that teach a philosophy programme. Female percentages of staff engaged in teaching and/or research in all academic disciplines are compared with those engaged in teaching and research in philosophy.*

Data Sources: DEEWR Higher Education Statistics (all disciplines), AAP Benchmarking Collection (philosophy)

from DEEWR. Only two types of degrees are considered here, namely bachelor degrees and doctorates by research. Student load is defined as Equivalent Full-Time (EFT) students studying philosophy. Thus one student taking a philosophy unit, which counts as 25% of the credit points for that year, is counted as one-quarter of an EFT student. A student enrolled half-time in a Ph.D. programme counts as half an EFT student.

Figure 4 displays student loads and completions in bachelor degree programmes for males and females between 2001 and 2008. There is a statistically significant increasing trend in student load for each gender, and the two trends are parallel. Thus, between 2001 and 2008, the student load increased, on average, by 74 (±18) males and 74 (±18) females each year,[3] with females consistently outnumbering males by about 236 EFT. Completions on the other hand show no statistically significant trend, although males always outnumber females.

On average over the eight years, female bachelor degree completions in a philosophy programme were about 44% of the total of such completions, while

---

[3] We can say with 95% confidence that the average annual increase in each sex is between 56 and 92 EFT.

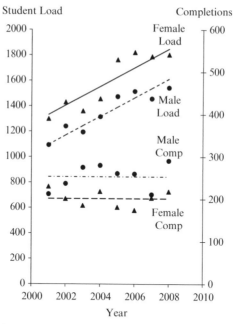

FIGURE 4 *Undergraduate EFT student load and bachelor degree completions by gender for philosophy programmes at Australian universities, showing fitted models as solid lines and actual numbers as points.*

Data Sources: DEEWR Higher Education Statistics (all disciplines and philosophy)

about 54% of the student load, i.e., students taking philosophy units, was made up of females.

It appears from these figures that more women than men are interested in studying some philosophy, but more men than women are serious about it, in the sense of majoring at the undergraduate level. Further investigation is required to see why the female percentage of completions is so much lower than the female percentage of undergraduate load, and possible reasons have been explored elsewhere in this volume.

Further evidence that women are not completing bachelor level philosophy programmes in the same numbers as men, while still taking more philosophy courses overall, can be gained by following cohorts of undergraduates enrolled in one or more units of philosophy from first year to third year. The data obtained by AAP contained numbers of students enrolled in one, two, and three or more undergraduate philosophy units at each year level in each of 2005, 2006, 2007, and 2008. A pseudo-cohort for the 2005 intake was constructed by comparing the number of students of each gender enrolled in first year units in 2005 with the number enrolled in second year units in 2006 and the number enrolled in third year units in 2007. A similar pseudo-cohort was constructed for those taking first year units in 2006.

Figure 5 shows the two pseudo-cohorts by gender; figure 5a has cohorts studying one or more units while figure 5b has cohorts studying two or more units at each level. There is a sharp decrease in numbers from first year to second year for both males and females followed by a shallower decrease to third year. But the decrease for females is steeper than for males. A similar trend between first and second year was also found for the 2007 intake (not shown). Third year data were not available for this pseudo-cohort.

Table 2 shows that the percentage of females decreases with increasing year level. This provides further evidence that female students are more likely than males to want to study some philosophy but are less likely to major in it.

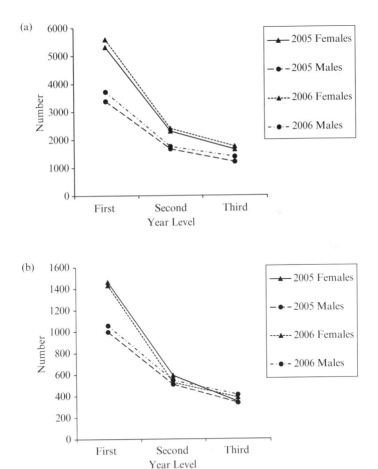

FIGURE 5 *Numbers of males and females studying philosophy units at first-, second-, and third-year levels for 2005 (solid lines) and 2006 (dotted lines) intakes. a: one or more philosophy units at each year level b: two or more units at each year level*

Data Source: DEEWR Higher Education Statistics (philosophy)

TABLE 2 Percentage of females at each year level for three pseudo-cohorts studying one or more units of philosophy, corresponding to 2005, 2006, and 2007 intakes

	2005 Intake	2006 Intake	2007 Intake
First Year	61%	60%	61%
Second Year	58%	58%	57%
Third Year	58%	56%	

Does the same trend occur in higher degrees? Figure 6 shows numbers of EFT students and numbers of completions for research doctorates by gender. There was a significant upward trend in male student load over the period 2001 to 2008 with total male load increasing by an average of 7.4 (±4.6) each year. The steepest increase was between 2001 and 2004. Although there does appear to have been some increase in female student load in 2001 to 2004, there was a decrease in subsequent years so that overall female student load was flat over the

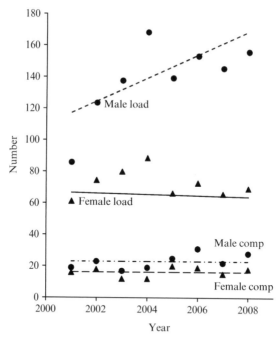

FIGURE 6 *Doctoral student load as expressed in number of EFT students and number of completions for research doctorates in philosophy programmes at Australian universities, by gender for the years 2001 to 2008. Fitted models are shown as lines while actual values are shown as points.*

Data Sources: DEEWR Higher Education Statistics (all disciplines), DEEWR Higher Education Statistics (philosophy)

period. For males, completions increased slightly at a rate of 1.3 (±1.1) per annum while completions for females were flat.[4]

While on average females constituted 34% of student load during the years 2001 to 2008, they made up 41% of completions during that period. Thus they were somewhat overrepresented among completions. We do not have data on completion rates by males and females.

In contrast with the bachelor degree completions, the percentage of completions of doctorates by females is higher than the percentage of female student load. It appears that the women who enrol for a doctorate are a little more dedicated than their male counterparts. This hypothesis needs further investigation.

In summary, the picture of women students of philosophy in Australia begins with more than 60% of those initially interested at the start of university study being female, dropping to about 44% of the philosophy major bachelor completions being female and 41% of doctorate completions. Among students, it appears that women are being lost during the undergraduate years.

3. New Zealand

The data presented in this section could not be obtained in the same way as for Australia and, therefore, were assembled from the calendars and websites of six universities[5] for 2008, 2009, and 2010.

In addition to a different method for obtaining data, different criteria[6] for counting staff were used in New Zealand universities.

Figure 7 shows the pooled results for the six universities. Because the numbers are small, there are limits to how much can be read from this graph. Overall the number of males at any given level exceeds the number of females, on average by a factor of 3:1. There has been a small improvement in the number of female readers/associate professors, changing from two to four from 2008 to

---

[4] We are 95% confident that the average annual increase in male completions is between 0.2 and 2.4, i.e., more than zero, whereas the interval for average annual increase in female completions was not significantly different from zero.

[5] Those universities were University of Auckland, Victoria University of Wellington, Waikato University, Massey University, University of Canterbury, and University of Otago.

[6] Included: philosophers who have retired from full-time positions but who are retained on fractional research and teaching positions. Excluded: non-permanent or fractional positions held by people who have never held a permanent full-time research and teaching position in philosophy; tutors or senior tutors, whether these are fixed-term or permanent positions. Counted as 1.0: fractional appointments; deans and other administrators who have been included among the regular philosophy staff on websites; new permanent full-time research and teaching staff who arrived before the end of a calendar year.

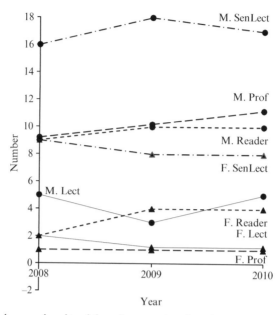

FIGURE 7 *Numbers employed in philosophy research and teaching positions in six New Zealand universities at lecturer, senior lecturer, reader/associate professor, and professor levels by gender for the years 2008, 2009, 2010.*

Source: Collected by A. Rini.

Key: Prof–full professor, Reader–reader or associate professor, SenLect–senior lecturer, Lect–lecturer, F–female, M–male.

2009. This did not result in any net change in numbers of females because this gain was countered by a corresponding decrease in the number of senior lecturers. Compare this with an increase of four males at the upper levels and maintenance of numbers at the lower levels from 2008 to 2010.

In 2010, there were 43 men and 14 women in full-time research and teaching positions. Men are more heavily represented at the highest level; for instance at the full professorial level, men outnumbered women by 11:1 in 2010.

No women were appointed to full-time permanent positions, at any level, between July 2005 and December 2010. However, 12 male appointments to full-time permanent positions were made during this period, covering all levels from lecturer to full professor.

These generally negative results for women fly in the face of earlier positive gains. To the best of our knowledge, in 1993, for example, there were only five women in New Zealand philosophy, whereas there were 14 by 2010, making up 25% of the regular research and teaching positions.

With no new hires, the only net change in the number of women since 2005 is a loss of one.

4. Canada

The Canadian Philosophical Association has conducted two equity surveys of philosophy departments at Canadian universities, one for the period 2001 to 2005 (Daigle, McDonald, and Lanoix, 2005) and another for the period 2007 to 2009 (Boileau and Daigle, 2009). While these surveys address several equity concerns, only results relating to women as a minority group will be discussed here.

For the first survey, responses were received from 30 departments of 67 to which the survey form was sent. For the second survey, forms were sent to 62 departments, and 30 responses were received. Only 19 responding departments were common to both samples. Because of the non-random nature of the selection of samples of departments and only partial overlap between the two groups, the numbers are not directly comparable. For instance, while the number of male full professors is about 145 in the first group and about 90 in the second group, one cannot necessarily conclude that the total number of male philosophy professors in Canada decreased from the first period to the second.

The first survey collected data relating to the academic years 2001–02, 2002–03, 2003–04, and 2004–05, while the second collected data for 2007–08 and 2008–09. Thus two years in the middle are missing. Given all of these constraints, we will comment on the two survey periods separately.

Figure 8 displays numbers of females and males holding academic positions by level for the two groups of years. Males outnumber females at every level, and three levels of males, excepting assistant professors, each outnumber every level of females.

It is interesting to examine whether hiring practices are attempting to address the low numbers of female academic staff. Table 3 shows the numbers of new staff hired by 22 philosophy departments in two years. Boileau and Daigle (2009) assumed that the remaining eight responding departments of the second sample did not hire anyone during the two-year period. While the number of male applicants is overwhelmingly larger than the numbers of women applying (14% and 21% of applicants were females in the two years), approximately equal numbers of men and women were eventually hired by these 22 universities.

We have no data about the levels to which these people were hired. If such data were available and also numbers of promotions by level, it would be possible to obtain a fuller picture.

Ten of the 30 departments responding to the survey indicated that they had a Ph.D. programme, and the numbers of degrees awarded are shown in table 4. The percentage of Ph.D. candidates who were females is 30%, whereas the percentage of degrees awarded to females is around 43%.

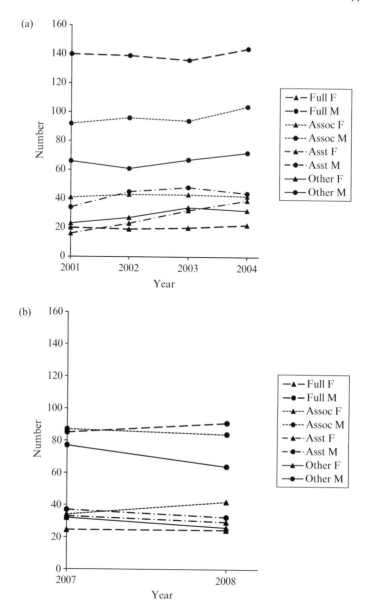

FIGURE 8 *Numbers of staff by level and gender at selected Canadian universities. (a) 30 departments reporting for academic years beginning in 2001 to 2004. (b) 30 departments reporting for academic years beginning in 2007 and 2008 on the right (19 departments report in both periods).*

CPA Equity Survey 2009 Report, CPA Equity Survey 2005 Report.

Key: Full–full professors, Assoc–associate professors, Asst–assistant professors, Other–sessional, adjunct, and limited term appointees, F–female, M–male.

TABLE 3 Numbers of men and women hired to academic positions in 22 Canadian universities in two academic years.

	2007–08		2008–09	
	Women	Men	Women	Men
Applications	101	617	302	1132
Long-listed	19	32	25	64
Short-listed	19	22	16	30
Hired	8.5	7.5	6	8

Sources: CPA Equity Survey 2009 Report

TABLE 4 Numbers of doctoral candidates and degrees awarded at 10 Canadian universities with a Ph.D. programme in philosophy.

	Women	Men	%Female
Ph.D. awarded 2007–08	7	9	44%
Ph.D. awarded 2008–09	9	12	43%
Degrees in progress	96	223	30%

Source: CPA Equity Survey 2009 Report

Figure 9 shows numbers of applications, numbers of offers made and numbers of actual entries to doctoral programmes by gender. There were 16 universities offering a doctoral programme in the 2001–2004 sample and eight provided data in the 2007–2008 sample.

Males outnumber females for applications, offers, and entries in every year shown with one exception. In 2007, the numbers of females and males entering doctoral programmes at eight universities were equal. In the years 2001 to 2004, the data collected from 16 universities offering doctoral programmes appear to show an increase over time for applications and offers to both males and females. However, with only four time-points and substantial annual fluctuations, the only statistically significant trend is for male offers, where the average annual increase is between 10 and 16.4.

However, as a proportion of applicants, there is no significant difference between males and females in terms of offers and entries. Statistical tests were performed for the 2008 data and showed that the proportion of applicants who were offered positions in Ph.D. programmes did not differ between males and females and neither did the proportion of offers that were accepted. See appendix 2 for details.

Unfortunately, we do not have access to bachelor degree completions or undergraduate numbers by year level that would allow us to examine whether trends are similar to those in Australia. Nor do we have access to relative frequencies of males and females in all academic disciplines for comparison.

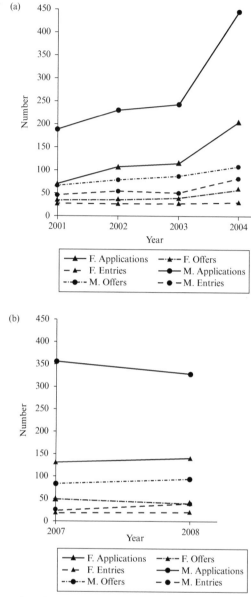

FIGURE 9 *Numbers of applications, offers, and entries to doctoral programmes at a: 16 Canadian universities (2001–2004) by gender and year b: eight Canadian universities (2007–2008) by gender and year.*

5. United States of America

Haslanger (2007) reports that of 100 associate and advisory editors of seven philosophy journals, only 17 were women in spring 2007. She also publishes gender ratios in tenure track positions for the 20 top-ranked philosophy departments in the U.S. In 2006, of a total of 412 people occupying these positions, 76 were women, or 19%.

Broader data collected by the U.S. department of education—figure 10—displays percentage females among academic staff at degree-granting institutions in the U.S. in 2003. It can be seen that the percentage of women employed in philosophy on a full-time basis was lower than in all other disciplines except engineering. For part-time staff, engineering and occupationally specific disciplines were the only disciplines with lower percentages of women than philosophy. The broad humanities discipline includes philosophy but has much higher percentages of women in both full-time and part-time employment.

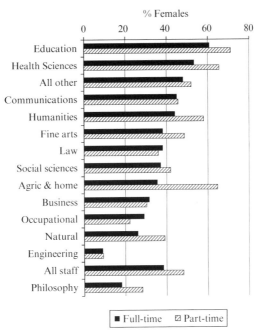

FIGURE 10 *Percentage females among academic staff, employed on either a full-time or part-time basis in 2003 at U.S. universities, by broad discipline areas and with all disciplines and philosophy shown at the bottom.*

Source: Derived from data published in U.S. Department of Education, National Center for Education Statistics, 2009 National Study of Postsecondary Faculty

Norlock (2006) notes that the American Philosophical Association (APA) has tried to gather data about women in the discipline by using surveys. Sending forms to 1,738 philosophy departments in the U.S. resulted in a 20% response rate. This is quite likely to be a biased sample, and the APA concluded that this did not constitute a sufficiently reliable sample.

Solomon and Clarke (2009) report that the "Committee on the Status of Women (CSW) requested in December 2006 that the APA office consistently follow up on the results of all positions advertised in Jobs for Philosophers (JFP)". They tabled results from jobs advertised in October and November 2007. Figure 11 shows the numbers of positions for which a philosopher was hired by type of position and gender. Altogether 515 positions were advertised and 294 were known to be filled with philosophers. Of these, 29% were females, with females filling 37% of the non-tenure track positions.

Solomon and Clarke also provide figures obtained from the National Opinion Research Center for numbers of Ph.D.s awarded in 2006 by gender and broad discipline, as well as for philosophy. These data are shown in figure 12. In 2006, only 29% of Ph.D.s in philosophy were completed by women. This proportion is much more similar to the physical sciences than to the humanities and also reflects the overall proportion of female academic staff in philosophy in 2003.

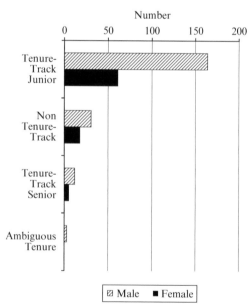

FIGURE 11 *Number of persons hired to fill positions advertised in Jobs for Philosophers in October and November 2007 by gender and type of position.*

Source: Solomon & Clarke (2009)

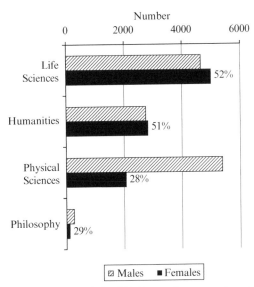

FIGURE 12 *Numbers of Ph.D.s awarded in 2006 by gender, comparing philosophy and broad disciplines, with percentage of females indicated.*

Source: Solomon & Clarke (2009)

It has been difficult to obtain data about undergraduates and bachelor degree completions or more recent data about staff.

The picture we have in the first decade of this century is that the proportion of female academic staff in philosophy is low, and the hiring practices do not appear to be overcoming this.

From the statistical point of view, a major issue confronting U.S. philosophers is the lack of recent data.

6. United Kingdom

The British Philosophical Association surveyed heads of U.K. philosophy departments during 2008–09 and 2009–10 (Beebee and Saul, 2011). There were 38 responding departments, including all the largest ones, from about 50 surveyed. Data for the two years have been combined in this report.

Figure 13 shows that males strongly outnumber females at all academic levels. There is some variation in the proportion of females at the different levels. These proportions were tested and found to be significantly different, mainly due to a much lower percentage of females at the professorial level. Full test results are shown in appendix 2. The overall percentage of females among philosophy academic staff at the surveyed universities is 25.4%. For philosophy professors at these universities, 15% are female and for all other levels combined 27.2% are female.

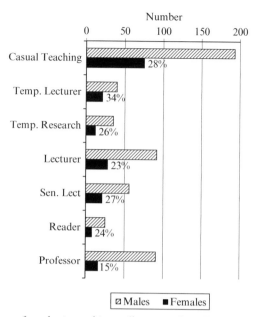

FIGURE 13 *Numbers of academic teaching and/or research staff at 31 U.K. universities in 2008–09 and 2009–10 by gender and level. The number of females as a percentage of the total at each level is indicated for each level.*

Data Source: British Philosophical Association survey

The numbers of students enrolled as undergraduates, taught and research masters, and Ph.D. candidates are shown in figure 14. Some of the categories are explained in the next few paragraphs.

In most philosophy departments in the U.K. (though not in Scotland), students select their degree programme at the application stage. 'Single honours' degree programmes are those in which philosophy is exclusively or nearly exclusively studied throughout the three-year programme (or, in Scotland, selected as the main subject in the third year of a three- or four-year degree programme).

Most U.K. universities run 'joint honours' programmes, with a 50/50 split between two subjects. Some others, here counted under 'joint honours', run combined programmes involving more than two subjects, e.g., philosophy, politics, and economics. Two institutions have extremely large joint honours programmes and account for nearly half of all joint honours students; excluding those two programmes, women rise to 51% of 'joint honours' students.

Taught masters degrees involving philosophy only are indicated as masters (phil) while interdisciplinary taught masters programmes that have a significant philosophy input are indicated by masters (other).

The only completion figures available in this data set are for Ph.D.s. Females made up 30% of the Ph.D. intake and 33% of the Ph.D. completions for the two years.

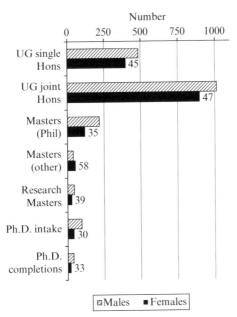

FIGURE 14 *Numbers of students enrolled in different degree programmes at 31 U.K. universities in two academic years, 2008–09 and 2009–10, by gender. The number of females as a percentage of the total in each programme is indicated.*

Data Source: British Philosophical Association survey

Key: UG–undergraduates, for single and joint honours, see text; Masters–Masters degree by coursework; Research Masters–by research

Figures 13 and 14 appear to indicate that there is a drop-off of women at each level of seniority. However, caution should be exercised when drawing conclusions from data collected over such a short time period. For example, the proportion of female honours students may have been higher in this period than when some of the other groups, such as Ph.D. completions and lecturers, were studying for honours degrees.

7. Comparisons and Summary

The overwhelming picture from all of the Anglophone countries is that, among academic staff, men outnumber women at all levels, with the estimated proportion of females ranging between 20% and 30%. Among the top 20 philosophy departments in the U.S.A., only 19% of tenure-track positions were occupied by women in 2006. These percentages are more comparable with physical sciences than with most of the other disciplines, particularly the humanities. All Anglophone countries exhibit a pattern of decreasing percentages of females for higher academic staff levels.

There are only limited data available on numbers and gender of new staff hired. We do know that no women were hired to full-time academic philosophy positions in New Zealand between 2005 and 2010. In other countries, there are either no data or the data are limited to specific years or specific universities.

These limited data show some variation among countries. For instance, in the U.S., 29% of the known outcomes of positions advertised on a philosophy website in late 2007 were filled by women. On the other hand, in Canada, the philosophy departments that responded to the question about hiring new staff appointed roughly equal numbers of men and women, despite male applicants overwhelmingly outnumbering female applicants. However, there is no information about the levels at which these new staff were hired. In Australia, 44% of academic staff hired to contract positions in a two-year period were women, mostly at the more junior levels.

In Australia, there is a pattern of more women than men wanting to study some philosophy at undergraduate level, but men outnumbering women in completing bachelor degrees in philosophy. In the U.K. also, men outnumber women in completing honours philosophy degrees. These two countries had similar proportions of female philosophy graduates at around 44–47%. In Australia, a sharp drop in undergraduate female participation in philosophy was observed from first year to third year. No data were available for undergraduates in the other countries.

At the doctoral level in Australia, the average proportion of females among degree completions, over an eight-year period, was 41%. In Canada, the proportion was 43%, but information was only provided by some philosophy departments. Canada and Australia also show a similar trend in that the number of males entering doctoral programmes is increasing, while the number of females entering remains flat. In Canada, this reflects the fact that the number of male applicants has been increasing. In the U.K. for two recent years, women made up 30% of the Ph.D. intake and 33% of the completions in a non-random sample of philosophy departments.

The most useful data are collected annually or biennially so that trends over time can be seen. The danger with considering cross-sectional data, collected in one year only, is that because numbers are often small, they can be variable, and the year studied may be idiosyncratic. For this reason, it is possible to gain a fuller picture of the situation in Australia and Canada than in the other countries discussed in this appendix.

Official statistical collections can give useful information if they are available at a sufficiently fine level. Official sources may provide data on academic staff broken down by level and gender, degree completions and student load, or enrolments by gender. These may only be available publicly at the broad disciplinary level, but it is often possible to purchase data at a finer level, such as philosophy, provided numbers are not so small as to breach confidentiality.

It is not necessary to take a census of all departments to gauge trends over time. However, there are problems with taking self-selected samples as representative. A statistically valid solution would be to take a sample, selected in a statistically random manner, each time and expend effort on obtaining a high response rate. An alternative would be to target the largest universities and obtain responses from them each time. The first method would allow us to make comments about all universities with a philosophy programme in the country of interest, while the second would allow us to examine trends for a specified group of universities.

If time and resources are to be expended on surveys to investigate further issues, thought should be given to the statistical validity of the survey design and measures to use to ensure a good response rate. These should include issues of form design, mode of delivery of the form, primary approach letters, follow-up of forms that have not been returned, and other inducements to get responses. Examples of inducements include the timing of the survey to fit in with academic workload and publicity that makes departments want to participate.

Acknowledgments

The authors would like to thank Katherine Norlock for providing data she obtained from the National Center for Education Statistics and Samantha Brennan for useful information about the CPA Equity Surveys. Special thanks also to Fiona Jenkins and Katrina Hutchison for involving us in this project.

References

Beebee, H. & Saul, J. (2011) Women in Philosophy in the UK: A Report by the British Philosophical Association and the Society for Women in Philosophy, http://www.swipuk.org/notices/2011-09-08/Women%20in%20Philosophy%20in%20the%20UK%20%28BPA-SWIPUK%20Report%29.pdf, September 2011.

Boileau, L. & Daigle, C. (2009) Summary of the equity survey for the CPA (2007-2009), available from Canadian Philosophical Association (last viewed on 31 March 2011), http://www.acpcpa.ca/documents/Survey%202009%20Final%20Report%20En.pdf.

Daigle, C., McDonald J., & Lanoix, M. (2005) Summary of the equity survey for the CPA (2001-2005), available from Canadian Philosophical Association (last viewed on 31 March 2011), http://www.acpcpa.ca/documents/2005%20Report.pdf.

Goddard, Eliza. (2008) Report B: Appointments by Gender in Philosophy Programs in Australian Universities, *Improving the Participation of Women in the Philosophy Profession* on behalf of Dodds, Sue, Burns, Lynda, Colyvan, Mark, Jackson, Frank, Jones, Karen, and Mackenzie, Catriona, report to the Australasian Association of Philosophy, http://www.aap.org.au/Resources/Documents/publications/IPWPP/IPWPP_ReportB_Appointments.pdf, March 2011.

Haslanger, Sally. (2007) Changing the Ideology and Culture of Philosophy: Not by Reason (Alone), available from the Society for Women in Philosophy (last viewed on 5 April 2011), http://www.mit.edu/~shaslang/papers/HaslangerWomeninPhil07.pdf.

Norlock, Katherine. (2006) Status of women in the profession. See the APA Committee on the Status of Women, available at http://www.apaonline.org/documents/governance/committees/Women%20in%20the%20Profession%20CSW.pdf/.

Solomon, M., & Clarke, J. (2009) CSW Jobs for Philosophers Employment Study, *APA Newsletter on Feminism and Philosophy*, Vol. 8, No. 2, 3–6.

{ APPENDIX 2 }

Statistical Analyses
Glenys Bishop

FIGURE 1 Analysis of number of philosophy staff at selected Australian universities by sex and year, indicating that there is no significant relationship between numbers of females and year and that number of males reduces by 7.1 on average each year. Analysis performed in GenStat.

Regression analysis

Response variate: Number
Fitted terms: Sex + (Year-2000).Sex

Summary of analysis

Source	d.f.	s.s.	m.s.	v.r.	F pr.
Regression	3	23258.	7752.8	1140	<.001
Residual	10	68.	6.8		
Total	13	23326.	1794.3		

Percentage variance accounted for 99.6
Standard error of observations is estimated to be 2.61.

Estimates of parameters

Parameter	estimate	s.e.	t(10)	t pr.
Sex F	36.86	3.12	11.83	<.001
Sex M	159.36	3.12	51.14	<.001
(Year-2000).Sex F	0.143	0.493	0.29	0.778
(Year-2000).Sex M	−7.107	0.493	−14.43	<.001

FIGURE 2 Analysis of Australian philosophy doctoral student load, indicating a significant linear relationship between load and year for males but not for females. Female load is best represented by the mean 73.58 while male load is best represented by a value 113 in the 2001 with an average increase of 7.37 effective full-time students per year thereafter. Analysis performed in GenStat.

Regression analysis

Adjust Year so that 2001 = Year 0

Response variate: Load

Fitted terms: Gender + Year.Gender

Summary of analysis

Source	d.f.	s.s.	m.s.	v.r.	F pr.
Regression	3	19955.	6651.6	29.32	<.001
Residual	12	2723.	226.9		
Total	15	22678.	1511.8		

Percentage variance accounted for 85.0

Standard error of observations is estimated to be 15.1.

Estimates of parameters

Parameter	estimate	s.e.	t(12)	t pr.
Gender Female	73.58	9.72	7.57	<.001
Gender Male	112.97	9.72	11.62	<.001
(Year-2001). Female	−0.37	2.32	−0.16	0.877
(Year-2001). Male	7.37	2.32	3.17	0.008

FIGURE 3 Analysis of Australian philosophy bachelor degree completions showing that there is no trend over time for either females or males and that on average male completions exceed female completions by 51.88 each year. Analysis performed in GenStat.

Regression analysis

Response variate:	Completions
Fitted terms:	Gender + Year.Gender

Summary of analysis

Source	d.f.	s.s.	m.s.	v.r.	F pr.
Regression	3	11759	3919.5	5.61	0.012
Residual	12	8387	698.9		
Total	15	20145	1343.0		

Percentage variance accounted for 48.0
Standard error of observations is estimated to be 26.4

Estimates of parameters

Parameter	estimate	s.e.	t(12)	t pr.
Gender Female	207.2	17.1	12.14	<.001
Gender Male	238.4	17.1	13.97	<.001
(Year-2001). Female	−1.71	4.08	−0.42	0.682
(Year-2001). Male	4.27	4.08	1.05	0.315

Test of Means

Sample	Size	Mean	Variance	Standard deviation	Standard error of mean
Male-Female	8	51.88	1562	39.53	13.98

95% confidence interval for mean: (18.83, 84.92)
Test statistict = −3.71 on d.f.
Probability = 0.008

FIGURE 4 Analysis of Australian philosophy bachelor degree load showing that the trend over time for males and females is parallel with an increase in each of 73.74 per year, with females starting in 2001 at an estimated higher level of 1,332 than the 1,096 males.

Regression Analysis

Response variate: Load
          Fitted terms: Constant + Year + Gender + Year.Gender

Estimates of parameters

Parameter	estimate	s.e.	t(12)	t pr.
Constant	1298.0	52.9	24.52	<.001
Year	83.6	12.7	6.60	<.001
Gender Male	−167.0	74.9	−2.23	0.046
Year.Gender Male	−19.6	17.9	−1.10	0.294

Parameters for factors are differences compared with the reference level:
Factor Reference level
Gender Female
Response variate: Load
Fitted terms: Adj Year + Gender

Summary of analysis

Source	d.f.	s.s.	m.s.	v.r.	F pr.
Regression	2	679159	339579	49.71	<.001
Residual	13	88806	6831		
Total	15	767964	51198		
Change	−1	−222359	222359	32.55	<.001

Percentage variance accounted for 86.7
Standard error of observations is estimated to be 82.7

Estimates of parameters

Parameter	estimate	s.e.	t(13)	t pr.
(Year-2001)	73.74	9.02	8.18	<.001
Gender Female	1332.4	43.0	30.98	<.001
Gender Male	1096.6	43.0	25.49	<.001

FIGURE 5 Analysis of Canadian doctorate applications showing that rates of offers and rates of entry are not significantly different for males and females in 2008. However, the number of offers to males is increasing by an average of 13.2 per year. Analysis performed in SPSS.

Rate of Entry

2008	Males	Females	Total
Offers	95	37	132
Entries	40	21	61
Total	135	58	193

H0: Rates of entry are the same for the two genders
P-value 0.367

Rate of offer

2008	Males	Females	Total
Applications	328	140	468
Offers	95	37	132
Total	423	177	600

H0: Rates of offer the same for the two genders
P-value 0.675

Changes over Time: Male Offers

Model	Unstandardized Coefficients		t	Sig.
	B	Std. Error		
1 (Constant)	−26348.500	3216.492	−8.192	.015
Year	13.200	1.606	8.218	.014

258

Appendix 2

TABLE 1 Analysis of UK Staff Numbers

| | Analysis performed in Excel 2010 [3] | | | | | | |
| | Observed | | | Expected under H0 | | Contribution to result | |
	Males	Females	Total	Males	Females	Males	Females
Professor	91	16	107	79.8	27.2	1.56	4.59
Reader	25	8	33	24.6	8.4	0.01	0.02
Senior Lecturer	56	21	77	57.5	19.5	0.04	0.11
Lecturer	92	28	120	89.5	30.5	0.07	0.20
Temporary Research	35	12	47	35.1	11.9	0.00	0.00
Temp. Lecturer	40	21	61	45.5	15.5	0.67	1.96
Casual Teaching	193	75	268	200.0	68.0	0.24	0.71
All	532	181	713				

H_0: males and females distributed the same at all levels
$\chi^2 = 10.17$, 6 degrees of freedom P-value = 0.118
Permanent non-professorial staff make very little contribution to this result and can be combined.

TABLE 2 Analysis of UK Staff Numbers with broader categories

| | Observed | | | Expected under H0 | | Contribution to result | |
	Males	Females	Total	Males	Females	Males	Females
Professor	91	16	107	79.8	27.2	1.56	4.59
Permanent Staff	173	57	33	171.6	58.4	0.01	0.03
Temporary/ Casual Staff	268	108	47	280.5	95.5	0.56	1.65
All	532	181	713				

H_0: males and females distributed the same at all levels, where reader, senior lecturer, and lecturer have been combined to permanent staff, and temporary research, temporary lecturer and casual teaching have been combined.
$\chi^2 = 8.40$, 3 degrees of freedom P-value = 0.015
Conclusion: There are differences in proportions of males and females in various categories with females underrepresented at professor level and overrepresented among temporary/casual staff.

References

Excel 2010 distributed by Microsoft, http://office.microsoft.com/en-au/excel/, last accessed 8 January 2013.

GenStat software distributed by VSN International, http://www.vsni.co.uk/software/genstat, last accessed 8 January 2013.

Statistical Package for the Social Sciences distributed by IBM, http://www-01.ibm.com/software/analytics/spss/, last accessed 8 January 2013.

{ CONTRIBUTOR BIOGRAPHIES }

Michelle Bastian completed her Ph.D. in philosophy at the University of New South Wales. She is currently a Chancellor's Fellow at the Edinburgh College of Art, University of Edinburgh. Her work focuses on the use of time in social practises of inclusion and exclusion.

Helen Beebee is Samuel Hall Professor of Philosophy at the University of Manchester. She has published extensively on topics in metaphysics, epistemology, and the history of philosophy, including *Hume on Causation* (Routledge, 2006), *The Semantics and Metaphysics of Natural Kinds* (Routledge, 2010, co-edited with Nigel Sabbarton-Leary), and *The Oxford Handbook of Causation* (Oxford University Press, 2009, co-edited with Christopher Hitchcock and Peter Menzies), as well as articles in journals such as *The Journal of Philosophy, Philosophy and Phenomenological Research, Analysis* and *Noûs*.

Glenys Bishop is a statistical consultant at the Australian National University and, prior to that, worked for nine years as a statistical methodologist at the Australian Bureau of Statistics in the areas of survey design and analysis, data confidentiality, and data linkage. Bishop has held academic positions in statistics at the University of Adelaide and at Bond University, where she taught a variety of theoretical and applied statistics subjects, and has maintained a keen interest in technology-assisted learning techniques since the early 1970s. Bishop has a broad background in applied statistics in the areas of survey design and analysis, and experimental design and analysis. She has collaborated with agricultural scientists, medical researchers, and social scientists. Recent publications are listed at http://scu.anu.edu.au/staff/dr-glenys-bishop

Samantha Brennan is professor of philosophy at Western University Canada, where she is also an affiliate member of the Department of Women's Studies and Feminist Research, a member of the Rotman Institute of Philosophy, and a member of the graduate faculty of the Department of Political Science. Brennan was chair of Western's Philosophy Department from 2002–2007 and 2008–2011. Brennan received her Ph.D. from the University of Illinois at Chicago and a B.A. in philosophy from Dalhousie University, Halifax, Nova Scotia. She has published widely in ethics and political philosophy, and she has a special interest in issues of children's rights and family justice. You can find details of Brennan's publications at http://publish.uwo.ca/~sbrennan.

Susan Dodds is professor of philosophy and dean of arts at the University of Tasmania. She has been working as a philosopher in Australia since 1986, first as a tutor at Melbourne and La Trobe Universities, then for 19 years at the University of Wollongong before moving to Tasmania in 2009. Her research is in the areas of political philosophy and applied ethics, with current projects on the concept of vulnerability in ethics and bioethics; the role of deliberative democracy and development of defensible policy on ethically contested areas of medicine; and the challenges to applied ethics associated with developments in medical nanotechnology and bionics.

Marilyn Friedman is W. Alton Jones Professor of Philosophy, as well as professor of political science, at Vanderbilt University, U.S. She was a professorial fellow at the Centre for Applied Philosophy and Public Ethics at Charles Sturt University, Australia. She has published widely on feminist theory, ethics, and political philosophy. Her authored books include *Autonomy, Gender, Politics* (Oxford University Press), and her edited books include *Women and Citizenship* (Oxford University Press).

Eliza Goddard is a research associate in the Faculty of Arts at the University of Tasmania, working in the areas of feminist philosophy, political philosophy, and bioethics. She is currently completing a Ph.D. at UTAS through the Ethics Program of the ARC Australian Centre of Excellence for Electromaterials Science (ACES), where she works on the impacts of medical bionics on selfhood and social relations. Since 2006, Goddard has been the executive officer of the Australasian Association of Philosophy (AAP) and is the author of *Improving the Participation of Women in the Philosophy Profession* (2008), co-author of the ALTC report *Forward thinking: teaching and learning philosophy in Australia* (2010), and co-author (with Graham Priest) of the entry on the Australasian Association of Philosophy in *The Companion to Philosophy in Australia & New Zealand* (2010).

Katrina Hutchison is a postdoctoral research associate at Macquarie University. She is currently working on two nationally funded research projects on the ethics and epistemology of surgery. She completed her Ph.D. on free will at the Australian National University in 2010. She also has research interests in the role and value of philosophy beyond the academy, and in theories of higher education teaching as applied to philosophy, with a particular interest in assessment techniques.

Fiona Jenkins is a senior lecturer in the School of Philosophy, Research School of Social Sciences, Australian National University. In 2013–14, she is the convenor of the ANU Gender Institute. Her research includes a project on the significance of Judith Butler's notion of "ungrievable life", looking at equality and discrimination in a global context. Her recent publications from this project have appeared in journals including *Angelaki, Differences, Australian Feminist*

Law Journal, and *Australian Journal of Human Rights*. She has a co-edited book, *Allegiance and Identity in a Global World*, forthcoming, with Cambridge University Press in 2013. She also has a comparative project, "Gender and Feminism in the Social Sciences", looking at different disciplinary trajectories in philosophy, history, sociology, and political science to examine the relationship between an improved gender profile and mainstreaming feminist and gender scholarship.

Catriona Mackenzie is professor of philosophy and director of the Research Centre for Agency, Values and Ethics at Macquarie University, Sydney. Her research and teaching expertise spans ethics, moral psychology, feminist philosophy, political philosophy, and applied ethics. She is co-editor of several volumes, including *Relational Autonomy: Feminist Perspectives on Autonomy, Agency, and the Social Self* (Oxford University Press, 2000), *Practical Identity and Narrative Agency* (Routledge, 2008), *Emotions, Imagination and Moral Reasoning* (Psychology Press, 2011), and *Vulnerability: New Essays in Ethics and Feminist Philosophy* (Oxford University Press, forthcoming). Mackenzie has published in multiple edited collections and in such journals as *Australasian Journal of Philosophy*, *Hypatia*, *Journal of Applied Philosophy*, *Journal of Social Philosophy*, *Philosophical Papers*, and *Philosophical Explorations*. Her current research includes projects on autonomy, on the moral and political obligations arising from vulnerability, and on conceptions of the self.

Justine McGill currently teaches philosophy at the University of Melbourne. Much of her philosophical work has focused on concepts and problems of responsibility. She is interested in taking philosophical ideas beyond disciplinary and academic boundaries, and her publications include an essay on "Logic of a War Crimes Trial: Radovan Karadzic" in *Best Australian Essays 2009* (Black, 2009). With sociologist Craig Brown, she co-edited and contributed to an interdisciplinary collection entitled *Violence in France and Australia: Disorder in the postcolonial welfare state* (University of Sydney Press, 2011). More recently, she has begun to combine longstanding interests in Buddhist thought and meditation practice with exploration of Western philosophy of mind and psychology to delve into the mysteries of consciousness. Creative experiments in philosophical thought can be found on her Tango Philosophy blog: http://tangophilosophy.blogspot.com/.

Adriane Rini is a senior lecturer in philosophy at Massey University in New Zealand, where she started in 1999 as temporary contract teaching staff. In 2009, she was president of the AAP (NZ Division), and in 2011 she was secretary of the NZ Division. She is the author of *Aristotle's Modal Proofs* (Springer, 2010) and co-author of *The World-Time Parallel* (forthcoming). She has been awarded three separate Marsden Grants (2003, 2006, 2010) from the Royal Society of New Zealand, and during 2010, she was awarded a foreign fellowship from the Royal Flemish Academy for Science and the Arts in Brussels. Her main areas of research are in the history of logic (especially modal logic) and in the logic and metaphysics of time and modality.

Jennifer Saul is professor of philosophy and head of department at the University of Sheffield, where she has taught since 1995. Saul specialises in philosophy of language and feminist philosophy, and she is the author of three books: *Feminism: Issues and Arguments* (Oxford University Press, 2003), *Simple Sentences, Substitution, and Intuitions* (Oxford University Press, 2007), and *Lying, Misleading, and What is Said: An Exploration in Philosophy of Language and in Ethics* (Oxford University Press, 2012). She is director of the Society for Women in Philosophy, U.K.

Cynthia Townley works at Macquarie University in Sydney. She completed her Ph.D. in philosophy at the University of Tasmania and was previously employed at the University of Melbourne and at the University of Nevada, Las Vegas. Her research interests include epistemology, ethics and feminist theory, animal ethics, and medical ethics. She shares her household with a cat and a dog.

{ INDEX }

The letter *f* following a page number denotes a figure. The letter *t* following a page number denotes a table